Genre and Graduate-Level Research Writing

 **The Michigan Series on Teaching Multilingual Writers**

Series Editors
Diane Belcher (Georgia State University) and
Jun Liu (University of Arizona)

Genre and Graduate-Level Research Writing

An Cheng

Oklahoma State University

 The Michigan Series on Teaching Multilingual Writers

Series Editors: Diane Belcher and Jun Liu

Ann Arbor
University of Michigan Press

♾ Printed on acid-free paper

ISBN-13: 978-0-472-03706-3 (paper)
ISBN-13: 978-0-472-12454-1 (ebook)

2021   2020   2019   2018   4   3   2   1

Foreword

The University of Michigan Press has long been in the vanguard in producing much needed pedagogical materials for graduate students facing the demands of advanced academic writing in the disciplines (see the numerous publications that have emerged from the collaboration of John Swales and Christine Feak, such as Swales & Feak, 2000, 2012). An Cheng's addition to our Michigan Series on Teaching Multilingual Writers addresses a significant gap in the area of academic writing for graduate students—namely, a genre-oriented book-length treatment of the needs of current and future teachers of such writers.

In *Genre and Graduate-Level Research Writing*, Cheng provides genre theory–informed support for those tackling the daunting task of scaffolding graduate-level writers' efforts to navigate discipline-specific research genres that may be far from familiar to the writing teachers themselves. A prolific researcher in the field of English for Academic Purposes who also has a wealth of experience teaching graduate student writers, Cheng makes the tall task of easing graduate students' entry into advanced research writing appear increasingly more manageable with each succeeding chapter one reads in this eminently reader-friendly, practitioner-empowering volume. Readers of this book, especially those relatively new to such a pedagogical challenge, will very likely come away from it equipped with both a broader and deeper understanding of the why's and how's of a genre-based approach to teaching advanced research writing.

While this volume is a welcome, long-needed research-and-theory-based introduction to its topic, we suspect that, with its abundant best-practices examples, it will also be viewed as a resource that readers return to again and again as they further develop their own expertise as supporters of graduate-level research writers.

References

Swales, J., & Feak, C. (2000). *English in today's research world.* Ann Arbor: University of Michigan Press.

Swales, J., & Feak, C. (2012). *Academic writing for graduate students: Essential tasks and skills* (3rd ed.). Ann Arbor: University of Michigan Press.

Acknowledgments

My sincere gratitude goes first to the graduate students whom I have had the good fortune to work with and to continue to work with in multiple institutional sites and in various pedagogical formats. Many of these students supported me to formally collect, with IRB approvals, multiple sources of data from them. Similar to Swales (2009a) who prefers to call the graduate students in his classes "course participants" rather than "students," I see these individuals as more my co-learners than my students. To this day, I continue to read regularly the works they have submitted, including the data that have been transcribed, tabulated, and categorized, and I never cease to be in awe of the disciplinarily driven logics and modes of arguments they have revealed to me through their writing, the insightful comments they have provided on the genre samples they collected and analyzed, and the sometimes very poignant stories of challenges and uplifting accounts of success related to research writing that jump vividly out of the interview transcripts and their literacy narratives. They have helped deepen my interest in genre pedagogy and in research writing instruction. At the same time, they have turned me from feeling pretty certain at some point that I had already had this "genre pedagogy thing" all figured out to someone who realized that the only certain thing is that I do not and will never know enough (see Cheng, 2015a, for an example) and all I can do is to continue to learn and grow. To a large extent, this book is driven by this humble realization and is the result of me trying to continue to figure out this "genre pedagogy thing" and its relation to research writing. Seen in this light, I hope that this book can be a worthy dedication to them.

I would also like to thank the teachers and teacher educators with whom I have had the honor to communicate in various forms (via emails, Skype calls, or through face-to-face formal and informal discussions in the lobbies of conference hotels or in and outside the venues of the workshops I have given or attended). Their suggestions and questions to me as well as their answers to my questions have helped me rethink some of my assumptions, see the gaps in my knowledge, and enable me to make the best efforts to clarify to myself and to them some of principles and practice of genre-driven theory and pedagogy that result in this book.

I would also like to thank Kelly Sippell for supporting me in every stage of writing the book. Her suggestions, including her own as well as those by the anonymous reviewers that she had carefully and intelligently interpreted and clearly conveyed to me, have helped reshape almost all the chapters in this book. Some chapters have been rewritten in a drastically different, and, I hope, more effective manner. I am thankful for her comments, insights, and encouragement.

An Cheng
Stillwater, OK
January 2018

Grateful acknowledgment is given to the following publishers for permissions to reprint copyrighted materials.

American Psychological Association for the excerpt from "Incivility in the Workplace: Incidents and Impact," by L. M. Cortina, V. J. Magley, J. H. Williams, and R. D. Langhout, *Journal of Occupational Health Psychology*, 6, 64–80, Copyright © 2001.

Nature Publishing Group for the excerpt from "A Brain-Specific MicroRNA Regulates Dendritic Spine Development," by G. M. Schratt, F. Tuebing, E. A. Nigh, C. G. Kane, M. E. Sabatini, M. Kiebler, and M. E. Greenberg, *Nature*, 439, 238–289. Copyright © 2006.

The University of Michigan Press for the excerpt from Unit Seven: Constructing a Research Paper I, by J. M. Swales and C. B. Feak, *Academic Writing for Graduate Students: Essential Tasks and Skills (3rd ed.)*, p. 286, Copyright © 2012. Used with permission.

The University of Michigan Press for the table from Unit Seven: Constructing a Research Paper I, by J. M. Swales and C. B. Feak, *Academic Writing for Graduate Students: Essential Tasks and Skills (3rd ed.)*, p. 285, Copyright © 2012. Used with permission.

The University of Michigan Press for Figure 16 from Unit Eight: Constructing a Research Paper II, by J. M. Swales and C. B. Feak, *Academic Writing for Graduate Students: Essential Tasks and Skills (3rd ed.)*, p. 331, Copyright © 2012. Used with permission.

The University of Michigan Press for Figure 18 from Unit Eight: Constructing a Research Paper II, by J. M. Swales and C. B. Feak, *Academic Writing for Graduate Students: Essential Tasks and Skills (3rd ed.)*, p. 368, Copyright © 2012. Used with permission.

The University of Michigan Press for Task Nineteen from Introductions to Journal Articles, by C. B. Feak and J. M. Swales, *Creating Contexts: Writing Introductions across Genres,* p. 57, Copyright © 2011. Used with permission.

Every effort has been made to contact the copyright holders for permission to reprint borrowed material. I regret any oversights that may have occurred and will rectify them in future printings of this book.

Contents

Introduction

This book explores the context, theory, and practice related to working with graduate-level research writers in the classroom. Graduate-level research writing is broadly defined in this book as scholarly writing that graduate students, junior researchers, and, in some cases, senior undergraduate students need to learn to engage in peer-responsive written communication about their research. I argue that formal instruction on research writing is necessary for graduate-level research writers and novice academics, and writing instructors should build and continue to update their knowledge for working with graduate-level writers.

This book adopts genre as the theoretical lens for understanding research writing instructional practices because genre pedagogy has been noted as "one of the most highly theorized curricular orientations" in "addressing the very specialized discoursal needs of novice EAL [English as an Additional Language] graduate writers" and other graduate students (Belcher, 2012, p. 136). The book, thus, explores what genre is, how it has been conceptualized in the English for Specific Purposes (ESP) school of genre studies, why this particular school of genre theory and pedagogy may be especially suitable for guiding one's work with graduate-level research writers in the classroom, what genre analysis in this school may involve, and what the goal of genre-focused teaching should be.

Genre theory and pedagogy, then, drive the close examination of the topics in the rest of this book. These include a description of genre-focused learning materials, approaches to facilitating learner-driven inductive or task-based analysis of genre, making sense of disciplinary specificity in students' writing of research genres, and other topics.

This book primarily targets the needs of novice writing instructors in applied linguistics/TESOL or in writing studies graduate programs and the graduate faculty and teacher educators who work with these novice instructors. I hope that the close attention to genre and to the connections among context, theory, and practice that have been built into this book can enable these and other readers to reflect on their practices, to build and update their knowledge, and to use their reflections and knowledge to make theoretically informed and contextually responsive pedagogical decisions.

The comparatively sharper focus on genre in the ESP tradition and its impact on graduate-level research writing instructional practices affords this book the space to look closely at how genre plays out in concrete practices in contexts where a clearly defined, unique student population with "very specialized discoursal needs" learn research writing (Belcher, 2012, p. 136). Seen in this light, I hope that this book will contribute to knowledge in genre studies and benefit the genre-focused scholarly community.

Chapters in This Book

Chapter 1 defines what graduate-level research writing is and offers six reasons why formal instruction on graduate-level research writing is necessary for novice research writers and why it is important for writing instructors to build or to update their knowledge of graduate-level research writing instructional theory and practice.

Chapter 2 looks closely at rhetorical consciousness-raising, which was proposed by Swales (1990) and has since been adopted by other practitioners as the preferred instructional objective in graduate-level research writing classes. Because rhetorical consciousness-raising is often discussed together with the concept of genre, the chapter elaborates on the definitions of genre and introduces several approaches to genre analysis. The chapter then expands on the notion of rhetorical consciousness-raising to include two interrelated learning objectives: (1) to develop students' awareness of genre analysis as a conceptual framework or tool that can be applied to the analysis of any genre in the graduate-level research writing classroom and beyond (genre awareness) and (2) to increase students' awareness of discipline-specific features in the target genres (awareness of genres) through guiding students to become increasingly proficient in applying the genre analysis framework to the genre samples in their fields.

Chapter 3 concentrates on various forms of genre-focused instructional materials applicable to the graduate-level research writing classroom. Among them are published textbooks that have adopted the genre-focused approach to teaching graduate-level research writing, practitioners' program- or course-specific instructional materials, and learner-contributed genre samples. Of special interest in this chapter are my perspectives on how to guide students to build their reference collections.

Chapter 4 discusses two methodologies especially applicable to genre-focused instruction on research writing: the explicit in-class discussions of genre exemplars and learners' genre analysis tasks outside of class.

Chapter 5 looks at the four dimensions of writing tasks in the graduate-level research writing classroom. I explore how these four dimensions can be built into the same writing task and how they can help facilitate instructors' understanding and evaluation of students' discipline-specific writing.

Chapter 6 elaborates on five areas potentially useful for building and updating one's knowledge of research writing instruction. These areas include becoming familiar with second language (L2) and English for Academic Purposes (EAP) instructional approaches to writing, learning about research writing pedagogical initiatives targeting English as a first language (L1) writers, understanding students' learning as well as their practices of research writing in non-classroom settings, educating oneself about the discipline-specific nature of research writing, and learning to conduct action research in the research writing classroom.

Chapter 1

Six Reasons to Know about Genre and Graduate-Level Research Writing

This chapter defines what graduate-level research writing means and explains why developing a sophisticated understanding of research writing is important for graduate students, early career academics, and, to a smaller extent, senior undergraduate students as well as writing teachers who work with these groups.

Graduate-Level Research Writing: Definitions and Importance

Graduate students, or postgraduate students as they are often called in countries and regions outside the United States, and novice academics form a distinct group of nascent scholars and learners of research writing. Although not yet well-established, well-published faculty, yet no longer novice undergraduates, these groups are being acculturated into their disciplines through the process of writing about their research. Consistent with this observation, graduate-level research writing is broadly defined in this book as scholarly writing that graduate students, junior researchers, and, in some cases, senior undergraduate students need to learn to engage in, or to prepare to participate in, peer-oriented written scholarly conversations about their research. These written conversations are often through genres such as journal articles or theses/

dissertations that meet, or aspire to meet, the expectations of these students or scholars' respective discourse communities. As a result, these writers must acquire "the expertise in the academic genre set that orchestrates" their chosen fields, such as course papers, thesis proposals, theses or dissertations, grant proposals, conference proceedings, journal articles, and academic support documents, to name a few examples (Swales & Lindemann, 2002, p. 105; see also Curry, 2016, for a list of the genres graduate students are expected to learn).

More specifically, compared with beginning undergraduate students, graduate students and junior academics are "all under pressure to communicate in increasingly sophisticated ways to increasingly sophisticated audiences" (Freeman, 2016, p. 223). To do so, they need to master a larger body of discipline-specific vocabulary and sentence patterns suitable for the valued genres. They need to show greater breadth and depth of mastery in disciplinary conventions as manifested in the patterns in their target research genres. More important, they must increase their rhetorical awareness of how the target research genres are situated within various disciplinary networks (Tardy, 2009). With such an awareness, they can then learn and practice the disciplinarily sanctioned ways of constructing new knowledge often embedded in these genres. For example, they often must learn to critique previous knowledge claims, highlight one or several gaps in the literature, and argue that their research addresses the gaps and contributes to the construction of new knowledge through the journal article genre (Swales, 1990, 2004). They also must use various valued research genres to address the needs of different audiences, including the graduate school admission committee members, classmates and professors in their subject-matter courses, readers of their qualifying exams/papers, dissertation committee members, conference panels, grant proposal reviewers, journal referees, and many others.

In some universities, especially those in the United Kingdom, senior undergraduate students are also often required to write an undergraduate dissertation that discusses the research literature thoughtfully, adopts the disciplinarily preferred research methods correctly, and aspires to engage in scholarly conversations with professional peers through presenting and discussing one's findings coherently and confidently (see, for example, Naoum, 2013, and Parsons & Knight, 2015, for their guidebooks on writing undergraduate dissertations in construction and in geography as well as the project by Robinson, Stoller, Costanza-Robinson, and Jones, 2008, to teach research writing to undergraduate students in chemistry). Graduate-level research writing, as discussed in this book, applies to this and other similar student populations.

Although graduate students, early career academics, and, to a lesser extent, senior undergraduate students need to develop a sophisticated understanding of the important genres in their disciplines, is formal instruction necessary for these students? By extension, is it necessary for writing instructors to build and increase their knowledge related to the teaching and learning of graduate-level, discipline- and peer-oriented research writing? In the rest of this chapter, I highlight six reasons why I believe the answer to both questions is yes. I hope that these and other related reasons will help convince the readers of this book of the importance of increasing their knowledge about genre and about the learning and teaching of graduate-level research writing.

Six Reasons to Know about Genre and Graduate-Level Research Writing

Reason 1: The Pressure Felt by Scholars to Engage in Research Writing in English

An obvious reason for enhancing one's knowledge of the context, principle, and practice of graduate-level research writing instruction is related to the increasing number of L2 graduate students studying in English-speaking countries. These students must learn and produce graduate-level research writing in English in order to complete their degree study and to advance their careers (Belcher, 2012). The United States has been as an illuminating example. According to the Institute of International Education (IIE), which is an independent, not-for-profit organization that promotes research and policy dialogues on global higher education, international students enrolling in U.S. universities reached a record high of 1,078,822 students in the 2016–2017 academic year (IIE 2017 *Open Doors* Data and Fast Facts at www.iie.org). Among these students, 391,124 were graduate students, with many of them in fields such as business, engineering, and computer science.

Outside of English-speaking countries such as the United States, the United Kingdom, Australia, New Zealand, and Canada, graduate students are also increasingly being required to study for their degrees in English (e.g., Kuteeva & Negretti, 2016). For example, graduate students in China are not only being asked to write their theses and dissertations in English, but are also required to publish research papers in English, sometimes in high-profile Science Citation Index (SCI) journals, before graduation (Curry, 2016; Flowerdew & Li, 2009; Li, 2017). In fact, some have noticed that much of the work reported in the internationally indexed papers by Chinese scientists has been conducted by doctoral students (Cargill, O'Connor, & Li, 2012). The requirement to publish English research articles in indexed journals before graduation has also been reported in Taiwan (Huang, 2010, 2014), Korea (Cho, 2009; Kim & Shin, 2014), and Indonesia (Cargill, O'Connor, Raffiudin, Sukarno, Juliandi, & Rusmana, 2017).

In addition, the "article-compilation" PhD thesis or dissertation in which a doctoral candidate is expected to have an article or two published in English-medium international journals before graduation is becoming increasingly popular in countries such as the Netherlands (Burrough-Boenisch, 2003), Japan (Gosden, 1995), China (Li, 2006), and the U.S. (Kittle Autry, Carter, & Wojcik, 2016), among others. Such a trend has, undoubtedly, added to the pressure for graduate students to write up and publish their research in English before or during the degree-earning process.

For L1 students, the pressure to learn research writing has also increased. With the number of graduating students far surpassing the number of jobs available each year in the United States, for example, L1 graduate students "clamor to produce publications while completing coursework, exams, and theses/dissertations" because "having a scholarly identity [through publications] before entering the job market feels essential," and to produce publications "may be a great source of stress and anxiety" (Brooks-Gillies, Garcia, Kim, Manthey, and Smith, 2015; see also Curry, 2016, for a similar observation). Apart from the pressure generated by the job market, the changing landscape of graduate education has also led to the need for L1 graduate students to learn research writing expediently and effectively. In a journal article that targets mainly English composition scholars who work with L1 students, Tauber (2016) argues that many previously practice-based professions that graduate students aspire to enter have become increasingly "educationalized" (p. 640). Consequently, graduate students entering a profession- or occupation-oriented graduate degree program today are expected to engage in the academic activity system with its demands for scholarly production and research writing. Such an expectation has added to the pressure for these students, similar to their peers in more traditionally research-oriented graduate programs, to learn research writing well. These and other reasons have led L1 graduate students to seek the type of EAP support offered to L2 speakers of English, as noted by Feak (2016).

After graduate students earn their degrees, the pressure to produce research writing in English often intensifies because English is the dominant language of academic publication (Curry & Lillis, 2017a, 2017b; Hyland, 2015a). In many geographical locations, acceptable target journals have been identified as those included in high-status citation indexes, which are often published in English (Burgess, 2017; Cargill & Burgess, 2017; Curry & Lillis, 2017a, 2017b). Given the growing prominence of English as the vehicle for communicating research findings, ministries of higher education, universities, and research centers around the world have, unsurprisingly, made policies that encourage researchers and scholars to publish in English-medium international journals, especially those with a high-impact factor (Burgess, 2017; Curry & Lillis, 2017a, 2017b; see also Englander, 2014). Selected countries around the world that have adopted this kind of policies include Spain, the United Kingdom, China, Brazil, Korea, Malaysia, Chile, and Sri Lanka, among others (Burgess, 2017; Kim & Shin, 2014). For example, as part of the effort to internationalize China's higher education system, the Chinese government has adopted Western criteria in measuring the credibility of scholarly publications and has encouraged academics to publish in high-status Western-based English-medium journals through incentives such as "cash prizes, housing benefits, or other perks" (Qiu, 2010, p. 142; Tian, Su, & Ru, 2016).

Reason 2: The Difficulties Encountered by Novice Research Writers

Due to the pressure to complete one's degree study through learning and producing various research genres in English and to advance one's career through publications, again, in English (see Reason 1), graduate students and junior scholars often feel the need to specifically learn research writing. Such a need becomes all the more salient if they encounter any difficulties with learning and using vocabulary, applying the correct grammar and sentence constructions, using reporting verbs, and other language problems that put these students and scholars at a disadvantage when writing their theses/dissertations (Rogers, Zawacki, & Baker, 2016) or when preparing and submitting their papers to English-medium journals (J. Flowerdew, 2015). Their research papers have been reported as sometimes rejected and criticized by journal reviewers and editors due to the perceived language problems (Duszak & Lewkowicz, 2008).

Some writers also lack a clear understanding of the disciplinary expectations behind the textual features that they are expected to learn (Casanave & Li, 2008) or may not have a solid command of the scholarly registers that involve, for example, a skillful mastery of discipline-specific citation language or metadiscourse that signals one's commitment to an argument (Kwan, 2010).

As a result of any of these difficulties, these students and scholars may lack confidence in their ability to write in English and are often anxious about the prospect of having to publish in English (Tian, Su, & Ru, 2016). Some senior researchers also feel that their research writing abilities may not be strong enough to meet the demands placed on them, which include not only submitting research papers themselves, but also guiding their graduate students to produce research writing that meets the requirements of the discourse community (Cargill, O'Connor, & Li, 2012).

Just as both L2 and L1 graduate students feel strong pressure to engage in research writing (see Reason 1), these difficulties apply to both L2 and L1 writers. As some have argued, research English is no one's first language, graduate-level research writing is far from a universal skill, and both research English and graduate-level research writing must be acquired through prolonged education for L2 and L1 writers alike (Hyland, 2015a; 2016). Indeed, the "increased communicative demands placed on [graduate students] by the generic academic ladder" could be as overwhelming to L1 as they are to L2 writers, as noted by Swales and Luebs (2002, p. 150) who describe an episode in which they offered a workshop on literature searches and reviews at the University of Michigan. More than 200 people showed up, "a clear majority being apparently native speakers of English." Many of these L1 doctoral students, as noted by Swales and Luebs (2002), were "close to being traumatized by the unknown exigencies" of the literature review part-genre (pp. 150–151).

Although this episode happened many years ago, the problem persists, as described in more recent accounts of curricular efforts to help L1 graduate-level writers (e.g., Fairbanks & Dias, 2016; Ritter, 2017) and in blogs that target L1 graduate-level research writers (see the blog *Patter* by Pat Thomson at https://patthomson.net/, for example). In fact, L1 graduate students' struggles with writing are not just "traumatizing" in general, but could also cause them to fail graduate school, as pointed out by the authors of *57 Ways to Screw Up in Grad School: Perverse Professional Lessons for Graduate Students* that targets a primarily L1 audience (Haggerty & Doyle, 2015).

Moving beyond degree study to look at scholarly publication, Hyland notices that many well-educated L1 speakers "lack the necessary know-how and experience to produce publishable papers." As a result, the enculturation into the norms of academic rhetorical practice could be "painful and protracted" for both L1 and L2 users of English, as argued by Hyland (2015a, p. 62; 2016).

Possibly due to such a realization, Swales and Feak (2011) claim that, when it comes to academic writing, the more valid and valuable distinctions nowadays are between senior researchers and junior researchers, regardless of their L1 backgrounds (see Swales, 2004, for a more detailed presentation of this argument). In fact, Curry calls the dichotomy between "native" speakers and "nonnative" speakers of English in terms of graduate-level research writing "reductionist" and "unhelpful" (2016, p. 79).

At a more technical level, researchers have noticed that some of the problems experienced by L1 writers, such as difficulties with citation, academic conventions, genre expectations, argumentation, word choice, cohesion, sentence structure, and writer identity, are not very different from those encountered by L2 writers (e.g., Aitchison, Catterall, Ross, & Burgin, 2012; Paltridge, 2016). Rogers, Zawacki, and Baker (2016), after surveying 428 doctoral students (362 L1 writers and 66 L2 writers), found "a high degree of similarity" in some of the items pointed out by both L1 and L2 writers as highly challenging (p. 57). These include "translating ideas into written form," "organizing and structuring chapters and sections," "planning and prewriting," and "choosing the most appropriate words," among others (p. 57). Similarly, Fairbanks and Dias (2016) noticed that the U.S.-educated students who came to the writing center at Claremont Graduate University in the United States were very excited when they were introduced to the model for research paper introductions, possibly because of their lack of the knowledge of the effective framework for writing such a part-genre.

For these reasons, some graduate-level communication programs have started to target L2 and L1 students "equally and without distinctions" as "a matter of general policy for graduate communication" programs (Tierney, 2016, p. 275). Such a policy has also been borne out by actual pedagogical practices. Sundstrom (2016), for example, describes how the courses developed in the Graduate Writing Program at the University of Kansas (U.S.) initially served only international students. After these courses were offered several times, the enrollees turned out to be "70 percent native speakers and 30 percent nonnative speakers" (p. 193). Similarly, Phillips (2016) expected that L2 speakers would comprise most of the clientele at the graduate writing and research center directed by her at Ohio University (U.S.) and was quite surprised to find that 50 percent of the consultation sessions at her center have typically been with monolingual domestic L1 speakers of English.

Reason 3: The Problems with Mere Immersion- or Apprenticeship-Based Learning of Research Writing

The previous two sections have described the pressure and challenges for novice writers to engage in graduate-level research writing during and beyond their degree study. The pressure and challenges described have attracted the attention of researchers in writing studies and in English for Academic Purposes (EAP) who have examined how graduate-level research writers navigate the sociocultural networks surrounding their writing activities and how such writers participate in, or aspire to participate in, their respective discourse communities through their writing (e.g., Belcher, 1994, 1997; Casanave, 2002, 2014). Using the theoretical framework of "community of practice" and the related concepts of legitimate peripheral participation and situated learning (Lave & Wenger, 1991; Wenger, 1998), these scholars have highlighted the situated nature of graduate-level research writing and the importance of having access to experts in real time and in contexts outside of formal instructional settings. Instead of focusing on, or merely looking at, the cognitive processes these writers engage in or the ways they acquire and produce rhetorical organizational patterns or lexico-grammatical features in valued genres, scholars adopting the framework of legitimate peripheral participation are more interested in these writers' participation in academic communities and the social relationships through which these writers define themselves. By extension, scholars adopting such a theoretical lens often consider academic and research genres to be a form of situated cognition embedded in and, consequently, best learned through participating in disciplinary activities (Berkenkotter & Huckin, 1995). In other words, in the views of these scholars, those new to research writing can best improve their ability to control genres and writing through participating in the writing and writing-related activities of different communities of writers and through the formation of various trajectories of disciplinary enculturation (Belcher, 1994; Casanave, 2002; Paltridge, Starfield, & Tardy, 2016).

Studies on graduate-level research writers have also been informed by the theoretical frame of academic literacies. This theoretical frame views research writing as a sociocultural practice occurring within a complex social system that incorporates issues of epistemology, power, and identity as student writers strive to create meanings and construct knowledge as burgeoning or active participants in the academy (Lea, 2004). Such a theoretical frame often invokes the concepts of voice and identity to interpret the different perspectives of those who play the "game" of graduate-level research writing (e.g., Aitchison et al., 2012; Casanave, 2002). It has given rise to a multitude of studies that examined the struggles and achievements of graduate-level research writers (see a critical review of many of these studies in Chapter 5 and Chapter 7 in Paltridge, Starfield, & Tardy, 2016).

Most of the studies in these categories focus more on graduate-level research writers *outside,* rather than *inside,* the writing classroom, although the distinctions between the two may not be as clear-cut as often assumed (see Tardy, 2009). Even though studies on learners outside classroom settings have offered valuable insights into the struggles of graduate-level research writers, they have, indirectly and quite ironically, foregrounded the importance of formal instruction on research writing and, by extension, of enhancing teachers' knowledge of the classroom-based learning of research writing. As noted by Belcher (2006), most EAP theorists and practitioners would agree that immersion and legitimate peripheral participation are helpful and even essential for developing graduate students' target discourse expertise. They would agree that onsite learning can enable, for many students, the expertise in graduate-level research genres. At the same time, EAP proponents would probably contend that immersion is not enough, especially for students and junior scholars facing the academic and linguistic hurdles previously described. Specifically, colleagues or faculty advisors/supervisors may be eager to teach novice writers in naturally occurring sociocultural contexts of research writing but may be ill-equipped to provide the scaffolded apprenticeship that these writers need (Cargill, O'Connor, & Li, 2012; Tauber, 2016). Basturkmen, East, and Bitchener (2014), for instance, describe how the supervisors of student theses they studied often found it difficult to offer constructive feedback on the drafts of the Results sections in their supervisees' theses. Although these supervisors or faculty members were likely to have implicit knowledge of how to write this section, they may not necessarily have the explicit knowledge of the rhetorical patterns or the linguistic features in research writing to guide their students' writing (see also J. Flowerdew, 2016) or may simply have difficulty articulating, or lack the training to articulate, their tacit expert rhetorical knowledge to their students (see also Blakeslee, 1997; Starfield, 2016).

In addition, even where senior scholars have well-developed skills themselves for writing and publishing in English and are eager to impart wisdom about research writing to younger colleagues and students, their efforts are often hampered by their overwhelming workloads, including a large number of research students they supervise, their own research activities, and the absence of effective teaching materials, among other factors (Cargill et al., 2017; Starfield & Mort, 2016).

Possibly because of these and other reasons, EAP specialists argue that, for those at linguistic or other disadvantages, much more explicit, guided "immersion" is called for than normally available *in situ*, and classroom instruction could serve as a form of such explicit guidance. Such a view, indeed, has been supported by reports of faculty and graduate students who had expressed quite strongly the need for explicit writing instruction on research writing at the graduate level. For example, the overwhelming majority of the faculty members surveyed at a major research university in Korea felt that the only available research writing course for graduate students offered should be a required course for all graduate students (Kim & Shin, 2014).

In fact, scholars and practitioners in EAP and writing studies have argued that not only should students be taught explicitly the graduate-level discoursal and research writing practices, their advisors could benefit from training on how to mentor their students explicitly in the meaning-making processes of their fields (Paltridge, Starfield, & Tardy, 2016). Such an observation is, again, not limited to those who work with L2 students. Brooks-Gillies et al. (2015) and Ritter (2017) both argue that graduate students need instruction and support, both formally and informally, especially since they notice that the academic communities that graduate students aspire to enter have rarely integrated into the curriculum any systematic instruction on research writing to initiate these newcomers consciously into the written conventions of their respective discourse community. This point was reflected in a comment by James Potter (2001), a scholar in communication studies who, when addressing an L1 audience, said that "in graduate school the focus of our education is almost exclusively on research . . . ." and "we almost never receive instruction in writing" (see a similar, more recent observation in Ritter, 2017). Potter (2001) also talked about how many graduate students and novice academics learn the writing part of publishing in "the School of Hard Knocks" when their manuscripts are rejected and insisted that there must be a better way than "learning through rejection" (p. 13).

Reason 4: The Prominence of Genre Analysis as an Approach to Analyzing and Teaching Research Genres

Partly because of the belief in the value of teaching and learning graduate-level research writing explicitly in classroom settings, scholars have analyzed many research genres and the recurrent organizational patterns and textual features in them, often with pedagogical applications in mind. Scholars adopting the ESP approach to genre analysis have contributed tremendously to this line of research. In the ESP tradition, genre is often defined as "a class of communicative events" with "communicative purposes" recognized by "the expert members of the . . . discourse community" (Swales, 1990, p. 58; 2004). The most familiar ESP genre analytic framework is the one established by Swales (1990, 2004); his original framework is characterized by the analysis of *moves*, or the "defined and bounded communicative act that is designed to achieve one main communicative objective" (Swales & Feak, 2000, p. 35). To use the relatively familiar graduate school admittance letter as an example, *On behalf of the Dean of the Graduate School, I congratulate you on being accepted to the program in Aerospace Engineering to begin study at the master level* is one move, the purpose of which is to deliver the good news of the student having been admitted into the program. Following this move is another possible move such as this: *This letter is your official authorization to register for Fall 20XX. As a reflection of the importance the Graduate School places on the ability of its students to communicate effectively, the Graduate School requires all new students whose native language is not English to have their English evaluated.* The purpose of this move is to explain the necessary administrative matters that the letter receiver should be aware of or should comply with (Swales & Feak, 2012a, p. 9). To use a more academic example, *We interviewed 52 postpartum mothers at the Bronx Lebanon*

Hospital Center within 5 days of delivery and determined the presence of psychiatric symptoms using the 29-item Psychiatric Symptom Index constitutes a move in the research article abstract. The purpose of this move is to describe the methods and materials adopted in the study (Swales & Feak, 2009, p. 9).

The framework is later enriched by socially informed theories of language and has generated numerous descriptions of the "regularities of purpose, form, and situated social action" (Hyland, 2003, p. 22) of various discipline-specific genres and the genre-specific features in them. For example, ESP researchers have studied such highly valued research genres as research articles (e.g., Kanoksilapatham, 2015; Swales, 1990), graduate theses and dissertations (e.g., Paltridge, 2002; Soler-Monreal, 2015), grant proposals (e.g., Feng & Shi, 2004), book reviews (e.g., Motta-Roth, 1998), calls for papers (e.g., Yang, 2015), conference presentations (e.g., Rowley-Jolivet & Carter-Thomas, 2005), and academic support genres (e.g., Wang & Flowerdew, 2016), among others.

The smaller parts within a research genre, or part-genres, such as abstracts (e.g., Samraj, 2005), introductions (e.g., Swales, 1981, 1990), literature reviews (e.g., Kwan, 2006), methods (e.g., Peacock, 2011), results or findings (e.g., Basturkmen, 2009), discussions (e.g., Cotos, Link, & Huffman, 2016), conclusion (e.g., Bunton, 2005), and acknowledgments (e.g., Hyland & Tse, 2004a) in journal articles or dissertations have also been the subjects of studies.

Within a genre, recurrent textual, or lexico-grammatical, features have also been closely examined; these features have included, among others, imperatives (e.g., Neiderhiser, Kelley, Kennedy, Swales, & Vergaro, 2016), hedging and boosting (e.g., Hyland, 1998), metadiscourse (e.g., Hyland & Tse, 2004b), stance markers (e.g., McGrath & Kuteeva, 2012), citation practices and reporting verbs (e.g., Harwood, 2009), signaling nouns (e.g., Flowerdew & Forest, 2015), pronouns (e.g., Harwood, 2007), and lexical bundles (e.g., Cortes, 2013).

ESP genre-based researchers and teachers have also turned some of the descriptions of discipline-based genre exemplars into pedagogical materials (e.g., Cheng, 2007a). Most prominent among these are a series of genre-driven textbooks by Swales and Feak (e.g., 2012a) that are described in detail in this book. In these books, Swales and Feak adopt an analysis-focused and rhetorical approach by asking users to "apply their analytical skills to the discourses of their chosen disciplines and to explore how effective academic writing is achieved" (2012a, p. ix). They emphasize "rhetorical consciousness raising," which can be achieved through the cycle of "Analysis→ Awareness→Acquisition→Achievement" (p. ix). Other notable genre-based books for teaching and learning graduate-level research writing include Paltridge and Starfield's (2007) resource book for academic advisors supervising L2 research students and Bitchener's textbook that teaches students in applied linguistics to write a thesis or dissertation (2010) (see Chapter 3).

These and other efforts have turned genre pedagogy into "one of the most highly theorized curricular orientations" in "addressing the very specialized discoursal needs of novice [English as an additional language] graduate writers" and other graduate students (Belcher, 2012, p. 136). The prominence of genre analysis as an approach to analyzing and teaching graduate-level research writing means that those working with, or interested in working with, graduate-level research writers should become familiar with the basic principle and practice in this approach, regardless of whether they plan to adopt it.

Reason 5: Increasing Accounts of Pedagogical Practices

The recognition of the importance of formal instruction on research writing (see Reason 3) and the efforts to describe graduate-level research genres and to translate some of the results of genre analysis into pedagogical materials (see Reason 4) have led to various graduate-level research writing pedagogical practices as reported in the literature. A few examples are described briefly, and these and other examples will be analyzed in detail in the subsequent chapters. The English Language Institute of the University of Michigan (hereafter Michigan) offered a longitudinal EAP curriculum designed to help international students meet the communicative demands of graduate education. The curriculum included courses such as Research Paper Writing and Dissertation and Prospectus Writing. Swales and Lindemann (2002) described an exercise for the Dissertation and Prospectus Writing course that they developed to teach the literature review part-genre to 11 graduate students and two visiting scholars. They showed how graduate-level research writing courses can help learners become "more observant readers of the discoursal conventions of their fields and . . . can deepen their rhetorical perspectives on their own disciplines" (p. 118).

In another research writing course at Michigan, Swales, Barks, Ostermann, & Simpson (2001) developed several assignments to target the needs of a group of L2 Master of Architecture students. These assignments helped highlight a range of issues related to the teaching and learning of graduate-level research literacy, including the role of the discourse analytical approach in graduate-level research writing courses, the value of a critical approach in teaching research-oriented speaking and writing, and the constraints facing teachers of graduate-level research-related literacy skills.

Outside of the United States, Charles (2012) reports on a course in the Oxford University Language Center where students from multiple disciplines and language backgrounds used two corpora and a language analysis software to study how thesis writers often defend against potential criticisms of their research. Charles incorporated discourse-based tasks to help her students recognize the rhetorical move thesis writers often make to defend their research. She also developed corpus tasks for her students to carry out controlled, context-sensitive corpus searches that focused on lexical and sentence-level, or lexico-grammatical, issues related to the rhetorical functions of defending one's research against possible criticisms. She argues that the combination of the top-down discourse analysis that focuses on rhetorical functions and the bottom-up corpus searches that zoom in to the lexico-grammatical features performing such functions provides the enriched input necessary for her students to connect the rhetorical purposes, the rhetorical moves, and the lexico-grammatical choices in their learning of the thesis genre.

In another course on thesis writing, Paltridge (2003) describes how he familiarized Master of Education students (both L1 and L2) with the conventions and expectations of the master's dissertation (or master's thesis in the United States) genre and helped the students develop their strategies for writing their own dissertations. To achieve these goals, Paltridge (2003) included topics such as the context of dissertation writing, attitudes to knowledge and different levels of study, differences between master's and doctoral degrees, the roles and responsibilities in dissertation writing, online genre analysis of sample dissertations, and planning and writing individual chapters. Paltridge reports that the student feedback on the course was overwhelmingly positive.

In Sweden, Kuteeva (2013) reports on a course entitled English for Academic Research aimed primarily at master's students at the faculty of humanities in a Swedish university. The course prepared its participants to write a research proposal and a master's thesis. It focused on the analysis of different genre-specific features in the model texts in the course participants' fields of research. The course ran over a period of six weeks, with a three-hour seminar every week. Kuteeva introduced additional online genre analysis tasks to complement in-class genre analysis activities. Each student reported the results of his or her genre analysis in a short forum post.

Other than semester-long courses, instructors of research writing have also offered short workshops (e.g., Fairbanks & Dias, 2016). For example, Cargill and O'Connor (2012; see also Cargill, O'Connor, & Li, 2012; Cargill et al., 2017) gave a series of workshops that they called Collaborative Interdisciplinary Publication Skills Education to train novice academics in multiple cities in China to publish their scholarly work. Their workshops incorporated the contributions of experienced scientists who were journal editors, journal referees, authors of scientific articles in English as well as those who were research communication teachers/applied linguists. Their workshops aimed to develop participants' skills in three components: genre analysis of published sample journal articles, awareness of the journal publication process, and the abilities to package information in an audience-sensitive manner.

Lynne Flowerdew has also described various workshops she offered to science and engineering research students at a university in Hong Kong (2015, 2016). For example, she developed a two-part voluntary workshop. In Part 1 of the workshop, she guided her students to analyze printed extracts of the Discussion sections from theses and to identify prototypical organizational patterns. She then asked her students to complement these top-down, genre-focused pen-and-paper activities with bottom-up corpus-enabled tasks designed to familiarize her students with search strategies for identifying useful lexicogrammatical patterns for particular rhetorical functions. In Part 2 of the workshop, she guided her workshop participants to attend to the variations in the rhetorical organization in the Discussion sections of theses and dissertations. She also introduced concordancing tasks that focused on problematic areas identified in students' drafts of the Discussion sections of their own theses.

Swales and Feak (2012a) notice that, when the first edition of their textbook *Academic Writing for Graduate Students* was first published in 1994, the number and range of courses in academic writing for graduate students were both rather small and largely restricted to entering international students. When the third edition was published in 2012, both the number and the range of these courses, they point out, have increased as graduate students move around the world in growing numbers, bringing with them their recognition of the importance of learning and teaching graduate-level research writing (e.g., Yakhontova, 2001). Swales and Feak (2012a) also point out that the number of these courses has increased due to the growing realization that L1 speakers of English would welcome, for various reasons, some assistance with their research writing, a point that some composition scholars and writing studies scholars have also agreed upon (e.g., Brooks-Gillies et al., 2015; Ritter, 2017).

Such an observation is supported by a plethora of examples of pedagogical practices, some of which will be analyzed in more detail in the subsequent chapters (e.g., Frederickson & Mangelsdorf, 2014; Gustafsson, Eriksson, & Karlsson, 2016; among many others). Apart from these published accounts of graduate-level research writing courses or workshops, unpublished syllabi, such as those available on the resource section of the Consortium on Graduate Communication (https:// www.gradconsortium.org/), a professional community serving instructors of graduate-level academic writing, have also showcased the variety of available courses on graduate-level research writing. The accumulating literature on pedagogical practices means that those interested in working with graduate-level research writers need to become familiar with these practices, including understanding the theoretical underpinnings, the actual practices, and any implications of these practices for their own pedagogical settings. Where at one point they may have been unaware of models that align with their course needs, it's now clear that many models and contexts exist and are available as resources and roadmaps.

Reason 6: The Documented Challenges Facing Novice Instructors

The prominence of genre analysis as an approach to analyzing and teaching research writing (see Reason 4) and the growing literature on pedagogical practices (see Reason 5) have pointed to the existence of a body of knowledge related to graduate-level research writing instruction, knowledge that those interested in working with graduate-level research writers need to build or to continue to update.

Such a need becomes all the more salient when teaching graduate-level research writing continues to be perceived as challenging by many. For example, Norris and Tardy (2006) describe a course offered at Purdue University in which the teacher, "Christine," grappled with a variety of issues typically encountered by instructors of graduate-level research writing.

Christine describes her uncertainty about her abilities to teach the graduate-level writing class this way:

> Perhaps ironically, one of the most difficult parts of teaching 002 [the writing class for graduate students] for me was my uncertainty about my own qualifications for teaching the course. First, as a doctoral student in an English department, I was teaching a course to my fellow graduate students in other university departments. Second, I was a student in the humanities teaching students who were, for the most part, from the sciences and working on projects that were completely foreign to me. (Norris & Tardy, 2006, p. 271)

Christine's feelings turn out to be quite common for many other novice or even experienced instructors teaching discipline-related research writing classes to graduate students or to junior academics (e.g., Cortes, 2011; Min, 2016; Prior & Min, 2008; Sundstrom, 2016). For example, drawing on the data she collected from an ESL writing program at a large university in the midwestern region of the United States, Min (2016) describes a situation in which first-year students in a Master's in Teaching English as a Second Language (MATESL) program became instructors of two L2 graduate writing courses in which many doctoral students from other disciplines were enrolled. The first-year MATESL students, both L1 and L2 speakers, lacked teaching experience and disciplinary expertise in their students' fields, so it was unsurprising that many of these MATESL students felt unprepared to teach graduate students and reverted to what they were familiar with—treating the graduate writing course the same way they would the undergraduate writing courses. They also made problematic assumptions about the transfer of writing skills across disciplines and genres. Min (2016) describes these novice instructors' experience as a "schizophrenic" experience (p. 169): the experience was too disorienting to help these novice instructors develop any lens to correlate theory, practice, and reflection.

Indeed, even though various factors may be contributing to the challenges experienced by novice instructors, the multi-disciplinary mix of students in graduate-level research writing classes often stands out as a particular challenge for instructors, as seen in Christine's comment (Norris & Tardy, 2006) and in Min's observation (2016). Graduate-level research writing classes or workshops are often populated by students from a wide range of disciplines across the campus. These classes have been reported as including students from multiple different disciplines in one section, and these disciplines "may or may not share methodologies" and may "differ considerably" in writing style, format, and even the genres students need to learn (Starfield, 2016, p. 187; see also Starfield & Mort, 2016).

Take myself as an example. When I was pursuing my doctoral degree, I was a graduate teaching assistant with independent instructional duties. Even though I quite eagerly requested to teach the two sections of the one and only graduate-level writing course offered by the university's applied linguistics program due to my research interest, this course seemed intimidating to me at times, in part due to the fact that the students were not only doctoral and master's students but were also from all over the campus in terms of disciplines.

For example, in one of the sections in which I collected data on student learning that led to my dissertation, 11 course participants were engineering majors of various kinds, and the other students were from accounting, finance, physics, agriculture, information systems, and other fields. When I asked them to collect journal articles from their fields for in-class discussions and out-of-class analysis (see Chapter 3 and Chapter 4 for more details about asking students to collect journal articles for analysis), the articles they submitted to me came from journals as diverse as the *Journal of Structural Engineering, Atmospheric Environment, Journal of the Acoustical Society of America, Journal of Microelectromechanical Systems, European Journal of Operational Research, Journal of Experimental Botany, MIT Sloan Management Review,* and *Journal of the Philosophy of Sport.* The sections of the same course preceding and following my data-collection sections had the same diversity of field representation.

After I earned my PhD degree, I collected new data about students' genre-focused learning in another graduate-level research writing course in another university, and the diversity of field representation was the same: The 16 students came from 12 fields, including engineering, animal science, biology, marketing, education, sociology, and even one student from TESOL. Past and future sections of the same course at this university also had the same type of multidisciplinary mix. Additionally, when I offered summer workshops on research writing to both L1 and L2 graduate students at a neighboring university, I noticed that the workshop participants represented multiple disciplines and sometimes there were more than 15 disciplines in each workshop series.

Others have reported on a similarly diverse disciplinary mix of students in their classes. A dissertation writing class offered by Belcher (1994) included students from Chinese literature, applied mathematics, and human nutrition studies. A graduate-level writing class by Douglas (2015) consisted of students from chemistry, geology, geography, forestry, wood science, physics, psychology, chemical engineering, electrical engineering, human and community development, biology, political science, and public health. Badenhorst, Moloney, Rosales, Dyer, and Ru (2015) noticed that the students in their graduate writing course were from poetry, the esoteric, music anthropology, and philosophy from the humanities group and electrical, computer, civil, ocean and naval architecture, and mechanical in the engineering group. Kuteeva (2013) points out that "a very wide spectrum of epistemological traditions is represented, ranging … from lab-based osteoarchaeology to logic-driven philosophy to source-based history or musicology to emerging inter-disciplinary fields such as fashion studies or performing arts" in the graduate-level writing class she offered (p. 86; see reports of similar situations in Charles, 2014; Cortes, 2011; Fredericksen & Mangelsdorf, 2014; Gustafsson, Eriksson, & Karlsson, 2016; Hirvela, 1997; Lee & Swales, 2006; Norris & Tardy, 2006; Paltridge & Woodrow, 2012; Starfield, 2016; Starfield & Mort, 2016; Swales & Lindemann, 2002).

The climate of economic austerity and the general lack of institutional resources (Starfield, 2016), tradition (Norris &

Tardy, 2006), or the institutional division of labor (Tauber, 2016) may be some of the factors leading to many, if not most, graduate-level research writing classes reported in the literature containing a multidisciplinary mix of students in them.

In fact, a single-subject writing course may look discipline-specific on paper but variations within the discipline may be so great that the class may need to be taught the same way that a multidisciplinary one would. When I taught a writing for publication class to the graduate students in my own department, I assumed that it would resemble a single-subject writing class; in reality, the students represented graduate students in the fields of TESOL, composition and rhetoric, professional writing, English education, and communication studies. In the Introduction to Graduate Studies course that I teach regularly to the students in the TESOL/Linguistics program and professional writing program at my university, some of the principles and strategies described in the rest of the book are used; the papers collected by students for study and analysis (see the details of this assignment in Chapter 3) are very different due to their research interests (phonology as opposed to ESP) or their research methods (corpus analysis vs. narrative inquiry). The discipline-specific writing tasks they are required to do (see Chapter 5) are, consequently, very different even though these students are from the same program. Swales and Luebs (2002) also noticed that the students' target genres in a writing class turned out to have very different genre-specific features even though the students were all from psychology. One can also imagine the disciplinary or sub-disciplinary differences within a School of Engineering or a School of Geology.

Therefore, the multidisciplinary mix of students in the graduate-level research classroom will be a reality for most institutions (e.g., Fairbanks & Dias, 2016). Such a pedagogical reality may pose special challenges when it comes to learning to set learning objectives, select or develop materials, design learning tasks, and evaluate student writing, especially when novice instructors may themselves be graduate students or contingency instructors in English or applied linguistics (see examples in Starfield, 2016; Norris & Tardy, 2006, and Min, 2016).

Researchers and practitioners have also noticed that instructors unfamiliar with effective approaches to teaching graduate-level writing may have already influenced students' learning negatively. For example, in a book chapter on the resources and strategies that an international L2 graduate student adopted to become a successful writer, Phillips (2014) reports that the student seemed to have benefitted minimally from a cross-disciplinary graduate-level writing course designed for international multilingual writers. For example, the student received little positive feedback from his teacher, a faculty in TESOL; the feedback he received seemed overly critical and general. Phillips (2014) observed that the instructor identified problems like "lang. [language] is non-idiomatic" and "sentence structure" is problematic but rarely offered the student alternative language or any particularly constructive comments towards revision or future writing projects (p. 78).

Given these findings, it is unsurprising that some directors of programs that target the communication needs of graduate students have noticed that "the single biggest requirement for success [of programs and courses that aim to meet the needs of graduate-level research writing and communication] is to find and keep good teachers who are able to teach advanced graduate students well" (Freeman, 2016, p. 237). Others have argued that the ad hoc preparation systems for training instructors of graduate-level research writing that mainly rely on pre- and in-service training and professional development workshops "should develop into more systematic programmatic (degree-bearing) training for graduate writing specialists" (Sundstrom, 2016, p. 202). Such arguments, together with the stories of uncertainties and challenges, add an additional reason for teachers and other related parties to build and update their knowledge of graduate-level research writing instruction.

This chapter has argued why learning about genre and about research writing instructional practices are important for novice teachers and for all others working with graduate-level research writers. Helping teachers and others increase their knowledge of the research and practice related to learning and teaching graduate-level research writing can begin with a set of concrete questions. In fact, when reflecting on the problems and feelings of uncertainties experienced by Christine, the instructor of one section of the graduate-level academic writing course at Purdue University, Norris and Tardy (2006) raised a series of questions that they believe novice instructors of graduate-level research writing may be grappling with:

1. Should the class follow a traditional full-class discussion model?

2. How can one teach the multidisciplinary mix of students in the same class?

3. Would a discipline-specific writing class better address students' needs?

4. How should the instructor of a graduate-level writing class balance the requirements in the writing class and his or her rather heavy workload as a graduate student?

5. How should an instructor guide his or her students to read and write discipline-specific texts in a graduate-level research writing class when the instructor may only have training in applied linguistics or writing studies, if any?

I would also add these to the list:

1. What should be the goals in graduate-level research writing classes?

2. How can instructors choose what pedagogical materials to use, and how can instructors develop their own pedagogical materials?

3. How should instructors provide feedback on students' research texts, an issue brought up by Phillips (2014) in her discussion of the problematic case?

4. How can instructors continue to develop or to update their knowledge related to graduate student writers and research genres so as to continue to grow as a practitioner and as a researcher of graduate-level writing instruction?

Given the prominence of genre-focused theory and pedagogy, those working with graduate-level research writing may also need the answers to questions such as:

1. Genre has been considered as a conceptual and curricular building block "of the right size" (Swales & Luebs, 2002, p. 136; see also Reason 4). What does genre mean in this sense?
2. How should researchers and practitioners analyze research genres?
3. What are moves and lexico-grammatical features?
4. What are the goals of genre-focused teaching?
5. How should genre-focused teaching typically play out in research writing courses, especially those with students from multiple disciplinary backgrounds?

The rest of this book will address these and many other related questions.

Questions for Reflection and Discussion

1. This chapter lists six reasons for instructors to build and to continue to update their knowledge related to the teaching and learning of graduate-level research writing. Can you think of any additional reasons for instructors to build and to increase their knowledge in this area?
2. The chapter points out that research writing is difficult for L1 speakers of English as well. In fact, some have argued that the traditional distinctions between L1 and L2 users of research English are collapsing (see Swales, 2004). When it comes to today's educational settings, a more valuable distinction may be that between senior researchers (who are more experienced in research writing in English) and junior researchers (who may still be relatively new to the game of research writing, regardless of their L1 backgrounds). What do you think of such an argument? Have you, for example, noticed any challenges that are unique to L1 graduate-level research writers

that may not be so significant to L2 writers? Have you noticed any challenges that are unique to L2 graduate-level research writers that may not be so significant to L1 writers?

3. Reflect on your own experience of learning research writing as well as the experience of students you have worked with. What do you think of the argument that, when it comes to learning graduate-level research writing, formal instruction is necessary, as argued in this chapter? Do you know of any writers who succeed in research writing without any formal instruction? What may be the reasons for their success? Do you know of any writers who have benefited tremendously from attending classes or workshops in research writing? How have these classes or workshops helped them?

4. When elaborating on Reason 6, I point out that a typical graduate-level research writing class often has a mix of students across the disciplines in it. What may be the advantages for instructors of having a multidisciplinary mix of students in a research writing class? What may be the benefits for students of having peers from other disciplines in the same research writing class? What may be some of the challenges that instructors and students have to overcome in a graduate-level research writing class with a multidisciplinary mix?

5. This chapter ends with a series of questions that novice instructors of graduate-level research writing may need to grapple with in order to succeed in the classroom. Can you think of any other questions that you feel should be added to the list? Why? Do you notice any questions from the list that may not be so significant to you? Why?

Chapter 2

Rhetorical Consciousness-Raising, Genre Awareness, and Awareness of Genres

This chapter first examines rhetorical consciousness-raising, which was proposed by Swales (1990) and has since been adopted by other researchers and practitioners as the preferred instructional goal for the graduate-level research writing classroom. Since rhetorical consciousness raising is often discussed together with the concept of genre, three approaches to genre analysis will be introduced. Because many students need to learn discipline-related genre-specific features, the notion of rhetorical consciousness-raising is used with regard to two interrelated instructional objectives: (1) to develop students' awareness of genre analysis as a conceptual framework (genre awareness) for guiding their further examination of genre samples in the graduate-level writing classroom and beyond and (2) to increase students' awareness of discipline-specific features in research genres (awareness of genres, the plural form, or discipline- and genre-specific features) through guiding them to become increasingly proficient in applying the genre analysis framework to their analysis of genre samples valued in their respective disciplines.

Defining and Applying Rhetorical Consciousness-Raising

In what some (e.g., Lancaster, Aull, & Escudero, 2015) consider to be the most influential book on graduate-level research writing, *Genre Analysis,* Swales (1990) draws our attention to "the pedagogical value in sensitizing students to rhetorical effects, and to the rhetorical structures that tend to recur in genre-specific texts" (p. 213). He believes that participants in graduate-level research writing courses can benefit from our teaching if we guide them to learn to "schematize the structures of the sections [in research genres such as journal articles] themselves and so further develop an understanding of what it is that allows them to recognize a section as Method or Discussion" (p. 213). He elaborates as to why he believes sensitizing students to the rhetorical effects of important discipline-oriented research genres should constitute the instructional objective in the graduate writing classroom: By focusing on the rhetorical effects of texts, we sidestep the problem of heterogeneous content interests due to the multidisciplinary mix of students in a typical graduate-level writing class (see Chapter 1). Instead of arguing about disciplinary content, course participants are in the position of focusing on a common goal—making sense of how recurring genre-specific textual features may have certain rhetorical effects on them as readers and writers. Discussing the rhetorical effects of research texts in class can also help develop course participants' increasing control of the metalanguage for discussing texts, such as "negotiation of knowledge claims," "self-citation," and "metadiscourse," among others (p. 215). Developing the necessary metalanguage, Swales argues, provides course participants with a certain analytical perspective to help them critique their own and others' writing.

In addition, reflecting on the rhetorical effects of textual features can add a "novelty" value to graduate-level writing class, according to Swales (1990, p. 215), and can help distinguish such a class from those content courses in students' own disciplines. Similarly, focusing on the rhetorical elements in research texts, such as the communicative purposes and the relationships between readers and writers, is likely to add to an instructor's credibility, presenting the instructor as having something unique to contribute to students' learning of research writing. In particular, Swales (1990) found that "colleagues from other discourse communities are both surprised and impressed when the English instructor arrives armed with lines of inquiry that show sensitivity to ... that community's central genres" (p. 216; see also Swales, 2004; Swales & Luebs, 2002). Overall, Swales argues that raising students' rhetorical consciousness benefits both students and instructors and creates a unique socio-rhetorical situation and a shared goal in the graduate-level writing classroom.

In subsequent publications, Swales expands on this theory. For example, Swales and a former student (Swales & Lindemann, 2002) have described an activity for teaching the literature review part-genre in which students and junior scholars "become more observant readers of the discoursal conventions of their fields and thereby deepen their rhetorical perspectives on their disciplines" (p. 118). They show how rhetorical consciousness-raising deepens students' perspectives on their own disciplines.

Rhetorical consciousness-raising has very clearly been stipulated as the instructional goal in the series of textbooks Swales coauthored with his colleague Christine Feak (Feak & Swales, 2009, 2011; Swales & Feak, 2000, 2009, 2011, 2012a). In the third edition of the widely adopted *Academic Writing for Graduate Students: Essential Tasks and Skills*, for example, Swales and Feak (2012a) ask their readers to "apply their analytical skills to the discourses of their chosen disciplines and to explore how effective academic writing is achieved" (p. ix), a goal that is consistent with that of rhetorical consciousness-raising. In the other volumes, they advocate for the cycle of "Analysis→Awareness→Acquisition→Achievement" as essential in this regard (Swales & Feak, 2009, p. xiii). This cycle asks users to carry out linguistic and rhetorical analysis by comparing certain features of a text from a different field with what they know or can discover from texts in their own areas because "these comparisons lead to a greater awareness and understanding of how research English is constructed, which then provide a platform for further acquisition of specific writing skills" (Swales & Feak, 2009, p. xiv). Again, rhetorical consciousness-raising as the instructional objective is believed to be able to lead to learners' deepened understanding of their chosen field as well as their possible acceptance into the discourse community they aspire to join.

Rhetorical consciousness-raising as an instructional objective has been accepted by other practitioners of graduate-level research writing instruction. Starfield (2003), for example, describes how a thesis-writing course for both L1 and L2 students raises students' awareness of the linguistic and the genre-specific structuring of theses/dissertations in the social sciences and humanities. Starfield (2003) highlighted the Creating a Research Space (CaRS) framework (Swales, 1990; Swales & Feak, 2012a) that often appears in the introductory sections of research articles and theses/dissertations to her students and then annotated the moves and sub-moves in the introductory sections of some sample theses. Through "deconstructing" the sample theses this way, Starfield (2003) aimed to raise her students' rhetorical consciousness of how "the texts they are reading are constructed and contextualized and, at the same time, through exposure to a number of different theses, offer them a range of strategies for the construction of their own theses" (p. 143).

In another course titled Research Writing and Presentation, Starfield also set the goal of developing "students' awareness of the structure of texts within their own discipline" because "explicitly raising awareness of these features will enable students to adopt or adapt them to their own writing." She attributes such a goal to Swales' notion of rhetorical consciousness-raising and believes that such a goal is "in line with current thinking in writing pedagogy" (Starfield, 2016, p. 183). She also noticed that her students' feedback at the end of the course showed that they valued such a goal highly.

Hyland (2002) also argues for rhetorical consciousness-raising as an instructional objective in ESP teaching in general and in graduate-level research writing instruction in particular. Hyland has pointed out that a major problem of heterogeneous classes is finding enough common ground among students for class discussions and activities. One solution to this problem, he believes, is to take advantage of the opportunities that such classes offer to contrast the class participants' disciplinary experiences and expectations. He argues that activities aimed at rhetorical consciousness-raising not only satisfy students' demands for personal relevance in graduate-level writing classes, but also develop their awareness of the functions of texts and how these functions are conventionally accomplished.

Others have seen rhetorical consciousness-raising to have pedagogical applications due to the language learning histories of the students in graduate-level communications classes. Tierney (2016), for example, describes how the many years of English language courses in their home countries and the resulting English language proficiency enables graduate students to contribute actively in class and to provide valuable feedback in groups. As a result, according to Tierney, "awareness-raising and metacognitive strategies" have been adopted as the instructional goals and teaching technique in the graduate-level communication courses at Yale University where Tierney directs the graduate communication support program (p. 275).

In 1995, Belcher and Braine used a different term to expand on this notion: "academic discoursal consciousness-raising" (p. xv). In their view, this term involves developing in students the explicit awareness of "the texts, subtexts, and contexts of academic discourse" for students to "join the collectivist endeavors that academic community are" (p. xv). Note that Swales also talks about rhetorical consciousness-raising as important for helping students to understand discipline-specific discoursal conventions. Belcher and Braine (1995) seem to have expanded on this notion to emphasize how academic discoursal consciousness-raising can also help develop in students a sense of the sometimes hidden rules of what some call the *games* of academic writing and the strategies academic insiders often adopt to play such games (Casanave, 2002, 2014).

Hirvela (1997) has also identified as a goal of his graduate-level writing course to help students penetrate the invisible discourse of their fields. He describes the learning objectives in his academic writing course for international graduate students as aiming to acquaint the students with what Belcher and Braine call the "subtexts and contexts" (1995, p. xv) of academic writing and sensitize them to the subtleties that constitute the invisible discourse they must learn to recognize and control if they are to acquire full membership in the discourse community they have elected to join (Hirvela, 1997). Similarly, Gustafsson, Eriksson, and Karlsson (2016) described the objective of their graduate-level research writing course that targets journal article writing at the Chalmers University of Technology in Sweden as aiming to "direct students' attention to the rhetorical assumptions of the various communities in the [multidisciplinary] group to highlight the kinds of givens used to legitimize practice in the respective disciplinary discourses" (p. 262).

Rhetorical consciousness-raising also seems to have been perceived or accepted by relatively novice instructors as seen in the case of Michele reported in Tardy (2009).

In sum, starting with Swales (1990), scholars and practitioners of graduate-level research writing have identified rhetorical consciousness-raising as the suitable learning objective in their classroom. Such an objective includes raising students' awareness of the "rhetorical structure" in "genre-specific texts" and the rhetorical effects of the rhetorical structure and its attendant linguistic features (Swales, 1990, p. 213). It encompasses deepening students' awareness of the discoursal conventions in students' respective fields and their perspectives on their chosen disciplines (Swales & Lindemann, 2002; see also Belcher & Braine, 1995; L. Flowerdew, 2016; Gustafsson, Eriksson, Karlsson, 2016; Hirvela, 1997; Hyland, 2002; Starfield, 2003, 2016; Tierney, 2016). Rhetorical consciousness-raising has also been conceptualized as raising students' awareness of the critical skills to read the rules of academic writing privileged by insiders of academic communities and raising students' awareness of the "subtexts and contexts" of academic writing (Belcher & Braine, 1995; Swales et al., 2001).

Raising Rhetorical Consciousness through Genre Analysis

When scholars have argued for the importance of rhetorical consciousness-raising, they often invoke the concept of genre. Swales (1990) has discussed sensitizing students to the rhetorical effects of *genre*-specific features as part of this process; he has cited some students' failure to "call upon useful expectations as to how the introduction [in a journal article] might be rhetorical constructed" as the reason to raise their awareness of the rhetorical structure in key research *genres* (p. 214; emphasis added). He refers to the importance of presenting "prototypical examples of relevant *genres*" (p. 213; emphasis added) and to raise students' awareness of the discoursal conventions of students' fields (Swales & Lindemann, 2002). Similarly, Belcher and Braine refer to the awareness of forms of academic discourse, or genres, as part of raising students' rhetorical consciousness (1995).

In fact, in a review of the status of L2 writing research and practice, Belcher (2012) points out that "interest in addressing the very specialized discoursal needs of novice EAL [English as an Additional Language] graduate writers has helped motivate … one of the most highly theorized curricular orientations in L2 writing, namely, genre pedagogy" (p. 136; see also Hyland, 2004b; Paltridge, 2001). Referring to supporting graduate-level writing in general (rather than just L2 writing), Sundstrom (2016) points out that "*genre* and rhetorical approaches and methodologies have been tested and shown to work in interdisciplinary settings with skilled instructors" (p. 201; emphasis added).

Since scholars and instructors of graduate-level research writing often discuss rhetorical consciousness-raising in conjunction with genre, it would be important to explore what genre is, what genre pedagogy often entails, and why genre pedagogy is considered to be a "highly theorized" curricular orientation especially suitable for raising rhetorical consciousness and believed to have been "tested and shown to work" in the graduate-level research writing classroom.

Arguably, the most influential definition of genre, at least to those analyzing discipline-specific research genres and teaching research writing through a genre-focused approach, comes from Swales (1990):

> A genre comprises a class of communicative events, the members of which share some set of communicative purposes. These purposes are recognized by the expert members of the parent discourse community, and thereby constitute the rationale for the genre. This rationale shapes the schematic structure of the discourse and influences and constrains choice of content and style. Communicative purpose is both a privileged criterion and one that operates to keep the scope of a genre as here conceived narrowly focused on comparable rhetorical action. In addition to purpose, exemplars of a genre exhibit various patterns of similarity in terms of structure, style, content, and intended audience. (p. 58)

Other ESP and EAP scholars have expanded on this definition of genre. Ann Johns and Diane Belcher have both highlighted the socio-rhetorical dimensions of genre, with Johns defining genre as "responses by speakers or writers to the demands of a social context" (2002, p. 3) and Belcher calling genre "socially agreed-upon ways of achieving communicative purposes" (2012, p. 136). Aiming for a more comprehensive definition of genre that emphasizes texts, subtexts, and contexts (see Belcher & Braine, 1995, and Hirvela, 1997, for their discussions of the three), Flowerdew defines genre as "a multifaceted construct characterized by a range of features including social action, communities of practice, power relations, text, and intertext" (2011, p. 120).

Genre-oriented scholars have identified three broad, interrelated approaches to genre by citing major differences in how genre is defined, how the research focus varies, and how research findings of target audiences differ (Hyon, 1996; see also Bawarshi & Reiff, 2010; Flowerdew, 2011; Hyland, 2004b; Johns, 2002; Paltridge, 2001). Systemic Functional Linguistics (Halliday, 1995) has been adopted by researchers examining the broad genres or rhetorical modes, such as description, narration, and argumentation (Paltridge, 2001). The New Rhetoric approach is used mostly by rhetoric and composition scholars in North America who are especially interested in the social and ideological implications of genre (e.g., Bawarshi, 2003; Devitt, 2004; Devitt, Reiff, & Bawarshi, 2004). The English for Specific Purposes (ESP) approach (Swales, 1990, 2004) is often favored by researchers and practitioners interested in genre as a tool for teaching discipline-specific and peer-oriented writing to L2 users, including graduate-level research writers and beyond, in academic and professional settings.

Despite the distinctions among the three approaches, the divisions "have become much less sharp—even if they have not entirely disappeared" (Swales, 2009c, p. 4). "Consolidating trends" among the three schools have, in Swales' view, pointed to a "more nuanced approach to genre awareness-raising and genre acquisition" (p. 5). As Swales (2009c) sees it, "The work of genre is to mediate between social situations and the texts that respond strategically to the exigencies of those situations" (p. 14). Therefore, genre analysis should focus on the interactions between social situations and texts, i.e., to track "textual regularities and irregularities and explain them in terms of the relevant and pertinent social circumstances and the rhetorical demands they engender" (Swales, 2009c, p. 14).

Despite this argument, novice practitioners interested in teaching research writing to graduate student writers may find it useful to start with the ESP approach to genre for at least three reasons: (1) the close attention given by the ESP approach to both the textual and the contextual aspects of genre, (2) the comparatively accessible analytical framework practiced by those adopting the ESP approach, and (3) the rich pedagogy-relevant research findings on research genres generated by those adopting the ESP approach to genre analysis.

The ESP approach to genre study has been noted as increasingly bridging the linguistic and rhetorical traditions in genre, thus exemplifying the "consolidating trends" Swales (2009c) suggests. This approach to genre "is becoming increasingly context-driven, and the overlap between the New Rhetoric. . .

and ESP research and theory . . . becomes greater every year"
(Johns, 2003, p. 206). The connections between the linguistic
and the rhetorical or, in Swales' words, between "the texts"
and the "social situations," in the ESP approach can be seen
in its emphasis on the role of discourse community, with its
shared communicative purposes, in identifying, analyzing, and
teaching genres (Swales, 2009c, p. 14).

More specifically, genre is often defined as structured communicative events engaged in by specific discourse communities whose members share broad communicative purposes
(see Swales, 1990). This definition has led many ESP genre-
focused researchers to closely associate genres with *discourse
communities*, such as the various academic disciplines that
students in graduate-level research writing classes are part of
or will be part of. Genre researchers have also closely associated genre with the communicative purposes recognized by
the discourse community because "the issue of writer purpose
is essential to genre theory" (Johns, 2008, p. 239). The close
attention to the purposes of a genre as recognized by its discourse community has also led ESP genre-focused scholars
to use the nomenclature of these communities, such as the
research article and grant proposal, to identify highly valued
genres or part-genres, or the smaller parts within a genre, for
scholars to analyze and for students to learn (Johns, 2003).
The connections among a discourse community, its communicative purposes, and the rhetorical organizational and
lexico-grammatical features in its valued genres often result
in a "deeper and multilayered textual account" that strives
to assess rhetorical purposes, unpack rhetorical structures,
and identify syntactic and lexical choices in a discourse community's valued genres, all with the needs and assumptions
of the target discourse community in mind (Swales, 1990, p.
3). The emphasis on the connections among discourse community, communicative purposes, and organizational and
lexico-grammatical features, thus, has great potential to help
instructors and learners of graduate-level research writing to
track "textual regularities and irregularities" and link them
to "the relevant and pertinent social circumstances and the

rhetorical demands" in a coherent and systematic manner (Swales, 2009c, p. 14).

Additionally, the ESP approach to genre analysis offers a comparatively accessible analytical approach that teachers and learners of graduate-level research writing can adopt to engage in the "comparison and contrast" and "episodic dissection" of the target genres, which have the potential to lead to students' heightened rhetorical consciousness (Swales, 2009c, p. 15). In fact, genre in the ESP tradition has been "widely recognized as conceptual and curricular building blocks of 'the right size'" (Swales & Luebs, 2002, p. 136). More simply put, genre analysis involves, among other things, examining the genre's rhetorical organization or schematic structure. The rhetorical organization is revealed by looking at the "moves"—a primarily functional, rather than formal, unit that performs a "bounded communicative act that is designed to achieve one main communicative objective" (Swales & Feak, 2000, p. 35). For example, a letter of admittance issued by the graduate school of a university would often include these moves: to acknowledge the relation between the writer and the letter receiver, to deliver the good news, to provide administrative details, and to close the letter in a welcoming tone that point to the future (see Swales & Feak, 2012a, for more details). In a research article abstract, there are likely these moves: to provide the background/introduction/ situation to the project/paper, to present the research purpose, to explain the methods/materials/subjects/procedures, to provide the findings/results, and to offer discussions/conclusions/implications/recommendations (see Swales & Feak, 2009).

The analysis of the moves can then proceed to the linguistic (style, tone, voice, grammar, and syntax), or lexico-grammatical, features that help perform a particular rhetorical move or to bring it into its linguistic realization. For example, the lexico-grammatical features for delivering the good news of admittance would involve verbs such as *congratulate*, and closing a letter of admittance in a welcoming tone would include using phrases such as *look forward to*. In a similar vein, the "to explain the methods" move in an abstract is often performed by verbs used in the past tense.

Although actual samples of a genre may vary in how they are perceived to be representative examples of the genre by members of the target discourse community, the often conventionalized rhetorical organizational and lexico-grammatical features give teachers and students something to identify and to discuss. Note that these conventionalized rhetorical organizational and lexico-grammatical patterns are recognized by members of the discourse community as helping to achieve the rhetorical purposes valued by that discourse community. Therefore, the analysis of rhetorical organizational and lexico-grammatical features should always be driven by one's attention to the target discourse community and its sanctioned or valued communicative purposes. After all, "It is communicative purposes (defined in relation to a discourse community's shared goals) that gives rise to and provides the rationale for a genre and shapes its internal structure," as explained by Bawarshi and Reiff (2010, p. 46). At the same time, a deeper awareness of these patterns furthers one's understanding of the discourse community and its communicative purposes, thus allowing instructors and students to see the constant interactions between the textual and the rhetorical situational aspects in research genres.

The analysis of a genre should, therefore, be driven by attention to the "prototypical ... conventions of the genre" and "an understanding of the genre's intended purposes and an awareness of the dynamics of persuasion within a socio-rhetorical context" (Tardy, 2009, p. 21). The first part develops formal knowledge of the genre while the second builds rhetorical knowledge of the genre. Paying close attention to the interactions between the textual and the rhetorical aspects of genre and aiming for the simultaneous and coherent development of students' formal and rhetorical knowledge can raise students' rhetorical consciousness (see Cheng, 2011b, for how the attention to the textual and the contextual could become mutually enriching in students' analysis of genre samples).

To recap, the ESP approach to genre analysis proceeds from a genre's rhetorical organizational pattern to the lexico-grammatical features that help bring such a pattern into realization, all the while closely attending to the genre's communicative purposes and the values and expectations of the discourse community that drive the genre's rhetorical organizational pattern and the associated lexico-grammatical features. Attending to all three forms a circle of potentially meaningful and productive analysis and provides instructors and learners of graduate-level research writing with a comparatively accessible framework, or at least the starting point, for analyzing target genres.

However, the actual analysis may become more complicated and possibly messier than it has been described here, as noted by Paltridge (1994) and Pho (2008), who have questioned whether the relationship between the top-down analysis of the rhetorical organization and the bottom-up analysis of the lexico-grammatical features in a genre is as straightforward as believed by researchers. Nevertheless, there is evidence that this framework is an accessible entry way into the analysis of a research genre. By practicing applying the framework, students can increase the sophistication of their analysis and can then carry the framework beyond the classroom to continuously heighten their rhetorical awareness and learn new genre-specific features. This process will be explained in detail in Chapter 3 and Chapter 4.

Finally, the ESP approach to genre analysis has produced descriptions of many discipline-specific research genres and part-genres. Some are genres directly related to what learners of graduate-level research writing need—journal articles, research proposals, dissertations—as well as their inherent genre-specific rhetorical organizational and lexico-grammatical features. As discussed in Chapter 1, some of these analyses of genres have led to pedagogical materials targeting graduate-level research writing (e.g., Swales & Feak, 2012a) or can be adapted for these purposes. Chapter 3 takes a closer look at materials and Chapter 4 explores other pedagogical applications.

In sum, the three reasons that the ESP approach to genre analysis is particularly applicable to the graduate-level research writing classroom are: (1) the close connections between the textual or the formal on the one hand and the contextual or the rhetorical on the other in the ESP approach to genre; (2) the relatively accessible analytical framework that covers the rhetorical organization, the lexico-grammatical features that support the rhetorical organization, and the rhetorical contexts underpinning the two in an interactive and synergistic manner; and (3) the availability of pedagogy-relevant findings from genre analysis studies on research genres or part-genres that have been translated into materials development or pedagogical applications for in- and out-of-class genre analysis.

An Expanded Understanding of Rhetorical Consciousness-Raising: Raising Genre Awareness and the Awareness of Genres

The wide acceptance of rhetorical consciousness-raising as a suitable instructional objective in the research writing classroom and the ways that genre and genre analysis, particularly in the ESP tradition, assist in raising students' rhetorical consciousness have been discussed. But how can rhetorical consciousness-raising be compatible with learners' need to learn discipline-specific features in research genres? Participants in graduate-level research writing classes or workshops are typically pursuing research degrees in a diverse array of disciplines but will each need to write up and even publish their current or future research in a way that meets the expectations of their respective fields (Belcher, 2012). And we know that working with a multidisciplinary mix of students in the same class can be a challenge for novice instructors (see Chapter 1). So, does raising students' rhetorical consciousness mean heightening their awareness of the target genre/genres covered in a course as a discipline-neutral, general model of research writing? Or does it also mean that instructors should make students aware of the disciplinary variations based on the disciplines of course participants—such as looking at journal articles in chemistry as well as those in biology together with articles in a range of other disciplines represented in the same class? If the latter is the choice, then what would be the relevance of these tasks to students in that class who are not in chemistry, in biology, or in any discipline unrelated to them from which a particular genre sample has been selected for in-class analysis? For example, would a graduate student in chemistry find the in-class discussion of a biology paper irrelevant and vice versa? To what extent should an instructor focus on the consciousness-raising of any possible disciplinary variations in a particular target genre in question?

These questions are both challenging and pressing given the misgivings expressed by some researchers about the feasibility of learning about genre in writing classes in general and about addressing disciplinary specificity in instructional settings in particular. For example, Freedman (1994) questions whether or not genre—with its complex rhetorical considerations—could be taught successfully in the classroom to begin with, let alone the possibility of covering all the disciplinary variations within the same target genre (see responses to Freedman's argument in Devitt, 2004; Hyland, 2002; Johns, 2008).

Most students in graduate-level writing classes are already juggling schedules to fit the writing class into their schedules because they are often taking a full load of disciplinary courses and are likely working as a teaching or research assistant (see Basturkmen, 2010; L. Flowerdew, 2016, Freeman, 2016; Norris & Tardy, 2006; Swales & Lindemann, 2002). As Tierney (2016) points out, unless the courses for graduate students pay attention to "genres that are highly discipline specific in which students have not had adequate instruction," graduate students "simply will not attend" them (p. 276).

For these and other reasons, raising students' rhetorical consciousness of not only the target genres as discipline-general models or frameworks of writing, but also emphasizing the disciplinary variations within each of these genres should be a goal in the research writing classroom if instructors strive to meet two important learning objectives. One of these instructional objectives is to help course participants improve their awareness of genre analysis as a conceptual framework that can be repeatedly applied to any genre. Instructors can guide course participants to analyze multiple discipline-specific examples of a target genre. These analyses should lead to students' ultimate realization that the ability to consider "the audience for and the purpose of a particular text, and how best to communicate rhetorically in that instance" (Beaufort, 2004, p. 140) is something that they can do for any example of any genre in any discipline. The process of carefully analyzing these discipline-specific genre examples offers opportunities for students to see how genre analysis is a productive and generative framework focused on the socio-rhetorical contexts (i.e., the immediate contexts, the roles of readers and writers, the discourse communities, and the communicative purposes). It also directs attention to the rhetorical organization in the genre and the lexico-grammmatical features that undergird that organization. It helps students develop their genre awareness.

A second learning objective is the flip side of the first. Becoming aware of, and proficient in, genre analysis as a heuristic or a conceptual framework (the first objective) becomes the means that serves the goal of deepening one's rhetorical perspectives on the concrete textual features in the genre-specific features in one's own discipline (the second objective). In this way, students learn to produce discipline-specific texts within and beyond the writing class. I call the second objective awareness of genres. Though I distinguish between these two learning objectives (Cheng, 2007b; 2011b), they are intended as always interconnected, perpetually interacting, and mutually enabling. One serves as the means to the other, and vice versa. Specifically, the first learning objective—the development of rhetorical and genre awareness—helps students to achieve the second—the awareness of the characteristics of concrete features in the research genres in one's field. In turn, being aware of, and learning to constantly update, one's knowledge of the distinctive details in the research genres in one's field (the second learning objective) furthers the goal of enriching one's rhetorical knowledge and reinforcing one's knowledge of genre analysis as a conceptual, heuristic framework. The two goals form a mutually propelling cycle (developing genre awareness leads to developing awareness of genres, which leads to furthering one's genre awareness, which leads to further enhancing one's awareness of genres, etc.) with the two elements feeding into each other in an ever-evolving manner.

In the literature on academic writing instruction, distinctions between these two goals have been proposed. For example, Johns (2008) distinguishes between two basic goals for a course: *genre acquisition*, a goal that focuses on students' ability to "reproduce a text type, often from a template, that is organized, or 'staged' in a predictable way" (p. 238), and *genre awareness*, which can assist students in developing the rhetorical flexibility necessary for adapting their socio-cognitive genre knowledge to ever-evolving contexts. Johns argues that a carefully designed and scaffolded program that focuses on genre awareness, as opposed to genre acquisition, is ideal for novice students and for other students as well.

In my discussion of genre awareness and awareness of genres, the two are mutually supporting, and one is not necessarily more "ideal" than the other because neither can be achieved without the other. In addition, genre awareness, in my view, has a distinct conceptual aspect to it. In other words, genre awareness means cultivating learners' awareness of genre analysis as a conceptual framework that could be applied across multiple genres or across multiple discipline-specific examples of the same genre. By becoming familiar with genre analysis as a conceptual framework, learners develop the kind of "rhetorical flexibility necessary for adapting their socio-cognitive genre knowledge to ever evolving contexts" (Johns, 2008, p. 238). Finally, the awareness of genres in the framework proposed does not imply the kind of separation between the textual and the rhetorical. In other words, awareness of the concrete genre-specific features, as seen in the disciplinarily varied samples within the same genre, necessarily entails awareness of how these features have been affected by their rhetorical contexts. These distinctions become important when we look at how genre awareness and awareness of genre*s*, or the awareness of genre-specific features in discipline-specific writing, may play out in materials and concrete learning tasks.

Questions for Reflection and Discussion

1. What does the word *rhetorical* mean in the term *rhetorical consciousness-raising*? Has your understanding of this word (*rhetorical*) changed in any way after you have read this chapter? If yes, how so? If no, why not? In your own words, explain to a novice instructor what *rhetorical consciousness-raising* means and what it typically entails.
2. Can you think of any additional reasons why rhetorical consciousness-raising is a suitable learning objective in the graduate-level writing classroom? Conversely, can you think of any reasons why rhetorical consciousness-raising may not be the most suitable goal to you? If so, what should be the suitable instructional objective in the graduate-level writing classroom, in your view?
3. This chapter introduces the concept of genre. To what extent has this chapter changed or updated your understanding of genre?
4. This chapter offers three reasons why I believe the ESP genre analytical framework is especially suitable for the graduate-level research classroom: (1) the close attention given by the ESP approach to both the textual and the contextual aspects of genre, (2) the comparatively accessible analytical framework practiced by those adopting the ESP approach, and (3) the rich pedagogy-relevant research findings on research genres generated by those adopting the ESP approach to genre analysis. Which one is especially appealing or convincing to you? Can you think of any additional reasons why the ESP approach to genre may be especially relevant for the graduate-level research writing classroom?

5. Explain to a novice instructor the differences between the concepts of *genre awareness* and *awareness of genres* as discussed in this chapter. You may want to consider this scenario to help your explanation: You are teaching a graduate-level writing class with students from multiple disciplines. Two of the students in this class are in chemistry, and the other eighteen students are from various disciplines unrelated to chemistry. If you analyze a sample from a journal article in chemistry in class, how would this activity help develop the genre awareness as well as the awareness of genres in the eighteen students in the same class who are from disciplines unrelated to chemistry? If you feel that you still cannot offer a perfectly clear explanation at this point, don't worry. After reading Chapters 3 and 4, try your explanation again to see if you can do a better job.

Chapter 3

Materials That Guide Genre-Focused Learning of Research Writing

If genre awareness and the awareness of genres constitute two suitable learning objectives that contribute to the overall objective of raising learners' rhetorical consciousness in the graduate-level research writing classroom, then how can we achieve them? This and the next chapter address this question from multiple angles: designing pedagogical materials (Chapter 3) and guiding students' genre analysis (Chapter 4).

Genre-Focused Textbooks for Teaching and Learning Graduate-Level Research Writing

Once the learning objectives have been determined, instructors of graduate-level research writing classes often face the question of what input materials or teaching materials are suitable for developing students' awareness of genre as a conceptual framework as well as their awareness of the interrelated contextual, rhetorical organizational, and lexico-grammatical features in discipline-specific research genres.

This question about pedagogical materials is important given what some have noticed as the challenge in producing suitable teaching materials for their graduate-level research writing classes or workshops. In fact, the challenge may be the reason behind the non-existence of published textbooks for graduate-level research writing that led to Swales and Feak's effort to write the textbooks reviewed in this section (K. Sippell, personal communication, 2017 July 26). Swales later describes the "desperate feeling of 'I can't find the perfect text for what I want to do in class'" that leads to "hours. . .of leafing through textbooks, manuals, journal articles or websites," which may have motivated him to write the textbooks he coauthored with Feak reviewed in this section so that other instructors do not have to go through such a "desperate feeling" (2009b, p. 5). Given this and other dilemmas, such as the time-consuming process of producing EAP materials for one's classes in general (Anthony, 2011; Dudley-Evans & St John, 1998), instructors of graduate-level research writing classes may often feel the need to review and adopt published textbooks targeting this instructional setting. In fact, doing so is consistent with Swales' argument that an access route for the designer of a language learning program, including a program in teaching graduate-level research writing, is "the well-established and sensible practice of reviewing available instructional materials" (1990, p. 69). This section, thus, looks at some published textbooks that adopt a genre-based approach and target graduate-level research writing courses.

The Swales & Feak Volumes: Content and Pedagogical Applications

Arguably, the most influential published textbooks for the teaching of graduate-level writing have been the volumes written by John Swales and Christine Feak and published by the University of Michigan Press: *Academic Writing for Graduate Students* (Swales & Feak, 1994a, 2004a, 2012a); the *Commentary for* Academic Writing for Graduate Students (Swales & Feak, 1994b, 2004b, 2012b); *English in Today's Research World* (Swales & Feak, 2000); *Abstracts and the Writing of Abstracts* (Swales & Feak, 2009); *Telling a Research Story: Writing a Literature Review* (Feak & Swales, 2009); *Creating Contexts: Writing Introductions across Genres* (Feak & Swales, 2011); and *Navigating Academia* (Swales & Feak, 2011). These textbooks, by the authors' very understated admission, have achieved "some resonance in the scholarly literatures devoted to discussions of academic discourses and the acculturation of students to those discourses" (Feak & Swales, 2014, p. 301) as well as "commercial and critical success" (Swales, 2009a, p. 190).

Academic Writing for Graduate Students: Essential Tasks and Skills

The book with the longest history in the series is *Academic Writing for Graduate Students: Essential Tasks and Skills* (hereafter *AWG*), now in its third edition (Swales & Feak, 2012a). According to Swales and Feak, *AWG* grew out of the first-year and second-year writing courses developed at Michigan's English Language Institute dating back to the late 1980s (Feak & Swales, 2014). The initial audience was international graduate students "with limited experience writing academic English," but later editions have also targeted proficient L2 users of English and L1 speakers of English (Swales & Feak, 2012a, p. ix).

The first unit of the current edition asks students to reflect on their "positioning" so as to write "academically" as competent members of their chosen academic disciplines (Swales & Feak, 2012a, p. 1). This positioning can be achieved through attention to six "considerations" in research writing—audience, purpose, organization, style, flow, and presentation (2012a, p. 3). A series of tasks then illustrates what is meant by each consideration and why each is important. For example, Task 3 in this unit asks the readers to compare and contrast two passages on the same topic. After presenting the two passages, Swales and Feak ask a series of questions to draw their readers' attention to how the differences in vocabulary, in the level of details, and in the use of definitions may be among the various resources one could use to target different audiences who may be differentially familiar with the topic. Attending to audience's needs and reactions is an integral part of analyzing and understanding the rhetorical context of any given genre or part-genre (Bawarshi & Reiff, 2010) and is part of raising students' rhetorical consciousness (Swales, 1990). Numerous other tasks in the series similarly focus on drawing students' attention to audience's expectations and needs, as will become clearer later.

In fact, noticing the different dimensions of genre becomes apparent very early in the book. For example, the letter of admittance (the good news letter) and the letter of rejection (the bad news letter) in Task 6 that are presented to show students the importance of recognizing the organizational patterns in writing are very useful in teaching students the concept of rhetorical moves. The letter of rejection often works especially well because the paragraph boundaries have been purposefully collapsed. Removing the paragraph boundaries as Swales and Feak do in Task 6 emphasizes the point that a move is "a functional term that refers to a defined and bounded communicative act that is designed to achieve one main communicative objective" (Swales & Feak, 2000, p. 35). Because a move "can range from a single finite clause to several paragraphs" (Swales & Feak, 2000, p. 35), the task very effectively conveys to students the point that they should not rely on, or merely rely on, sentence or paragraph boundaries to decipher what a move is. Instead, they should look closely at how a stretch of text constitutes a rhetorical move only when the segment of text "does a particular job" or performs a unified communicative purpose (Swales & Feak, 2009, p. 5). As shown in Chapter 2, developing genre awareness usually entails developing an awareness of the rhetorical organization, lexico-grammatical features, and the underpinning communicative context in the genre one focuses on. Therefore, helping students to develop their conceptual understanding of what a rhetorical move is, as Task 6 does so effectively, is crucial because students need to learn to recognize how the overall rhetorical organization in any research genre is made up of various rhetorical moves.

The task also effectively shows how a move and its lexico-grammatical features are driven by the readers' projected response, which is part of the rhetorical context of any given genre, thus driving home the message that any analysis of genre should focus on all three interconnected dimensions: the rhetorical organization, the lexico-grammatical features, and the underlying rhetorical context. It also shows students how a seemingly similar move may be written very differently when the underpinning communicative purposes are different, thus highlighting the need to recognize the close connections among the three dimensions of genre analysis (see Chapter 2). The "to close the letter" move shows how we can guide our students to recognize how lexico-grammatical features are driven by communicative purposes. In the good news letter of admittance, this move is written in a welcoming tone that points to the future, as seen in this sentence: "We look forward to welcoming you to Midwestern University and wish you success in your academic career" (Swales & Feak, 2012a, p. 9). The same move in the bad news letter of rejection, by contrast, closes the letter in a way that discourages any possible future communication: "I trust you will be able to pursue your academic interests elsewhere and wish you luck in your further endeavors" (Swales & Feak, 2012a, p. 10).

The focus of Unit Two is General-Specific (GS) and Specific-General (SG) texts. Swales and Feak (2012a) point out that the GS pattern can be used to answer an examination question or to provide the background to an analysis or discussion, among serving other rhetorical purposes. They illustrate how a GS text can begin with some general statements, with statistics, or with definitions, and they provide multiple tasks to guide their readers to consider the rhetorical effects of each type of opening. They then discuss how definitions, including sentence definitions and extended definitions, can be written. Again, rhetorical considerations are invoked in such a discussion. For example, readers' possible unfamiliarity with a concept or "the lack of agreement on or some ambiguity surrounding the meaning" of a term between the readers and the writer or within the discourse community in general are brought up as factors affecting the decision to provide or not to provide a definition (p. 67). Swales and Feak (2012a) note that the SG organization is frequently used in fields such as history and arts and in some medical or legal genres, such as case reports and case notes.

Unit Three focuses on the problem-solution pattern and the description of process often embedded in research genres such as research articles, research proposals, and case reports in certain fields. As is the case in other units, the authors present multiple sample passages, each with a series of discussion questions for readers to analyze in terms of the problem-solution and process-description patterns. For example, in Task One (pp. 101–103), after presenting a passage on the difficulties with research writing that some novice researchers in the sciences have encountered, they ask their readers to look at which sentences belong to which part of the four-part structure of the standard problem-solution text—situation, problem, solution, and evaluation, with the rhetorical purpose of each part listed. It is quite clear how a task like this continues to exemplify the genre-focused approach to teaching and learning research writing through guiding students to identify the rhetorical purposes and the resulting rhetorical moves in research texts.

Unit Three also consistently draws attention to many of the move-performing lexico-grammatical features through multiple tasks that ask students to recognize and practice such features. These include -*ing* clauses to indicate cause and effect (e.g., "*researchers worldwide are increasingly pressured to publish in English language journals, thus leading to a decline in publications written in languages other than English*") (p. 115; original emphasis); the passive voice in process descriptions (e.g., "*the three virus strains are then combined to create the vaccine, blended with a carrier fluid and dispensed into vials*") (p. 120); the -*ed* participles to help the flow of process descriptions (e.g., "*after the plants have been allowed to grow for some time, they are harvested and either incinerated or composted to recycle the metals*") (p. 128); active voice verbs that indicate a change of state in process description (e.g., "*the bean fractures when the load upon it becomes too great*") (p. 131); and direct and indirect questions used to problematize issues, cases, and other problems in problem-solution texts (e.g., "*however, is the data reliable?*" vs. "*however, there remains the issue of reliability*") (p. 135 and p. 136).

The unit on data commentary (Four) is a favorite among users because of its direct applicability to the findings and discussion part-genres in journal articles. I have frequently used this part with undergraduate students in the technical writing classroom to teach the Discussion section in technical reports and in teacher training courses or professional development workshops with instructors.

According to Swales and Feak (2012a), the communicative purposes in a data commentary are to "highlight the results of research; use the data to support a point or make an argument; to assess theory, common beliefs, or general practice; to compare and evaluate different data sets; to assess the reliability of the data; to discuss the implications of the data; and to make recommendations" (pp. 140–141). They then lay out the basic rhetorical organizational pattern of a data commentary that often includes three moves: to locate the data/to provide a summary statement of the data; to highlight a certain data point; and to discuss the "implications, problems, exceptions, recommendations, or other interesting aspects of the data" (p. 144). When they use discussion questions to draw their readers' attention to these moves in this rhetorical organizational pattern, they ask a series of questions that draw attention to the purposes behind a certain move (e.g., *What are the purposes of Sentences 1–3?* and *Which sentence contains the author's key point?*), the overall rhetorical organization made up by multiple moves (e.g., *How is the commentary organized overall?*), and the rhetorical purpose of data commentary in general (e.g., *On pages 140–141, we listed seven common purposes for data commentaries. In which category (or categories) does this one fall?*) (p. 143).

The unit also provides multiple tasks that focus on the lexico-grammatical features that can help research writers provide data commentaries:

- location statements and summaries—for example, *Table 5 shows... vs. ... are provided in Table 5* (p. 147)
- indicative vs. informative summary statements—for example, *Table 4 shows the types of internet misbehavior common among university students* (indicative) vs. *Table 4 shows that illegal downloading of music or films is common among students* (informative) (p. 149)

- verbs that can be used with indicative *vs.* informative summary—for example, *the verb* provide *cannot be used in an informative summary with a that clause that follows the verb* (p. 150)
- linking *as* clauses—for example, *as shown in Fig. 1...* (p. 152)
- ways of modifying or qualifying a claim—for example, *it is clear that...* vs. *it is possible that...* (p. 160)
- sentence patterns that deal with unexpected outcomes or problems, such as *may be due to ...* (p. 174)
- prepositions of time when dealing with chronological data, such as *from the 10th to the 45th minutes....* (p. 183).

Unit Five turns to writing summaries; here Swales and Feak begin with some preliminary steps in writing a summary—such as skimming texts, understanding the genres of the source texts, and taking notes—and then present a sample source text on the topic of energy drinks to illustrate an important point: an academic writer's summary of a source text should depend on the claim the writer aims to support. The unit covers a range of issues related to writing summaries, such as preventing plagiarism and learning to paraphrase by using synonyms and by changing the grammar, and introduces linguistic resources such as using certain verbs in their correct tenses to identify sources (e.g., *Barinaga claims that...*) and synthesizing multiple sources by using cohesive devices (e.g., *similarly, in contrast to,* and *to differ from*). Because many of the textual resources introduced in this unit are applicable to many types of students and because of the close attention to the strategies for preventing plagiarism, for paraphrasing, and for citing sources, this unit is full of content for teaching summary writing to different student populations.

Writing critiques is the topic of the next unit (Six). Because of the inherent disciplinary variations in critiques, this unit works especially well given the multidisciplinary mix of students in these types of courses (see Chapter 1). For example, Swales and Feak point out that "critiques are a regular part of take-home examinations" in some fields but are rarely assigned in other fields (2012a, p. 228); they also discuss how different fields have varying accepted standards of judgment regarding critiques and that what is "fair and reasonable" or what should be emphasized in critiques are field-specific (p. 228). The tasks in this unit focus on three genres—book reviews (for publication and for class), published article evaluations, and reaction papers; for each, samples and discussion questions are provided. As in other units, the move-performing lexico-grammatical features in the book review genre are explored.

The final two units, in Swales' and Feak's view, "consolidate many of the aspects of academic writing that have been stressed in earlier units" into research paper genre (p. 277)—in particular those focusing on students' pressing need to learn the Introduction-Methods-Results-Discussion (IMRD) pattern quickly. A unique feature in Unit Seven is a list (p. 286; see Appendix A in this book) in which they describe how the various organizational patterns in the previous units can fit into the different part-genres in the research article genre.

After describing the shape of a standard IMRD empirical paper and the rhetorical purpose in each section in this pattern (see Appendix B), Swales and Feak (2012a) look closely at the Methods section, raising disciplinary differences, including what the Methods sections are often called (*Methods, The Study,* or *Materials and Methods*) and what they often include in different fields (pp. 289–290). The seven moves often found in the Methods section are discussed and multiple samples presented, consistent with earlier units. The authors then move to the Results sections and the differences between data and results and those between results and discussions. Since the Results sections have a lot in common with data commentaries (Unit Four), they do not describe the organization of the Results sections in detail. They do, however, present different ways of commenting on data (*admitting difficulties in interpretation, citing agreement with previous studies, justifying the methodology,* and *pointing out discrepancies*). They draw upon from Thompson (1993) because they perceive commenting on data as remaining challenging for many novice research writers when they discuss their results.

In the final unit, Swales and Feak (2012a) look at the other parts of a standard empirical research paper: Introduction, Discussion sections, titles, abstracts, and acknowledgments. Here is where they present the famous Create a Research Space (CaRS) pattern often found in research article introductions. This pattern has three moves: establishing a research territory, establishing a niche, and occupying the niche, with each having multiple possible steps as seen in Appendix C (Swales & Feak, 2012a). They then present multiple samples and use questions similar to some of those described earlier to raise their readers' rhetorical consciousness of each of the moves and steps in the CaRS pattern.

After analyzing each of the moves in the CaRS pattern, Swales and Feak focus on the Discussion section. There, they look at how the Discussion section may fit within the research article genre in relation to the preceding Results section and the subsequent Summary and Conclusions sections. Consistent with the genre-based approach to teaching graduate-level research writing, they include multiple tasks to raise their readers' awareness of the rhetorical organizational pattern of the Discussion/Conclusion sections, which they summarize as including five moves (see Appendix D; Swales & Feak, 2012a).

Unit Eight concludes with some unfinished business, including the title, the abstract, and acknowledgments in a standard research article. As is their habit, they maintain focus on disciplinary variations, examining, for example, how titles are written differently for research papers in engineering, medicine, and applied language studies.

Abstracts and the Writing of Abstracts

AWG was originally followed by a single book in 2000 designed primarily for dissertation writers. In 2009 and 2011, some chapters were revised and expanded into small single volumes on specific part-genres: abstracts (Swales & Feak, 2009), the literature review (Feak & Swales, 2009), introductions (Feak & Swales, 2011), and academic support genres (Swales & Feak, 2011). Although the original 2000 volume was written as a follow-up to *AWG,* the small volumes were designed to be used in a variety of courses and settings—sometimes in conjunction with chapters in *AWG* and sometimes by themselves or paired with another of the small volumes. The approach to learning research writing adopted in these volumes is, according to Swales and Feak, the same as that adopted in *AWG*: "Analysis→Awareness→Acquisition→Achievement" (Swales & Feak, 2009, p. xiii). Many of the tasks are designed in the same spirit as those in *AWG* in that they all seem to aim to raise students' rhetorical awareness: their awareness of the rhetorical contexts, the rhetorical organizational patterns, and the lexico-grammatical features in research genres and part-genres. Therefore, the summary of each volume will be limited to unique aspects.

Abstracts and the Writing of Abstracts opens with a brief history and the rhetorical purposes of abstracts, which is followed by a "general analysis" of abstracts that starts with a sample abstract from one discipline and is accompanied by discussion questions. These questions cover what Swales and Feak (2009) perceive to be the important lexico-grammatical features in abstracts, such as the key clauses, the main verb tense, first-person pronouns, metadiscoursal expressions, and abbreviations, among others. One question taps into the rhetorical moves in abstracts. They present a five-move pattern and ask their readers to identify these five moves in the sample abstract: (1) background/introduction/situation, (2) present research/purpose, (3) methods/materials/subjects/ procedures, (4) results/findings, and (5) discussion/conclusion/implications/recommendation (p. 5).

Swales and Feak (2009) then analyze the five moves in the abstract part-genre (p. 9). For each of the moves, they, again, highlight certain useful rhetorical organizational and lexico-grammatical features. Unique in this volume is the examination of the structured abstracts where the moves are explicitly labelled as well as shorter abstracts in short communications, scientific letters, technical notes, research notes, and case studies in research journals. The volume also covers conference abstracts, a genre that many graduate students often need to write.

Telling a Research Story: Writing a Literature Review

Telling a Research Story: Writing a Literature Review, the most popular of the four volumes (K. Sippell, personal communication, 2017 July 26), opens with a detailed "orientations" section that directs readers' attention to the rhetorical context of the literature review part-genre, including the reasons for a literature review, the typical critiques by advisors of students' literature review, and how the literature review is normally written in their readers' fields. Reflection and discussion tasks are provided to raise their readers' awareness of these rhetorical contextual issues related to this part-genre. A particularly challenging aspect of writing a literature review is to "demonstrate that there is an organizing mind at work" behind the literature review (Swales & Feak, 2000, p. 119). Indeed, some dissertation advisors that Rogers, Zawacki, and Baker (2016) interviewed pointed out that their students often encounter difficulties in finding what their advisors would call an "anchor" or the "thread" that runs through the literature review. As a result, these students often relied on what their advisors described as the undesirable "so-and-so said this, and so-and-so said that" structure in their literature reviews (p. 63). Curry (2016) also points to the shift from summarizing to synthesizing/critiquing the literature when constructing a literature review as especially difficult for the doctoral students in her doctoral program of education.

Therefore, Feak and Swales' focused attention on how to impose a particular order serves the needs of many graduate students and junior scholars well. Feak and Swales point out several possible models by using the example of more than 25 published studies on the concept of discourse community. These studies, they suggest, could be organized according to publication date, origin of country, field, perspective on the concept, and type of publication, among other possible models of organization. They use tables and figures to show how these studies could be organized so that a particular order, anchor, or thread would become apparent to one's audience.

The rest of the volume addresses topics such as the Intro-duction-Body-Conclusion pattern in a literature review, writ-ing the first paragraph of the literature review, identifying the research sources for inclusion in one's literature review, and linking different sections of a review through the "cause and effect" or "symptom and effect" patterns. They also include examples of metadiscourse that reveal the organization of a literature review (e.g., *Part I of this review traces ....* and *the main purpose of this review has been to...*) (pp. 38, 40). Because literature cannot be reviewed without citations, they introduce various citation patterns, such as integral (author prominent) (e.g., *Muehlbach and Walsh [1995] examined....*) (p. 46) and non-integral (research prominent) citations (e.g., *research indicates that near to ... [Akerstedt, 1995]*) (p. 46). They also discuss issues such as avoiding ambiguity in cita-tions, using verb tense and aspect, and using reporting verbs correctly when citing others' studies.

After showing several examples of a literature review in a dissertation to emphasize the importance of drafting and revising, the volume includes issues such as taking a stance toward the literature through stance markers such as hedges, boosters, attitude markers, and personal pronouns. The volume ends with a discussion of how to use one's own words in a literature review through paraphrasing and summarizing.

Creating Contexts: Writing Introductions across Genres

Given that the literature review is often a part of the introduc-tion, *Creating Contexts: Writing Introductions across Genres* (Feak & Swales, 2011) focuses on introductions in research genres such as course papers, book reviews, journal articles, short research reports, proposals, and dissertations. This volume also opens with a "preliminary considerations" sec-tion (pp. 1–15) that looks at issues such as when to write the introduction section, the overall shape of the Introduction, and how to start the Introduction.

This orientation section is followed by a review of introduc-tions in course papers, book reviews, and reviews of journal articles and book chapters. Although learning to write the introductory sections in these genres well is important for graduate students and, in the case of course papers, undergraduate students, graduate-level research writers and their instructors may find the detailed look at the introductions in research articles (RAs)[1] especially relevant. In fact, the authors devote nearly 40 percent of this 136-page book to the introductory sections in RAs. They start their description of RA introductions by emphasizing the connections between the Introduction and the Discussion sections in a RA. After listing some of the frequent criticisms of poorly written RA introductions, they present five short introductions from general disciplines and ask their readers to describe the organization in each of these introductions.

They then usher in the well-known CaRS model, looking at both the moves, steps, and the specific lexico-grammatical features in these moves. Compared with the discussion in *AWG*, the discussion of CaRS in this volume seems to be more reflective; they point out that the model may seem "formulaic" as a "simplified" version "of what might be done in reality" and, thus, lacks specificity (Feak & Swales, 2011, p. 56). To support such an argument, they provide eight additional areas to include in JA introductions that may not fit neatly into the CaRS model, as uncovered by other researchers (Appendix E).

Like all their textbooks, they provide their readers with multiple tasks to analyze and practice a range of lexico-grammatical features that are important for performing the various moves in the introduction part-genre. These features include integral and non-integral citations, expressing agreement and disagreement with a cited study, gap-indicating statements, and gap-filling statements, among others. They end the book with a comparatively brief discussion of the introductions in proposals and in dissertations.

---

[1] Note that Swales & Feak use the term *research article* [RA] instead of journal article. Except when referring to articles as referenced in Swales & Feak, I use JA.

Navigating Academia: Writing Supporting Genres

In this volume, Swales and Feak (2011) focus on genres that are often publicly unavailable for study or analysis (e.g., occluded genres) such as the graduate school application Statement of Purpose, letters of recommendation, responses to journal reviewers, and various kinds of email messages. When discussing these genres, they, again, focus intensively on the rhetorical context, the rhetorical organization, and the lexico-grammatical features in these genres, similar to what they do in the other volumes. This volume is unique in being designed more for individual than course/workshop use.

Swales & Feak *Commentaries*

All of the Swales and Feak books have an accompanying *Commentary*. They are called this because of Swales and Feak have "rejected the traditional label of 'Instructor's Manual'" (Swales & Feak, 2012b, p. iii). The *Commentary for AWG* is sold separately but available to teachers who adopt the student textbook for their courses (it can also be purchased); it has also been adopted in some courses on the teaching of writing (L1 and/or L2) (K. Sippell, personal communication, 2017 July 26). For the small volumes, the commentaries are available online at www.press.umich.edu/script/press/elt/compsite/ETRW. These commentaries reiterate the point that the "aim throughout is to raise participants' perceptions and sensitivities to the language and structure of texts and to raise their awareness of likely audience reactions to those texts" (Swales, Feak, & Irwin, 2011, p. 1). Some of them include the perspectives of one of their research assistants, which creates a "dialogue between the tasks and the users of the book" (Swales, Feak, & Irwin, 2011, p. 2).

The Swales and Feak Volumes: Implications

Among the many reasons that these books are must-have resources for graduate-level research writers and their instructors are the details about important research genres and the genre-focused and disciplinarily responsive way these details are covered. The more than 800 pages of materials in the five books feature numerous details about a range of research genres and part genres. But it is also about how the details are covered. They are presented in a way that epitomizes the genre-oriented approach to teaching and learning research writing—that is, they are presented in a way that shows the close attention to all three interrelated aspects (rhetorical organizations, lexico-grammatical features, and rhetorical contexts) that those adopting the genre-focused approach to teaching research writing should attend to (see Chapter 2). Multiple tasks and the questions by design encourage discovery and raise the readers' awareness of the rhetorical organizations in various genres and part-genres. Tasks that highlight rhetorical organizations are almost always accompanied by tasks that draw the readers' attention to the lexico-grammatical features underpinning the rhetorical organization in question. Many examples, plus the more than 50 Language Focus boxes, point to the authors' close attention to the lexico-grammatical features that perform or enact various rhetorical moves in the genres and part-genres in question. The details about the rhetorical organizations and the lexico-grammatical features in key research genres have also been presented in a way that draws the readers' attention to the rhetorical contexts of the genres or part-genres in the book.

Apart from the genre-focused manner in which research genres are presented, the details about various research genres and part-genres have also been analyzed and discussed in a way that draws the readers' attention to disciplinary variations in research genres. The third edition of *AWG*, for example, includes texts from material chemistry, electrical engineering, communication, economic psychology, civil and infrastructural engineering, psychology, botany, nursing studies, and many other disciplines (see Swales & Feak, 2012a, pp. 412–414, for a list of the sources of these sample texts). The other volumes also include many examples from a variety of disciplines.

The use of a variety of disciplines then enables instructors and students to compare and contrast the samples from different fields. For example, the volume on writing introductions (Feak & Swales, 2011) presents five short introductions from the various fields (see the chapter on research article introductions). Readers are asked to describe the rhetorical organization and then to write about anything they find interesting or problematic in each. The readers are also asked to compare and contrast these samples with the published research articles in their own fields.

The attention to disciplinary variations can also be seen in the way some of the lexico-grammatical features are presented and analyzed in the series. For example, citing Hyland (1999), Swales and Feak show reporting verbs frequently used in different fields (2012a, p. 213; Feak & Swales, 2009, p. 55). Similarly, the volume on *Abstracts and the Writing of Abstracts* (Swales & Feak, 2009, pp. 6–8) presents several research article abstracts and asks the readers to analyze the key clauses, first-person pronouns, metadiscourse, acronyms and abbreviations, and other features in these discipline-specific samples.

The quantity of details related to the research genres in question, the genre-focused way that these details are presented, and the close attention to disciplinary variations when the details are discussed and analyzed have at least two implications: (1) the wide-ranging materials offer the potential for the textbooks to be used in different settings of research writing instruction and (2) they can be useful for self-study or the classroom.

In terms of different settings, instructors offering a whole course that focuses on the RA genre (e.g., Burgess & Cargill, 2013; Fairbanks & Dias, 2016; Huang, 2014; Gustafsson, Eriksson, & Karlsson, 2016; Starfield, 2016; Starfield & Mort, 2016) could base their teaching on Units Four, Seven, and Eight of *AWG* and supplement these units with materials from the relevant sections on RAs in *Abstracts and the Writing of Abstracts* and *Creating Contexts* (see Huang, 2014, for an example of using Unit Two in *AWG* to teach the writing of RA introductions in Taiwan). Those offering a workshop on preventing plagiarism to graduate or undergraduate students could draw on Unit Five in *AWG*. Faculty invited to offer workshops to help graduate students become professionalized may find that the Conference Abstracts unit in *Abstracts and the Writing of Abstracts* (Swales & Feak, 2009) or the unit on

Moving On to an Academic or Research Career in *Navigating Academia* offer plenty of insightful materials (Swales & Feak, 2011). The attention to disciplinary variations in the materials makes these materials suitable for classes or workshops with a multidisciplinary mix of students in them, as previously noted.

Second, instructors can use these volumes for self-study and professional development purposes as a way to continue to increase their knowledge of graduate-level research genres, their understanding of the genre-focused approach to teaching research writing, and their sensitivity to the discipline-specific nature of research writing. Some instructors of graduate-level research writing classes are often graduate students themselves in TESOL/applied linguistics (Min, 2016) or in writing studies (Norris & Tardy, 2006; Tardy, 2009) programs and may find themselves unprepared or underprepared when it comes to graduate-level research genres or discipline-specific writing (Min, 2016; Norris & Tardy, 2006; Tardy, 2009). In fact, they may not know enough about research writing to begin with. These volumes, with the numerous details on a wide range of research genres and part-genres, make them comprehensive and insightful teacher development resources for increasingly enriching instructors' knowledge of graduate-level research writing. I still remember how the discussions of unreal conditionals (e.g., *...would have been more persuasive* vs. *...would be stronger* ...) in Unit Six of *AWG* brought to my attention the different ways of critiquing others' works (Swales & Feak, 2012a) or how some of the tasks have helped me understand the CaRS model better as well as help me fill certain holes in my knowledge of writing journal article introductions (Cheng, 2015a).

Apart from a possible inadequate knowledge of research genres or part-genres, novice instructors of graduate-level research writing may also not know enough about how to use genre analysis as the vehicle to raise their students' rhetorical consciousness. They may not know enough about how to guide students in becoming aware of genre as a conceptual tool for analyzing any genre and of genre-specific features. It is quite clear that the volumes by Swales and Feak epitomize the genre-focused approach in a theoretically sophisticated, yet pedagogically accessible, manner. These books exemplify how to raise students' rhetorical consciousness through application of the ESP approach to genre analysis that covers all three interlocking components—the rhetorical contexts, the rhetorical organizations, and the lexico-grammatical features—when analyzing any research genre. Seen in this light, these materials deepen instructors' knowledge of the genre-focused approach to graduate-level research writing instruction and help them develop their own materials or guide their students' analysis of research genres in the classroom.

Learning to deal with disciplinary variations in research writing in classroom settings or even coming to terms with the discipline-specific nature of research writing may be daunting or intimidating to many novice instructors of research writing. Some, in fact, may still hold problematic assumptions about discipline-specific writing and field-specific knowledge-making practices (Min, 2016). Because the Swales and Feak volumes invoke many studies on discipline-specific writing and present tasks that direct the readers' attention to disciplinary variations in research genres, they will increase all instructors' sensitivity to, and knowledge of, disciplinary specificity in academic writing and enhance their skills at conducting comparisons and contrasts of discipline-specific genre samples in their classes.

Thesis and Dissertation Writing in a Second Language: A Handbook for Supervisors

Other published textbooks or handbooks based on the genre-centered approach to research writing instruction are also available. Paltridge and Starfield's *Thesis and Dissertation Writing in a Second Language: A Handbook for Supervisors* (2007) is one notable example. Although it is called a handbook, the authors believe that it is also suitable for courses or workshops on thesis and dissertation writing. Similar to the books of Swales and Feak and consistent with the genre-based approach, the book emphasizes all three dimensions of genre analysis. First, it delves into the rhetorical context, or the "social and cultural context in which the student's thesis or dissertation is being produced" (p. 3). It includes the readers and writers of this valued genre, the role of background knowledge and discourse community expectations in driving one's thesis, the attitudes to knowledge that one should adopt when writing a thesis, identity issues of burgeoning scholars/dissertation writers, and disciplinary variations in theses and dissertations. For instance, in one of the learning tasks, Paltridge and Starfield (2007) list the characteristics of high-quality and low-quality theses based on the research of Holbrook, Bourke, Lovat, and Dally (2004) who looked at 803 examiners' reports on 301 theses. "Expert use of the literature in design of the study and discussion of the findings," for example, is the characteristic of high-quality theses (Paltridge & Starfield, 2007, p. 19). They then present quotes from studies about the quality of theses from thesis examinations. For example, a research thesis ought to "tell a compelling story articulately whilst pre-empting inevitable critiques" (p. 20). They ask supervisors and instructors of thesis writing to discuss with students the implications of these criteria or quotes. The book also asks thesis supervisors and instructors to ask students to look for their university's guidelines and criteria for the examination of theses and dissertations so as "to consider these criteria while writing their research proposal and ... [consider] in what way their project fits with the university's criteria" (p. 57).

This book then examines the thesis proposal genre as well as the overall shape of a thesis before zooming in to every chapter in a typical thesis: the Introduction, the Background, the Methodology, the Discussion, and the Conclusion. Consistent with the genre-based approach to research writing instruction, they pay close attention to the rhetorical organization in each of these thesis chapters. Take their analysis of the Results/Findings sections as an example. Here, they present to their readers the "typical elements," or the typical rhetorical moves, in the Results sections of a thesis (p. 135) and introduce the specific steps or sub-moves within each. Using five excerpts from various disciplines to illustrate these moves and steps, the authors carefully label the moves and steps in the margins. In a learning task, they ask students to read two or three Results sections in recent theses and to identify the rhetorical organizational pattern by paying special attention to questions such as *how the research results are presented, whether the three moves as shown in Table 9.1 occur, in what order they occur, the extent of recycling of the moves,* and *the purpose of each of the moves* (p. 144).

Consistent with the genre-based approach to research writing instruction, Paltridge and Starfield (2007) also draw their readers' attention to "aspects of language use particular to thesis and dissertation writing" (p. 1). For example, when analyzing the Results/Findings sections in theses/dissertations, they highlight such features as the passive voice (*is considered, are referred to, are presented,* etc.), past tense verbs (*identified, was assessed*) and hedging (*should be viewed, is more than likely…., and … is a reasonable assumption…*) (pp. 138, 139, and 142).

Paltridge and Starfield (2007) also pay close attention to discipline-specific expectations and textual practices. They recognize that different disciplines often have their own preferred ways of doing things, so it is important to "make these as explicit as possible for students" (p. 80). To achieve this goal, they suggest that students look at several theses in their fields and analyze the rhetorical patterns and discipline-specific expectations. When analyzing the different chapters and sections in theses, they also look at samples in multiple fields to further emphasize the importance of studying discipline-specific textual practices. These fields are from education, architecture, cultural studies, dental science, physics, history, marine biology, dental sciences, linguistics, and engineering, among others.

The rich details about the thesis/dissertation genre, the genre-focused approach driving the discussion of the details, and the attention to disciplinary specificity in the book make this handbook suitable for both classroom instruction and for instructors' professional development. The book is based on the authors' many years of teaching thesis and dissertation writing in Australia, so it, quite understandably, includes primarily, though not exclusively, thesis samples from Australian universities. The theoretical framework and the scholarship the authors draw upon to analyze these thesis samples and the scholarship, however, come from the authors' own as well as the collective scholarship of EAP researchers from many geographical contexts. Consequently, the results of their analysis described in detail in their book are applicable to L2 writers of English theses or dissertations anywhere in the world.

Writing an Applied Linguistics Thesis or Dissertation: A Guide to Presenting Empirical Research

John Bitchener's *Writing an Applied Linguistics Thesis or Dissertation: A Guide to Presenting Empirical Research* (2010) is unique in focusing only on master's thesis writing in the field of applied linguistics, although Bitchener believes the book can be useful to those conducting and reporting empirical research in general. Bitchener's book also exemplifies the genre-centered approach to research writing instruction that aims to raise students' rhetorical consciousness. Bitchener adopts a relatively deductive approach in his analysis and presentation—that is, for each of the thesis chapters or sections, he explicitly lays out the moves and the sub-moves and then labels them in the corresponding chapter/section in a thesis that is used as a model throughout the book. For example, he points out that the Abstract includes introduction, purpose, method, product, and conclusion and that each includes multiple sub-moves. Then he analyzes the sample sentence by sentence, looking at the purpose in each and how these sentences, with their rhetorical purposes, constitute a certain move or sub-move. Since Bitchener is a disciplinary insider in applied linguistics, he is able to draw on his expertise when analyzing these sentences.

Consistent with the genre-oriented approach, Bitchener also highlights a range of lexico-grammatical features that perform the specific moves in question. For example, when analyzing the abstract, he focuses on verb tense as "the most important linguistic features ... when writing an abstract" (2010, p. 30). He points out how the present continuous (e.g., ... *is currently receiving an increasing amount of attention*), the present perfect (e.g., *the present study has continued that focus...*), past simple (e.g., *...who posited that ...*), and present simple (e.g., *the results of this study contribute to an understanding of...*) are used in various sentences to fulfill different purposes in the abstract genre (pp. 30–31).

Although Bitchener's book (2010) does not cover the rhetorical context part as extensively as the Swales and Feak volumes (e.g., 2012a) or as Paltridge and Starfield (2007) does, the discussions of the rhetorical moves touch on communicative purposes as well as the overall goals of empirical research in applied linguistics, thus again showing the attention to all three aspects of genre analysis that are critical for raising students' rhetorical awareness. Similar to Paltridge and Starfield (2007), the analytical framework used in Bitchener makes the results of analysis applicable to students writing theses in applied linguistics in a wide range of geographical contexts. In fact, Bitchener points out that the materials have been field tested in many countries.

In sum, throughout the history of English language teaching, textbooks have existed to provide a coherent syllabus and structure to the teaching and learning process, especially when teachers lack adequate training, the time/resources to develop materials of their own, or an acceptable level of proficiency in the language they are teaching. A look at these textbooks has shown how they have exemplified the genre-oriented approach to research writing instruction through their attention to the three dimensions of genre, through their references of existing research findings, and through their commitment to the goal of raising students' rhetorical consciousness. Therefore, these materials can not only serve the needs of various graduate-level research writing classes, but can also help novice instructors develop their professional expertise and pedagogical content knowledge as teachers of graduate-level writing.

"In-House" Topic-, Course-, or Program-Specific Genre-Focused Materials

Some instructors may prefer to develop their own materials that target the specific needs of their students. The literature has reported specifically on some "in-house" materials—that is, they were not published as a textbook or as part of a textbook that can be used directly in a graduate-level research writing class; instead, they are published as examples to support these authors/materials developers' discussions of various issues related to graduate-level research writing materials development in particular or to learning research writing in general. They are also "in-house" in the sense that they are usually program-, course-, or even topic-specific. Some are based on corpora, defined either in the loose sense of "an accumulation of texts used for study" (Swales & Feak, 2009, p. 3) analyzed manually by instructors and students or in the strict sense of a collection of computer-searchable materials. One example of such "in-house" materials is presented here to provide novice instructors with helpful perspectives on materials development specific for the graduate-level writing classroom.

Adopting a "genre-inspired" approach, Lynne Flowerdew (2016, p. 1) developed her own materials to teach a group of students in the sciences at a university in Hong Kong the grant proposal genre. She used a proposal on the topic of early detection of cancer to guide her students to analyze the typical rhetorical organization in the research grant proposal genre. The organization includes moves such as "territory," "gap/niche," "goal," "means," "achievements," "benefits," and "future recommendations" (L. Flowerdew, 2016, p. 5). She then used a proposal abstract from the Michigan Corpus of Upper-level Student Papers to show to her students certain rhetorical organizational patterns specific to the grant proposal genre, such as combining several moves in a sentence. For example, the sentence "my studies seek to profile..... by doing a transcriptome analysis," according to Flowerdew, combines the "goal" move, as seen in "my studies seek to profile," and

the "means" or "method" move, as seen in "by doing a transcriptome analysis" (2016, p. 6).

Consistent with the genre-based approach, Lynne Flowerdew's (2016) teaching of the research proposal genre also
shows her intensive focus on the lexico-grammatical features
that she believes to be "a valuable means of identifying particular move structures" (p. 8). To help her students build their
repertoire of useful phrases for performing various rhetorical
moves, she used text segments to ask her students to underline
phrases that signal specific rhetorical moves. These lexico-
grammatical features include phrases such as "the identification of subgroup of.... will allow a more effective ...." or "the
study of .... may lead to similar investigations on other human
cancers" to signal the "benefits + other potential applications"
move. They also include phrases such as "...since 1920s the
most important separation process used...... The importance
of flotation for providing....to the expanding metallurgical
industries is presently increasing rapidly..." to perform the
claiming "'real world' territory" move (p. 8 and p. 9; original
emphasis). When discussing the rhetorical organization, she
also consistently points out features that perform each of these
moves, such as "aims to" for the "goal" move, "will be used"
for the "methods" move, "we expect" for the "anticipated
results" move, and "in the near future, ...at other body site"
for the "other potential applications" move (p. 4).

Equally importantly, Flowerdew (2016) seems to have woven
her discussions of these organizational and lexico-grammatical
features unique to the research grant proposal genre into her
in-class analysis of the rhetorical contexts underpinning
these features. For example, when analyzing the rhetorical
organizational patterns, she asked her students to tap into their
responses as a reader as well as their understanding of the
role of discourse community in shaping the proposal genre by
asking them to explain whether they would fund the project if
they were a member of the research grants committee. When
explaining how grant proposal writers combine the "goal" and
the "method" moves, she drew her students' attention to the

grant proposal writer's intended rhetorical effect of implying that the approach, technique, or method adopted in a project is unproblematic by linking the approach/technique/method to the goal statement (Feng & Shi, 2004; Hyland, 2000; cited in L. Flowerdew, 2016, p. 6).

Other examples of "in-house" program-or course-specific materials include Charles (2007, 2012), Feak and Swales (2010), Eriksson (2012), Starfield (2003), Swales and Lindemann (2002), and others. These materials targeted different student populations (perinatology researchers in Feak & Swales, 2010, for example, as opposed to graduate student writers who have never written a grant proposal in L. Flowerdew, 2016). They focused on different genres or part-genres that needed to be covered (literature review in Swales and Lindemann, 2002, and thesis in Starfield, 2003). These teaching materials resulted from an instructor's own genre analysis of the samples used in class, as in the case of Starfield (2003) or L. Flowerdew (2016), or from corpus-driven, specialized searches, as in the case of Charles (2007, 2012), Eriksson (2012), and Feak and Swales (2010). The materials were also based on authentic texts (e.g., Feak & Swales, 2010; L. Flowerdew, 2016; Eriksson, 2012; Starfield, 2003), constructed texts (Swales & Lindemann, 2002), modified texts (Charles, 2007), or computer-driven searches or concordance results (Charles, 2007; Eriksson, 2012; Feak & Swales, 2010).

Despite these differences, they all share certain common characteristics: They focus on rhetorical contexts and communicative purposes (Charles, 2007; Swales & Lindemann, 2002), rhetorical organizations (Starfield, 2003; Swales & Lindemann, 2002) or a particular rhetorical function within a certain organizational pattern (Charles, 2007; Eriksson, 2012; Feak & Swales, 2010), lexico-grammatical features (Eriksson, 2012; Feak & Swales, 2010; L. Flowerdew, 2016; Starfield, 2003), or a combination of all three, thus adhering to and exemplifying the genre-focused approach to graduate-level research writing instruction.

Novice instructors can study these cases to learn to develop their own program-, course-, or genre-specific materials that cover the three important dimensions of genre analysis. Developing one's own materials successfully can add to a "sense of enjoyment and self-satisfaction" as practitioners of graduate-level writing instruction, as noted by Swales (2009b, p. 12).

Learner-Contributed Reference Collections as Pedagogical Materials

An additional source of pedagogical materials often consists of learner-contributed genre samples. Multiple accounts of instructors asking students to collect genre samples to be used as teaching materials have appeared in the literature (Charles, 2007, 2012; Cortes, 2007; Fredericksen & Mangelsdorf, 2014; Huang, 2014; Kuteeva, 2013; Lee & Swales, 2006; Starfield, 2016), showing that asking course participants to collect samples of texts from their disciplines to generate teaching materials has become a common pedagogical practice. However, in the literature, instructions or guidelines on how students should collect genre samples still seem to be rather vague, if existent. This section presents an assignment sheet based on previous research writing classes and workshops I have taught to offer some perspectives on the process of guiding students to collect their reference collections, with the hope of encouraging others to engage in comparable pedagogical practices.

As reported earlier (e.g., Cheng, 2015a and see Chapter 1), students in my graduate-level writing classroom often represented multiple disciplines as is often the case in graduate-level research writing. Aiming to use student-collected published research articles (RAs) as the teaching materials to achieve the objectives of developing students' genre awareness as well as their awareness of genres (see Chapter 2), I would customarily request students to each collect at least five published journal articles (JAs) from recent volumes of well-respected refereed journals in their respective fields to each build a reference collection, or "an accumulation of texts used for study and analysis" (Swales & Feak, 2009, p. 3). They would send me electronic copies of their selected JAs accompanied by a brief written explanation (one page in total) of why each was chosen. This process normally starts with an assignment sheet similar to that in Figure 3.1.

As shown in Figure 3.1, these guidelines aim to provide some details to help students build their reference collections. The assignment sheet in Figure 3.1 specifies that students should focus on the JA genre, as this genre is still considered the "pre-eminent genre of physical sciences, engineering, much of the social sciences and, increasingly, the humanities" (Hyland, 2015a, p. 113) and still the primary, or only, focus in some graduate-level research writing classes (e.g., Cheng, 2015a, 2015b; Gustafsson, Eriksson, & Karlsson, 2016; Huang, 2014).

Point 1 and Point 2 under "how should you select your JA samples" suggest that students collect samples from at least three well-respected journals in the field. Several suggestions in these two points are based on some previously noticed problems. For example, students who may be relatively new to their disciplines may not know what a "well-respected journal" is or what the well-respected research journals in their respective fields are. A PhD student in leisure studies, for instance, once selected a three-page thought piece called "Advocacy update: The fight to save Land and Water Conservation Fund (LWCF)" from a practitioner's magazine, rather than a research journal. (The Land and Water Conservation Fund is a state-level assistance program that helps local park land acquisition and recreational facility development across the United States.) The article explains why LWCF is important, why it is in crisis, and what the readers can do to save it (calling the state representatives is one of the suggested actions, for example). Another student selected some work-in-progress articles from a collection of working papers published by an academic department at a university.

Problems like these led to the suggestions that students consult the disciplinary experts or more experienced members in their areas (Point 1) because doing so would not only help

Figure 3.1: A Sample Assignment Sheet for Collecting JAs for a Reference Collection

---

ESL/ENGL XXXX (G):

Assignment sheet for collecting journal articles in your field for the genre analysis tasks

Why should you collect journal article samples?

From this week on, we will analyze additional genre-specific features in journal articles (JAs) in the fields represented in this class. To do so, I need you to each collect at least five JAs from your field. I will use these JAs to develop tasks for in-class genre analysis. You will also analyze the features in these articles out of class. You can then use what you have noticed in these JAs to help you write in this class and beyond.

How should you select your JA samples?

1. Select JAs from well-respected and widely read research journals in your field. These journals should be refereed or peer reviewed. If you are not sure about which journals are well respected in your field, ask your advisor, the professors in the subject-matter courses you are taking, or the more knowledgeable students in your program or in your research lab for their advice. The websites of the national and international professional associations in your area could also lead you to some well-respected journals. Some research methodology or writing guidebooks in your field may also point you to the frequently read journals.

2. Select your JAs from at least three different journals. The different journals may give you a sense of what JAs are like in different publication venues.

3. Select fairly recent JAs, preferably from the past three years. If you choose an older JA, explain why it is especially valuable for the class and for you to analyze it.

4. Select JAs with the "Introduction-Method-Results/ Discussion-Conclusion" pattern that we have looked at briefly.

5. Select JAs that are preferably closely related to your academic interests and research methods. Choose JAs that you see yourself writing and publishing in the future. However, collect these JAs with an eye for why they are especially suitable for your analysis as a writer, rather than merely as a researcher aiming to learn new ideas or research methods from these JAs.

Figure 3.1 (Continued)

> 6. Select well-written JAs. You may not have a clear idea of what "well-written" means yet. At this point, read through the introduction section of each article you plan to include in your collection quickly. Do the ideas flow from one sentence to the next and from one paragraph to the next quite logically? Can you understand and follow the authors' ideas relatively effortlessly even though the content may look unfamiliar to you? If the answer is yes to both questions, this article is possibly well written enough for your analysis. Again, if you are unsure, ask your advisor and other more experienced people for their advice. I could look at these articles and tell you what I think of them as well.
>
> 7. Select JAs with electronic or PDF copies that can be copied and pasted for in-class as well as out-of-class study and analysis later.
>
> 8. Feel free to switch to other JAs later if you find more suitable ones. Send me a copy of the new JAs.
>
> <u>What do you do after you have selected the articles?</u>
>
> A. Explain in a one-page memo why each of the JAs may be suitable for your analysis as a writer, rather than as a researcher aiming to learn new ideas or research methods from them. Use the reference style in your field to list the JAs.
>
> B. Upload the electronic copy of each JA to [the university's online course management system].

students identify suitable journals as the sources for their possible JA samples, but also help socialize them into their fields. The process of becoming familiar with the research journals in one's field is part of the process of understanding one's aspiring discourse community.

Consistent with the suggestions in Point 1, instructors could consult students' disciplinary advisors or professors, as students are advised to do, to identify well-respected journals in each student's field. In reality, however, doing so may not be feasible for many instructors, especially if the students in each section of a writing course are from multiple disciplines or if the instructor (who may be a graduate student or a adjunct faculty) does not have the institutional clout to elicit a positive response (see Charles, 2012, about a related observation).

Given this possibility, searching the websites of students' professional or academic associations is, sometimes, an effective source for instructors of graduate-level research writing to help students and, indirectly, help writing instructors themselves understand students' discourse communities and the representative journals. For example, after noticing the advocacy update opinion piece submitted by the student in leisure studies, I asked the student to stop by my office and asked her about the premier professional organization or organizations in her field (I offered AAAL and TESOL as the examples for me). I also conducted internet searches with her using terms such as "the well-respected academic or professional associations in leisure studies." The conversation with her and the new searches led to the website of the National Recreation and Park Association (NRPA) at www.nrpa.org (in fact, NRPA was mentioned several times in the advocacy opinion piece mentioned in the previous paragraph). The website included a tab called "Research" that led to another tab called "Journals." There, the three journals sponsored by NRPA and edited by university researchers were listed with the different focuses and intended audiences of each journal described in detail. The student said she would look at the articles from these three journals a little more closely and select JAs from them that would be more suitable for study and analysis. After the conversation, I continued to browse through the NRPA website and the journals, including some of the articles in them, to learn more about the disciplinary expectations, values, and topics in this student's field.

Another source for instructors is discipline-specific research or writing guidebooks. For example, a book on research writing in construction management lists sixteen journals read by scholars in the field, including five published by the American Society of Civil Engineers (Naoum, 2013). Some guidebooks list journals read by researchers in various sub-disciplines. For example, a handbook on dissertation writing in geography suggests that those deciding to work on periglacial geomorphology should read the journal *Permafrost and Periglacial Processes* (Parsons & Knight, 2015).

Given their potential usefulness in the article selection process, professional associations and discipline-specific guidebooks were suggested as resources for students to identify journals from which articles may be selected, as seen in Point 1. These resources, due to their relatively easy availability, especially compared with the sometimes unreliable, if available, access to students' subject-matter faculty, could be useful for instructors of graduate-level writing classes to learn about students' fields as well as to provide guidance to students who may still be relatively new to their respective disciplines.

Point 3 under "how should you select your JA samples" emphasizes the recent nature of the JAs. Many of the students are in the sciences or social sciences where recently published research often receives greater attention than older studies do, so this guideline hopes to add some face validity to the process by aligning the JA collection process with the common JA reading practice in students' own fields.

Point 4 guides students to focus on JAs that report on empirical data using some forms of the IMRD pattern, as other practitioners of graduate-level research writing instruction have similarly guided their students to do (e.g., Kuteeva, 2013; Swales & Feak, 2012a). Specifically, such a focus requires learners to steer clear of other journal publications, such as review articles, book reviews, editorials, or short communication, which they may need to learn to write much later in their academic careers (see Swales and Feak's discussion of these publications in 2012a). Also, on more than one occasion, some students have included review articles or meta-analyses in their reference collections. For example, a student majoring in TESOL once chose Diane Belcher's 2006 article titled "English for Specific Purposes: Teaching to perceived needs and imagined futures in worlds of work, study, and everyday life" published in *TESOL Quarterly* to include in her reference collection. Another student, in sociology this time, chose a paper titled "Explaining U.S. urban regimes: A qualitative comparative analysis" in the "New Directions" section of a journal entitled *Urban Affairs Review*. A third student, in business, picked an article called "Salesperson adaptive selling behavior and customer orientation: A meta-analysis" from the *Journal of Marketing Research*.

I explained that these articles would certainly help them become knowledgeable about their chosen areas of interest very quickly, but articles like these may not be good examples of the genre for their collections. An empirical article reporting on data or containing some form of data analysis may have more direct and immediate relevance to what they would be writing soon, either in the form of a dissertation or their first few JA publications.

Based on these previous problems and observations, Point 4 requires students to pick articles that report on empirical data with some form of an IMRD pattern in it. Of course, Point 4 is meant to be a general guideline rather than an absolute rule. As pointed out by Swales and Feak (2009), some fields, such as astrophysics, do not publish articles with empirical data because experimentation is impossible. In fact, two of my students in mathematics and physics, respectively, reported to me that they seldom read articles that follow an IMRD pattern. Given these findings, it would be advisable to work with students on a case-by-case basis despite what Point 4 requires.

Point 5 aims to address another potential problem: Here, students are encouraged to choose JAs closely related to their academic interests and their research methodology, as they may be more interested in analyzing these articles than articles unrelated to their academic work. For example, it probably would not be very motivating for a student interested in ESP research, to use an area within the field of applied linguistics as an example, to select or analyze a JA on the acquisition of the definite article that focuses on the reaction time in a controlled experiment that used eye tracking as the main method.

That said, a previously noticed problem is that some students did not draw any clear distinctions between readings that could serve as samples for genre analysis as opposed to those that seem to serve more as resources to increase their disciplinary knowledge about the research topics and the research methodologies in the field. In more than one instance, some students presented to me articles that they happened to be assigned to read in their disciplinary classes or some JAs published by the members of the research groups or research labs that they were affiliated with simply because they would like to increase their knowledge of the topic. The example of the student choosing Belcher's article (2006) falls into this category as well.

With this problem in mind, Point 5 was added to remind students to select JAs with an eye for why the articles are especially suitable for their analysis and their development of rhetorical knowledge, rather than just as a source for learning new ideas or research methods as part of developing their subject matter knowledge. Tardy (2009) has argued that both rhetorical and subject matter knowledge are important domains in learners' genre knowledge, but students may need to tackle different aspects of genre at different times. Students need to be reminded of the subtle distinctions between focusing on the rhetorical vs. the subject matter aspects of the JAs, distinctions that may require them to adopt, or to be trained to adopt, different stances toward the articles—as a genre analyst in the context of the writing class or as a researcher in the discipline. This point is reemphasized in Point A under "What do you do after you have selected the articles" where students are required to explain why they believe each chosen article is suitable for their study and analysis in the writing classroom, instead of in the subject matter classroom.

Somewhat related to Point 5, Point 6 requires students to select JAs that are well written. The challenge here is, because most course participants in research writing classes are not yet experienced or published writers, it may be difficult for them to determine whether an article is well written enough to serve as a worthy example for studying. In addition, many such students are L2 users and may feel unsure about the quality of the language in the samples they have collected (see a similar observation in Charles, 2012).

My suggested solution to this program is explained in Point 6. Specifically, students are asked to read at least a portion of each paper, preferably the Introduction, to develop a sense of whether the ideas in that portion of the text flow in a logical and accessible manner. At least two rationales are behind this suggestion: (1) Students at this point in a writing course have probably been introduced to the concepts of purpose, organization, flow, style, and presentation, so these concepts could at least serve as the criteria for students to evaluate the quality of writing in the possible JA samples; and (2) research writers who pay attention to these issues may be clear, coherent writers who may also be more aware of other larger organizational issues than other writers would, so their writing samples may have a better chance of serving as effective examples for course participants' study and analysis in and out of class.

Another line of defense, one that is mentioned very briefly near the end of Point 6, is that as the instructor, I read these articles quickly myself after they have been uploaded. I pay attention to the flow of ideas as seen through the authors' organization, style, and other issues that I often ask students to pay attention to. In addition, I pay attention to whether the Introduction contains some of the elements of the CaRS model. Some critics may argue that my attention to the presence of the CaRS pattern risks straitjacketing the students into it, resulting in the phenomenon of teaching the CaRS pattern too well for students to see other possibilities, as pointed out by Belcher (2009). My response to this concern is that a certain level of awareness of the CaRS model may point to an author's awareness of the audience-anticipated and disciplinarily sanctioned rhetorical organization not only in the introductory section, but also in other sections of a JA. Using the criterion of paying close attention to whether a JA author has an awareness of CaRS or the "deficiencies in past literature" model could at least help instructors and students rule out JAs of some highly digressive, rambling authors whose samples may not be especially beneficial to students, at least not at this stage when students are still being introduced to the basics of research genres.

I have kept Point 7 on the assignment sheet even though most journals today have an online presence with PDF files readily available.

Point 8 is derived from the observation that there can be a learning curve to the process of collecting JAs, and students should feel free to switch some articles out and add new ones later until a collection that is uniquely useful to each of them is built.

Despite some concerns, the process of working with students to collect genre samples can be a rewarding learning experience to instructors. The reference collections from previous students have introduced me to hundreds of research journals, some of them as "exotic" to me as the *International Journal of Clothing Science and Technology*, *Journal of Microelectronmechanical Systems*, or *American Journal of Physiological Cellular and Molecular Physiology*. I have found that a new journal from which an article was selected is always an opportunity to learn something new about discipline-specific writing in general and about a new field in particular. For example, after noticing two articles collected by two different students from the journal *Review of Scientific Instruments*, I went to the journal's website to check it out (http://scitation.aip.org/content/aip/journal/rsi/info/about). I was quite surprised to find that this journal had been publishing JAs every month since 1930. I could barely think of a similar journal in applied linguistics or in writing studies that has such a long history or that publishes this frequently (*ELT Journal* is the closest example). The fact that this journal regularly publishes the conference proceedings of two conferences is also something new to me. I explained to the students in one course section that, in some fields, conference proceedings, if published at all, are usually in the form of heavily revised journal articles appearing in a themed issue. In fact, noticing the place of conference proceedings in a field led me to pay special attention to the status of different types of publications.

Seen in this light, the professional life of a practitioner or researcher of graduate-level research writing instruction will never be boring, especially if one is willing to assume the role of a partner-in-learning with the highly intelligent students in the research writing classroom. With students contributing samples of JAs from different journals in different fields or samples from other research genres in every course section, there will always be opportunities to learn much about discipline-specific research writing.

Questions for Reflection and Discussion

1. Have you used any of the genre-focused textbooks reviewed in this chapter either as a teacher or as a student of graduate-level research writing? If not, what may be your reasons for that? If yes, what are the strengths of these textbooks, in your own view, apart from those raised in this chapter?

2. One point I make in this chapter is that the textbooks reviewed all pay careful attention to the three dimensions of genre analysis—rhetorical organization, lexico-grammatical features, and rhetorical context. Find one unit or chapter from any of the textbooks discussed. Study the genre samples, the questions, and the activities in this unit or chapter. Explain to what extent the unit has paid attention to all three dimensions of genre analysis.

3. Because this book is about genre and graduate-level research writing, this chapter only focuses on textbooks that adopt genre analysis as the underpinning theoretical framework. Are you, either as a teacher or as a learner of graduate-level research writing, familiar with any textbooks that focus on graduate-level research writing but do not adopt the genre-focused approach? What are the theoretical approaches in these textbooks? Compared with the genre-focused textbooks described in this chapter, what are the strengths and weaknesses of these other textbooks?

4. Have you developed any pedagogical materials for teaching graduate-level research writing? If yes, describe your materials. For example, what approach or approaches did you adopt to develop your materials? How does your approach compare with the genre-focused approach as described in this chapter? What kinds of samples did you use for your materials, and what questions or activities did you build into these materials? What are the reasons behind your decisions? If you have never developed any of your own materials, has this chapter given you a clearer sense of how to develop genre-focused materials that target all three dimensions of genre analysis? Why or why not?

5. Have you ever asked your students to collect genre samples for study and analysis? If so, what criteria and procedures did you use to guide students to collect genre samples? How are these criteria or procedures similar to, or different from, those described in this chapter? Did you encounter any of the problems described in this chapter? If so, what were your solutions to these problems, and how were these solutions different from, or similar to, those offered in this chapter?

6. Follow the suggestions in Figure 3.1 to collect five journal articles to build your own reference collection. Your reference collection could be either for pedagogical purposes or for enhancing your own learning of research writing. After you have collected all the articles you need, reflect on the suggestions in Figure 3.1. Which suggestion is the most helpful? Which one is not so helpful? Why?

Chapter 4

The Guided Inductive and Discovery-Based Analysis and Study of Genre

In the ESP and EAP literature, teaching methodology is sometimes defined broadly as "the nature of the interaction between the ESP teacher and the learners" (Dudley-Evans & St John, 1998) and as "what goes on in the [ESP] classroom ... and what the students have to do" (Robinson, 1991, p. 46). The question of an appropriate methodology applicable to the ESP classroom has been pointed out as "one worthy of consideration" (Flowerdew, 1993, p. 310; see also Hutchinson & Waters, 1987). Therefore, it would be worthwhile to explore this question in the context of the genre-focused graduate-level research writing classroom, which is considered by some as part of ESP teaching and learning (e.g., Basturkmen, 2010). Specifically, what would be the suitable instructional methodologies that can guide "what goes on in the classroom ... and what the students have to do" in graduate-level research writing classes (Robinson, 1991, p. 46)?

In-Class Explicit Analysis of Genre Samples

In a 1993 article, Flowerdew wonders how the concept of genre can help develop students' skills in learning any new genre and using it in any new situation. Flowerdew proposes six activities that he believes can increase students' sensitivity to "the subtle interplay between the various parameters affecting genre" and the impact of these parameters on "discourse structure and linguistic encoding" (1993, p. 309). One of these categories of activities is *metacommunicating,* or the *explicit* discussion of a genre sample in class. Metacommunicating of a genre sample can involve discussing rhetorical organizational patterns, or what Flowerdew calls "glossing the stages in the structural formula," and lexico-grammatical features, or "assessing . . . lexis" in Flowerdew's words (1993, p. 309), two of the three major dimensions inherent in the ESP approach to genre analysis (1993, p. 309).

Other instructors of research writing courses from Australia, New Zealand, Sweden, and the United States have described various classroom practices that seem to reflect the explicit analysis of genre samples as the main methodology in their classes (e.g., Basturkmen, 2010; Cortes, 2011; Kuteeva, 2013; Paltridge & Woodrow, 2012; Starfield, 2003, 2016). Even though these examples highlight the benefits of the explicit analysis of genre samples in the research writing classroom, the descriptions of in-class genre analysis tasks in these reports seem vague at times. As a result, novice and even experienced instructors of research writing may need additional details about how to discuss genre samples explicitly in class, details I provide in the next two subsections.

How to Conduct Guided Inductive Analysis of Genre Samples through a Set of General Questions

As discussed in Chapter 3, JA samples collected by instructors or by students are valuable sources of instructional and learning materials. Teacher-led discussions of these genre samples could adopt a "guided inductive approach" in which students are guided to comment on the genre samples "in their own words" (L. Flowerdew, 2016, p. 4). Such an approach, however, does not mean that an instructor should walk into a classroom, present a section from a genre sample to the class, and ask, "So, class, what do you think?" even though such a completely open-ended approach may also lead to insightful comments. An instructor could use certain questions to guide students to focus on the features in the chosen genre sample. For example, guiding questions could be designed in a way to apply to any sample from any section in any research genre or part-genre, such as those in Figure 4.1.

Figure 4.1 presents four categories of questions written to be applied to any sample for in-class discussions. These categories of questions can also be used to guide students' out-of-class genre analysis tasks, a point I will bring up later. These broad categories and the questions in them are, by no means, exhaustive. The categories and questions could be modified with questions added or taken out, depending on pedagogical contextual variations such as students' needs or their familiarity with a specific sample to be analyzed through these questions, among other factors.

That said, the questions in Figure 4.1 represent my attempt to develop a pedagogically accessible framework for analyzing research genres in classroom settings. The quest for such a framework was driven by what had been reported in the literature as well as by my pedagogical reflections.

Specifically, when I first taught graduate-level research writing as a graduate student myself many years ago, I tried to cover as many features as possible and made classroom discussions of the genre samples theoretically sophisticated because this was what I thought a proper analysis of genre should be, given that theorists' portrayal of genre and genre analysis is supposed to be inherently complex and nuanced (Hyon, 1996). My pedagogical reflections based on many sections led me to suspect that students often became overwhelmed and even sometimes disoriented, rather than well informed, as I hoped they would be through my analysis that strived for understanding the sophisticated and complex nature of genre. These considerations help me appreciate the validity of Tardy's (2009) suggestion that instructors in writing classes break genres into parts and help students build the parts into a whole, especially if doing so could help encourage instructors and students to engage in sustained genre analysis. They help

Figure 4.1: Genre-Analysis Questions

---

1. The rhetorical organizational pattern

(1a) What are the moves (and steps) that you have noticed in this sample? Use concrete action verbs to describe these moves and steps (e.g., "to argue for...," "to raise the research questions"). Pay attention to the communicative purpose behind each of the moves (and steps).

(1b) Do you feel that these moves (and steps) have flowed logically from one to the next? If not, why not? If yes, can you explain in detail how these moves (and steps) are logically connected?

(1c) Why are these moves and steps necessary? Should other moves (or steps) have been added here? Should some moves or steps have been taken out? Why?

2. The lexico-grammatical features

(2a) What are the words, phrases, sentences, and other features in this sample that have been used by the authors to perform each of the moves or steps that you have identified above?

(2b) Have these words, phrases, or sentences served the purposes in the moves (and steps) effectively? Have they met your needs as a reader? Why or why not?

3. The rhetorical context

(3a) What is the overall communicative purpose of this section of the text? In other words, what are the authors trying to do (vs. just say) in this section?

(3b) Have the authors achieved these purposes successfully? Have they met your needs as a reader? Why or why not?

4. The differences and similarities between the genre-specific features in the sample discussed in class and those in your own samples

(4a) How is this sample similar to, or different from, those in your collected JAs or in the JAs you have read in the past? Explain.

(4b) What might be the reasons behind the similarities or differences?

me realize the importance of using an accessible and manage-able framework of genre analysis, as suggested by Tardy, a framework attempted in the example in Figure 4.1.

Striving for an accessible framework, however, does not mean that instructors and students should settle for a watered-down version of genre analysis or should attempt to break genre into any artificial, insignificant, or unrelated parts for analysis. Compared with some existing guidelines for analyz-ing genre (e.g., Devitt, Reiff, & Bawarshi, 2004), the questions in Figure 4.1 may seem limited in scope and in number, but they are comprehensive enough to be able to help students uncover as much as possible about the rhetorical organizational pattern (see Category 1 in Figure 4.1), the lexico-grammatical features (Category 2), and the rhetorical contextual influences on the organization and lexico-grammatical features in the sample in question (see Category 3). Each of these categories could be unpacked, based on a specific chosen sample, to become as sophisticated as possible to engage students in as sustained an analysis of the genre exemplar as one wishes or is capable of.

The possibility to expand on the features that this acces-sible set of questions aspires to capture, of course, depends on instructors and students' knowledge of research writing as well as their effort or patience to analyze a particular sample. At the same time, such a possibility is enabled by the rich existing research findings on research genres. An argument for adopting the ESP approach to genre analysis in research writing instruction is the many studies on various aspects of research genres and part-genres available to instructors (see my reference to this point in Chapter 1 and Chapter 2). The find-ings from these studies could enable instructors with "applied aspirations" to "refashion these findings" in their classroom discussions of the genres and part-genres in question (Swales, 2009c, p. 4). As my descriptions of genre-focused pedagogical materials in Chapter 3 showed, Swales and Feak (e.g., 2012a) and others (e.g., Paltridge & Starfield, 2007) have exemplified the practice of drawing on existing research findings on various aspects of research genres to develop teaching points to guide their readers' understanding of these genres. Other instructors can follow such a practice to prepare teaching points related to the questions in the framework in Figure 4.1, but specific to the chosen sample, and use the teaching points to guide students' genre analysis.

An example is provided in Figure 4.2 and Figure 4.3 to illustrate what it means to use existing findings on research genres to develop pedagogical points to accompany the questions in Figure 4.1 to aid classroom discussions of genre samples. The example is based on a short literature review section from the Introduction of a JA on the topic of incivility in the workplace (see Figure 4.2). This JA was from the reference collection of one of the students in a series of writing workshops I gave at a nearby university. The short literature review section was presented with a set of questions resembling those in Figure 4.1 to the workshop participants, who analyzed the sample in a teacher-fronted discussion in one session of the workshop series.

As can be seen in Figure 4.2, sentence numbers are provided for the workshop participants' easy reference, similar to a common practice in the Swales and Feak series (e.g., 2012a). A few sentences preceding and following the "Incident Rates" section have also been provided in the handout given to the workshop participants so as to supply the necessary textual context for the sample even though only the "Incident Rates" section was analyzed closely in the workshop session.

The sample (Figure 4.2) is followed by a list of possible teaching points I developed based on my reading of the available findings from genre analysis studies as well as my own close analysis of the sample (see the teaching points in Figure 4.3). The teaching points were not presented to the workshop participants before the in-class analysis of the sample and were intended as points that could facilitate the in-class analysis of the sample using the questions in the framework described in Figure 4.1. No research writing textbooks were assigned to students in this and other similar workshop series even though I used the Swales and Feak series and other genre-focused writ-

Figure 4.2: Sample of the Literature Review Part-Genre

...., suggests that low-level, interpersonal mistreatment can engender organizational violence and damage individual psychosomatic functioning.

Partly because the concept is still so new, little empirical research has documented characteristics and effects of workplace incivility. Thus, our purpose was to address this dearth in the literature. We begin by briefly reviewing research on workplace psychological aggression, interactional injustice, unfairness, and bullying; although these constructs do not completely overlap with workplace incivility, they are related enough to inform hypotheses on the latter.

Incidence Rates

[1] Findings regarding rates of aggression, injustice, unfairness, and so on vary widely, largely owing to differing definitions, measurement instruments, and time frames. [2] Einarsen and Raknes (1997) learned that approximately 75% of Norwegian engineering employees had endured generalized, nonspecific harassment at least once during the previous 6 months. [3] Using a more conservative calculation of incidence, Bjorkqvist, Osterman, and Hjelt-Back (1994) found that 30% of male and 55% of female Finnish University employees described encounters with harassment at work at least occasionally during the previous half year. [4] By contrast, Cole and colleagues (Cole, Grubb, Sauter, Swanson, & Lawless, 1997) reported that only 19% of U.S. adults had experienced harassment at work in the previous year, and 13% reported being threatened with harassment or violence in the previous 5 years. [5] Research from various Scandinavian countries uncovered even lower rates of workplace bullying, ranging from 3%–4% (Leymann, 1992; Leymann & Tallgren, 1989, as reported in Einarsen & Skogstad, 19961) to 8%–10% (Einarsen & Skogstad, 1996; Matthiesen, Raknes, & Rokkum, 1989, as reported in Einarsen & Skogstad, 1996). [6] In sum, documented rates of behaviors related to workplace incivility vary dramatically, and rates of incivility itself are virtually unknown. [7] Thus, our first research question is purely exploratory: How prevalent is incivility in the American workplace?

Targets and Instigators of Incivility

Conceptualizing incivility as an inherently social phenomenon, Andersson and Pearson (1999) described it as an escalating exchange of behaviors between colleagues. Such a social-interactionist perspective implies that knowledge about individuals involved could advance research on the incivility process. Target
....

Source: Cortina, Magley, Williams, & Langhout, 2001.

ing textbooks as my own instructor's guides when preparing teaching points as seen in the citations in Figure 4.3.

Figure 4.4 is an additional example to show how to use existing research findings in genre studies to develop pedagogical points to accompany the questions in Figure 4.1 in order to facilitate classroom discussions of genre samples. This example comes from the Discussion section of a research article published in the journal *Nature* (Schratt, Tuebing, Nigh, Kane, Sabatini, Kiebler, & Greenberg, 2006; see Figure 4.4), and this JA was from the reference collection of a graduate student in biology. This short section is the whole Discussion section in the JA with 14 sentences in three paragraphs. Similar to the sample in Figure 4.2, it was presented to students with a set of questions resembling those in Figure 4.1, who analyzed the sample in a teacher-fronted discussion. Sentence numbers are provided in Figure 4.4 for ease of reference.

The sample in Figure 4.4 is followed by a list of possible teaching points I developed based on my reading of the available findings from genre analysis studies as well as my own close reading of the sample (see the teaching points in Figure 4.5). Once again, these teaching points were not presented to the students before the in-class analysis of the sample and were intended as points that could facilitate the in-class analysis of the sample through the questions in Figure 4.1. No research writing textbooks were assigned to students in this case even though I used the Swales and Feak series and other genre-focused writing textbooks as my own instructor's guides when preparing teaching points as seen in the citations in Figure 4.5.

As seen in Figure 4.3 and Figure 4.5, many of the teaching points are based on my reading of the literature on research genres, including the Swales and Feak volumes (e.g., 2012a), among others, as referenced in the two figures. Developing teaching points based on existing findings is quite common. In fact, Swales and Feak have referenced a range of studies when they cover various organizational, lexico-grammatical, and socio-rhetorical features related to different research genres in their materials. The same is true for Lynne Flowerdew (2016), Paltridge and Starfield (2007), and Charles (2007, 2012).

Figure 4.3: Teaching Points Related to the Literature Review Part-Genre

---

1. The rhetorical organizational pattern

(1a) What are the moves (and steps) that you have noticed in this sample? Use concrete action verbs to describe these moves and steps (e.g., *to argue for…, to raise the research questions,* …). Pay attention to the communicative purpose behind each of the moves (and steps).

- To <u>introduce</u> the findings in an area of research—Incidence Rates—reviewed in this introduction as seen in the topic sentence (Sentence 1)

- To <u>review</u> the specific findings related to this area (Sentences 2–5)

- To <u>critique</u> these existing findings (Sentences 1 and 6 and also throughout this paragraph)

- To help <u>raise</u> one of the research questions (Sentence 7)

- The literature review in this article is divided into three sections that use descriptive headings—Incidence Rates, Targets and Instigators of Incivility, and Effects of Incivility. Each section follows a rhetorical pattern similar to the one above: introduce the area to be reviewed, review the findings, critique the findings, and raise the research question corresponding to this area and its problem(s).

(1b) Do you feel that these moves (and steps) have flowed logically from one to the next? If not, why not? If yes, can you explain in detail how these moves (and steps) are logically connected?

- The general-to-specific (GS) pattern as well as the problem-solution (PS) pattern (Swales & Feak, 2012a) may be guiding how the steps flow logically in this section?

  - GS: a topic sentence (Sentence 1, general) is expanded into the specific studies reviewed (Sentences 2–5, specific) (see the shape of a GS text in Swales & Feak, 2012a, p. 56)?

  - PS: *Findings…vary widely* (Sentence 1) and *documented rates vary dramatically* with *rates virtually unknown* (Sentence 6) constitute a problem. The solution lies in Sentence 7—the research question?

Figure 4.3 (Continued)

- The logical flow could be illustrated as below where a partial GS pattern is embedded within a PS pattern?
  - ○ Introduce the problem
    - ▪ (General-topic sentence serves as both a general statement and a problem statement?)
    - ▪ Specific details?
  - ○ Restate the problem
  - ○ Introduce the solution
- Another pattern of logical flow can be seen in Sentences 2 to 5 where the authors start with the highest reported incidence rate to the lowest incidence rate, all to serve the argument that rates "vary" widely and dramatically.

(1c) Why are these moves and steps necessary? Should other moves (or steps) have been added here? Should some moves or steps have been taken out? Why?

- The communicative purpose is to raise the research question, so the pattern, with the subtle attention to the problems in the existing studies, is necessary.
- The last sentence in the preceding section does not explain or justify why "incidence rate" is an area that needs to be reviewed. Maybe the authors should have added a sentence at the beginning of the "Incidence Rate" section to explain why they need to focus on incidence rate?

2. **The lexico-grammatical features**

(2a) What are the words, phrases, sentences, and other features in this sample that have been used by the authors to perform each of the moves or steps that you have identified above?

- Move- or step-**specific** linguistic features:
  - ○ Reporting verbs: *learned, found, uncovered,* and *as reported….* (Feak & Swales, 2009; Hyland, 1999; Swales & Feak, 2012a)
  - ○ Citations:
    - ▪ Integral (author prominent) citations: *Bjorkqvist, Osterman, and Hjelt-Back (1994) found that…* (see Feak & Swales, 2009, p. 46)

Figure 4.3 (Continued)

- Non-integral (research prominent) citations: *Research from various Scandinavian countries uncovered even lower rates of workplace bullying, …* (Feak & Swales, 2009, p. 46)
- Citing a citation (indirect citations): *Leymann & Tallgren, 1989, as reported in Einarsen & Skogstad, 1996* and *Matthiesen, Raknes, & Rokkum, 1989, as reported in Einarsen & Skogstad, 1996* (Swales & Feak, 2012a, pp. 193–194)
  - Subtle criticisms of previous research: *using a more conservative calculation of incidence…?*
  - To show similarities and differences between literature items: *by contrast….* (Swales & Feak, 2012a, pp. 225–227)
- Move- or step-**general** linguistic features:
  - Imprecise expressions that expect readers to fill in the missing information: *And so on* (see Swales & Feak, 2012a, Unit One, p. 23)
  - Linking words and phrases: *by contrast, in sum, and thus* (see Swales & Feak, 2012a, Unit One, p. 37)
  - Writing about numbers: *approximately 75%…* and *only 19%*. The latter is a subtle criticism of findings reporting higher rates? (see Question 11 on page 144 of Swales and Feak, 2012a)
  - Adverbs and adverb positions: *virtually unknown, purely exploratory, at least occasionally* (Swales & Feak, 2012a, p. 24, pp. 105–106)
  - Set expressions: *vary widely* vs. *vary dramatically*

3. **The rhetorical context**
   (3a) What is the overall communicative purpose of this section of the text? In other words, what are the authors trying to do (vs. just say) in this section?
   - Doing the basic homework (Feak & Swales, 2009, p. 2)
   - To demonstrate how your current work is situated within, builds on, or departs from earlier publications (Feak & Swales, 2009, p. 2)
   - Calling attention to an issue so as to raise a research question (Noguchi, 2006; cited in Feak & Swales, 2009)

Figure 4.3 (Continued)

- Move 2a and Move 3b in a cyclical manner with each area reviewed generating Move 2a and Move 3b? (Feak & Swales, 2011; Swales & Feak, 2012a)
- A form of focused literature review? (Feak & Swales, 2009, p. 3)

(3b) Have the authors achieved these purposes successfully? Have they met your needs as a reader? Why or why not?

- I believe so, especially in light of the concerns often expressed about students' problematic literature reviews as described in Feak & Swales, 2009, Task 6. It seems that the authors of this literature review have addressed these concerns effectively.

4. **The differences and similarities between the genre-specific features in the sample discussed in class and those in students' own samples**

(4a) How is this sample similar to, or different from, those in your collected JAs or in the JAs you have read in the past? Explain.

- Refer to Task Two, Check Your Literature Review Knowledge, in Feak & Swales (2009, p. 5). Draw students' attention to the review of literature described there as possible points of differences.

The teaching points in these two examples (Figures 4.3 and 4.5), each with the respective samples, may seem more than can be covered in one session. It is often not necessary to cover all the teaching points or all the details in each point as seen in the examples here. Some of these points may have become familiar to students or may not be what they are interested in at a particular point. For example, although I was prepared to summarize what I have learned from Swales and Feak (2012a) and introduce to students the general-to-specific pattern and how it may be, in my view, embedded in the problem-solution pattern in the sample in Figure 4.2, the workshop participants seemed to have been quite satisfied with what they perceived to be the "topic sentence," "specific studies reviewed," "problems," "research question" pattern in the sample. Therefore,

Figure 4.4. A Sample of the Discussion Part-Genre

Discussion

[1] We have identified a dendritically localized miRNA that regulates the expression of the synaptic Limk1 protein, thereby controlling dendritic spine size. [2] We hypothesize that the association of Limk1 mRNA with miR-134 keeps the Limk1 mRNA in a dormant state while it is being transported within dendrites to synaptic sites (Fig. 6d). [3] In the absence of synaptic activity, miR-134 may recruit a silencing complex that has a key role in repressing Limk1 mRNA translation. [4] This then limits the synthesis of new Limk1 protein and restricts the growth of dendritic spines. [5] Upon synaptic stimulation, the release of BDNF may trigger activation of the TrkB/mTOR signalling pathway, which inactivates the miR-134-associated silencing complex by an as-yet-unknown mechanism, leading to enhanced Limk1 protein synthesis and spine growth. [6] Our preliminary finding that miR-134 moves to the polysome-associated mRNA pool upon BDNF stimulation (G.S. and M.E.G., unpublished observations) suggests that miR-134 itself may not dissociate from the Limk1 mRNA upon exposure of neurons to BDNF. [7] Instead, we speculate that BDNF alters the activity of other translational regulators within the miR-134-containing complex. [8] In addition to miR-134, other neuronal miRNAs have been predicted to bind the Limk1 30 UTR[38]. [9] Therefore, the combinatorial action of multiple miRNAs on the Limk1 30 UTR might explain our observation that miR-134 only partially inhibits Limk1 mRNA translation (Fig. 4).

[10] A recent bioinformatics approach predicted several additional neuronal mRNAs that may also represent miR-134 targets[39]. [11] Given that BDNF has important roles at multiple steps of synaptic development[40,41], it is possible that miR-134 regulates distinct sets of target genes involved in the formation, maturation or plasticity of synapses.

[12] We propose that miRNA regulation of the translation of a variety of neuronal mRNAs will be found to contribute in an important way to synaptic function[42]. [13] It is tempting to speculate that miRNAs act locally at individual synapses, thereby contributing to synapse-specific modifications that occur during synaptic plasticity. [14] A future challenge will be to identify the full complement of dendritic miRNAs as well as their target mRNAs, and to determine their role in synaptic development.

Source: from Schratt et al., 2006.

Figure 4.5: Teaching Points Related to the Discussion Part-Genre

1. **The rhetorical organizational pattern**

   (1a)   What are the moves (and steps) that you have noticed
          in this sample? Use concrete action verbs to describe
          these moves and steps (e.g., *to argue for…, to raise
          the research questions …*). Pay attention to the
          communicative purpose behind each of the moves (and
          steps).

   - To <u>summarize or report</u> key results (Sentence 1) (e.g.,
     Basturkmen, 2009; Yang & Allison, 2003)
   - To comment on the key results (Sentences 2–12)
     - To <u>revisit</u> the hypothesis guiding the study and
       relevant to the interpretation of the finding above
       (Sentences 2–5)
     - To <u>explain the key results </u>by explaining how the
       result fails to support or only partially supports
       the hypotheses outlined in the study (Sentences
       6–7; see Rudestam & Newton, 2001, p. 121, cited in
       Paltridge & Starfield, 2007, p. 146)
     - To <u>compare the key findings with previous findings,
       offering alternative explanation</u> for the key finding,
       especially in relation to the hypothesis (Sentences
       8–12; see, for example, Basturkmen, 2009; Yang &
       Allison, 2003)
   - To <u>make recommendations for future implementation
     and/or future research</u> (Sentence 14)

   (1b)   Do you feel that these moves (and steps) have flowed
          logically from one to the next? If not, why not? If yes,
          can you explain in detail how these moves (and steps)
          are logically connected?

   - Yes. The connection among the moves looks very
     logical. The authors highlight one key result. They
     then revisit the hypotheses so as to interpret what that
     result may mean in terms of the hypotheses. They then
     place the result within the larger picture in connection
     with other recent findings to develop some larger
     theoretical significance of the key result or to offer a
     satisfactory explanation for the result. Finally, they
     propose some areas for future research.

Figure 4.5 (Continued)

(1c) Why are these moves and steps necessary? Should other moves (or steps) have been added here? Should some moves or steps have been taken out? Why?

- These moves are necessary. Commenting on or highlighting some key results helps the researchers/authors work from "the inside out" and help them relate their results to previous work in their field (see Berkenkotter & Huckin, 1995, p. 41, cited in Basturkman, 2009, p. 248, and in Swales & Feak, 2012a, p. 369). The "to comment on the results" move, with the three steps in it, helps the researchers offer cognitively challenging novel explanations and increase the "news value" of their work (see Basturkmen, 2009, and Swales & Feak, 2012a).

- Two missing moves are "to offer background information (research purposes, theory, and methodology)" and "to state the limitations of the study." Even though the authors do not provide the "background information" move where they talk about the research purpose, theory, and methodology, maybe their elaboration on the hypotheses from sentences 2–5 has served the same purpose? The authors' *future research* move is quite short and vague (see Sentence 14). This vague statement, coupled with the lack of an explicit "limitation" move, points to Swales and Feak's (2012a) observation that, in some "big science" fields, researchers may not want to "give ideas to their rivals" (p. 369)?

2. **The lexico-grammatical features**

(2a) What are the words, phrases, sentences, and other features in this sample that have been used by the authors to perform each of the moves or steps that you have identified above?

- Move- or step-**specific** linguistic features:
  - The present tense when discussing key results (*.... that regulates..., ...that miR-134 moves to the ....*)
  - Hedges (*our preliminary findings...suggest that ....may not dissociate from...., therefore, the combinatorial action of ....might explain our observation that....only partially...., and given that...., it is possible that....*) (Hyland, 1998; Paltridge & Starfield, 2007, pp. 149–150; Swales & Feak, 2012a, pp. 159–164)

Figure 4.5 (Continued)

> - Move- or step-**general** linguistic features:
>   - *-ing* clauses to indicate cause and effect *(thereby controlling dendritic spine size, ...leading to enhanced Limk1 protein..., ... thereby contributing to ...* (Swales & Feak, 2012a, pp. 115–119)
>
> 3. **The rhetorical context**
>   (3a) What is the overall communicative purpose of this section of the text? In other words, what are the authors trying to do (vs. just say) in this section?
>   - The writing of the discussion section is about working from 'the inside out," with writers referring first to the study at hand before progressively widening the scope to include work by others (Basturkmen, 2009, p. 248)
>   - Discussions of results are evaluated "less on the actual results presented than the way the writer relates them to previous work in the field" (Hopkins & Dudley-Evans, 1988, p. 119)

I did not refer to the general-to-specific pattern that I drew upon from Swales and Feak (2012a) when guiding the discussion at that point even though the pattern was part of the teaching points I had prepared as seen in the bullet points under Question 2b in Figure 4.3. The message here is that instructors should strive to know as much as possible about the genre or part-genre in question, to analyze the chosen samples as closely as possible, and to develop as many teaching points as possible based on their knowledge to prepare to facilitate the in-class discussions of genre, at the same time knowing that not all the prepared teaching points need to be addressed.

To keep with the "guided inductive approach" to analyzing genre (L. Flowerdew, 2016, p. 5), teaching points prepared for a sample should preferably be brought up during or after, but not before, students' discussions. In other words, the in-class explicit analysis of research genres may be "guided" by instructors' knowledge of the teaching points corresponding to the sample under discussion, knowledge brought into a concrete form as a set of pedagogical points prepared beforehand based on the questions in Figure 4.1. However, such an analysis should preferably be "inductive" in the sense that students should be encouraged to bring forth what they may notice from the sample before any models or concrete features—again, as materialized in a set of concrete teaching points—are presented by the instructor. The inductive approach may be more conducive to raising students' rhetorical consciousness and is seen in many examples in the volumes by Swales and Feak (e.g., 2012a) and as noticed by Starfield who reported that her students appreciated the "focus on real examples and discussions rather than the typical 'lecture' format" (Starfield, 2016, p. 183; see also Basturkmen, 2010). Teaching points like those in the example could be brought up during class discussions to connect them to what the students have uncovered or to move the discussion along when the analysis may not be progressing as smoothly as one wishes (see Basturkmen, 2010, and L. Flowerdew, 2016). These teaching points could be brought up after class discussion to help synthesize what the students have brought up and to provide as systematic an understanding of the genre or part-genre in question as possible.

Note that some bullet points in Figures 4.3 and 4.5 end with a question mark because they are not meant to have definitive answers. Instead, they are supposed to be the instructor's often tentative understanding of what may be happening in the sample, as they are in my case, an understanding waiting to be enriched through students' comments and analysis. Doing so is part of the guided inductive approach to analyzing genres.

Although the categories of questions are in the order of moving from organizational pattern, to lexico-grammatical features, to rhetorical context as seen in Figures 4.1, 4.3, and 4.5, the discussion could start from any category or any question in it, depending on what the students may bring up in class.

Note that, in the list of questions in Figure 4.1, I intentionally do not start with the "context" or "purpose" questions in Category 3, as is often the case in other genre analysis guidelines such as that by Devitt, Reiff, and Bawarshi (2004). Although I agree with Tardy (2009) and others (e.g., Johns, 1997) about the importance of "link[ing] formal textual patterns with social context, obliging learners to address the question of why the samples they examine take on particular formal properties" (Tardy, 2009, p. 129), I believe that the discussion of context and purpose may be more meaningful when such a discussion is firmly anchored on, and situated in, the concrete rhetorical organizational patterns and the lexico-grammatical features noticed by students. In Cheng (2011b), I have looked at several cases of students who made sense of rhetorical contexts through the lens of textual features they chose to analyze. In my experience, talking about rhetorical context without anchoring such a discussion on textual features often results in superficial statements from students such as, "In my field, we always …," "We never….in [a field]," or "We should always … in the field of…." Statements such as these are less interesting to me than comments or questions from students such as, "Why do the authors say 'we speculate that BDNF alters the …'?", "To what extent is one allowed to 'speculate' when discussing findings in biology"? and "Is it a common practice to use 'unpublished observations' to support one's comments on one's results?" (see the use of the word *speculate* in Sentence 7 and the the inclusion of *unpublished observation* in Sentence 6 in Figure 4.4). Questions or comments like these show how readers' expectations, writer's assumptions, rhetorical purposes, the values of a discourse community, and other contextual issues may have been invoked more concretely through student's attention to the textual features that help materialize such contextual issues to begin with; this then makes the significance of the rhetorical contextual issues underpinning texts become more alive than just some generic statements about what the context or purpose of research writing presumably is or should be.

Another caveat is that, although the questions on rhetorical context and purpose are listed as a separate category of questions, they have also been woven into the why questions in Category 1 (see 1c in Figure 4.1) and Category 2 (see 2b in

Figure 4.1), which, again, shows my strong belief in discussing rhetorical contextual issues through the lens of organizational patterns and lexico-grammatical features (e.g., Cheng,
2011b, 2015a). At the same time, although the why questions
embedded in Category 1 and Category 2 in Figure 4.1 are
very important because they could urge course participants
to reflect on the rhetorical rationales behind any rhetorical
organizational and lexico-grammatical features, setting up
Category 3 as separate from Category 1 and Category 2 serves
as a strong reminder to students that genre analysis is not just
about understanding the various organizational and lexico-
grammatical configurations of texts, as important as these are.
It is, equally, if not more so, about the rhetorical rationales
behind the different configurations of organizational patterns
and lexico-grammatical features, an element that they should
always remember to incorporate into their own conceptual
framework and their development of genre awareness. The
separate category of purpose- or context-focused questions
would be useful as well when an instructor relies on these
questions to pull insights derived from the discussions of the
previous categories together near the end of a session.

This guided inductive approach to analyzing genre exemplars in class, which is driven heavily by a set of questions that
can be potentially used for any genre samples as well as by
students' and instructors' close reading of the sample in question, may work well because many students in graduate-level
research writing class are, as noted by Swales and Lindemann
(2002), "surprisingly useful and willing collaborators in various kinds of linguistic analysis" due to their "highly developed
analytical skills in their own fields and their commitment to
empirical evidence" (p. 118).

Although following this particular pattern of questioning as
seen in Figure 4.1 may seem monotonous at times, I noticed
that students often appreciated this relatively routinized
approach because they became increasingly familiar with what
to expect in each session and what to look for in each sample.
The relatively accessible framework also serves as a comforting

starting point, allowing room for making the analysis in class as sophisticated and complex as possible.

Logistically speaking, using these questions as laid out in Figure 4.1 to lead class discussions has the additional advantage of limiting the time commitment when novice instructors prepare their teaching materials and reducing the anxieties involved in having to develop tasks or questions specifically tailored to each sample analyzed in class. After all, these four categories of questions attend to all three dimensions of genre analysis and are potentially applicable to any section in any sample of a genre in question. Some, though definitely not all, of the teaching points developed for a sample could also be transferred to another sample of the same part-genre. For example, some of the teaching points in Figures 4.3 and 4.5 may also be applicable to another literature review sample (Figure 4.3) or another discussion sample (Figure 4.5), respectively.

How To Develop Genre Analysis Tasks Tailored to a Selected Genre Sample

Since some instructors may feel that they need a way to guide students to analyze research genres that is more specific to each sample presented in class than the framework in Figure 4.1 allows them to, we turn our attention there.

Swales (1990) defined a task as "one of a set of differentiated, sequenceable goal-directed activities drawing upon a range of cognitive and communicative procedures relatable to the acquisition of pre-genre and genre skills appropriate to a foreseen or emerging socio-rhetorical situation" (p. 76). Although tasks of Swales and Feak were discussed in Chapter 3, we will now see how some of their tasks were developed with the criteria of Swales' definition in mind. This is in hope that instructors will be able to develop their own specific tasks for guiding students to conduct genre analysis or to use the tasks in the Swales and Feak's series of textbooks more mindfully and effectively.

How to Create a Set of Goal-Oriented Activities in Genre
Analysis Tasks

The example Swales (1990) gives in his book to illustrate how
genre analysis tasks can be designed presents four related tasks
aimed to help students understand the rhetorical effects of the
academic request letter genre. Specifically, an academic request
letter is often written by a graduate student or junior scholar
to request a copy of the recent work by a more established
scholar. Swales first presents three sample academic request
letters. Each is worded differently. Task One asks students
to answer four questions: The first question asks students to
describe the similarity between the opening sentences in the
first two sample letters ("I have seen a summary of your work
on _____" and "I've come across a reference to one of
your publications which, unfortunately, is not available…..").
The second question asks students to consider the rhetorical
effects of the opening sentence in the third letter, including
the effects of bringing up the person who suggests the request
("_____ suggested that I write to you and request a copy
of some of your recent work, which by all reports would be
of much interest to me"). Questions 3 and 4 ask students to
continue to consider the rhetorical effects of the letters, such
as how the addressee may feel if the letter writer mentions a
third person that both the letter writer and the addressee know
or brings up the research interest shared by the letter writer
and the addressee (pp. 79–80).

In the second task, Swales reveals the rhetorical uptakes of
the three letters: One letter was answered promptly, another
slowly, and the third not responded to at all. Swales then asks
students to consider the possible reasons behind these outcomes and to redraft in pairs the two letters that do not elicit
the satisfactory rhetorical outcomes.

The third task asks students to consider the possibility of
adding an additional move to the request letters: to offer to
send a copy of the letter writer's recent work to the addressee.
The rhetorical purpose of such a move, according to Swales,
is to provide "an opportunity to show that you are an active

researcher in the field" (Swales, 1990, p. 80). Given the potentially face-threatening nature of such a move, Swales focuses on the lexico-grammatical features that can help one avoid sounding too "pushy" when performing such a move (p. 80). He presents four sentences that can perform this move with some sounding more "pushy" than the others do. Swales asks students to consider under which situations each of the four sentences would be used and why.

The last task asks students to check their own academic correspondence for any illuminating examples or for any important lessons to learn from the examples.

These tasks form a set of tasks directed to the goal of raising students' rhetorical consciousness of a particular research-related genre. When designing their own tasks tailored to a particular sample, instructors need to pay attention to how several tasks form a set and how the set of tasks achieves the end-goal of students' noticing key aspects of the research genre in question. This is an important tip for instructors whether using the Swales and Feak series or other textbooks.

How to Sequence Genre Analysis Tasks

One common way of sequencing tasks in Swales and Feak's volumes is to progress from tasks that emphasize rhetorical contexts to tasks that spotlight rhetorical organizational patterns and lexico-grammatical features. For example, in the first task in *Abstracts* (2009), users are introduced to the concept of the marketplace of ideas to stress the importance of a well-written abstract in assisting a manuscript to progress to the next stage in the review process. Various functions of RA abstract are given and then students rank the functions in terms of their importance to students and their fields.

This purpose- and context-focused task is then followed by one that highlights the lexico-grammatical and organizational patterns in RA abstracts, with several examples. Then Swales and Feak present eight discussion questions in Task Two (2009, pp. 4–5), seven of which draw attention to a range of lexico-grammatical features (the most common verb tense, citations, first-person pronouns, metadiscourse, and abbreviations or acronyms in abstracts (p. 4). This is followed by a five-move pattern that consists of "background/introduction/ situation—present research/purpose—methods/materials/subjects/procedures—results/findings—discussion/ implications/ conclusions/recommendations" and asks readers to determine how many of these moves are available in the sample. We can see how these two tasks have been sequenced by moving from rhetorical context to lexico-grammatical features, to the rhetorical organization that they would like their readers to pay attention to through the analysis of this sample.

When designing genre analysis tasks of their own, instructors can keep this method of sequencing tasks in mind, but should feel free to explore different ways of sequencing genre analysis tasks that can cover all three dimensions of genre analysis in an instructionally feasible and applicable manner.

How to Build Different Cognitive and Communicative Procedures into Genre Analysis Tasks

Swales (1990) lists cognitive and communicative procedures as a separate criterion to emphasize the fact that a set of tasks should employ different procedures. He does not spell out what these "cognitive and communicative procedures" are, but the first few tasks in *Navigating Academia* (Swales & Feak, 2011) reveal what these procedures may entail. The different communicative procedures in these tasks include posing a series of analysis questions to guide their readers to analyze the personal statement genre (Task Six), filling out a Likert-scale questionnaire with ten statements that aim to help the readers understand their own attitudes toward academic correspondence (see Task One), presenting a dialogue between a student and his writing tutor to direct their readers' attention to a variety of issues (Task Four). They follow up with a task that uses a different communicative procedure: asking their readers to rewrite the opening paragraph of the sample SOP to make it more memorable or draft a SOP of the reader's own (Task Five).

Although the frequently used communicative procedure of posing a series of analysis questions specific to a genre sample probably will remain a main tool in the genre-focused research writing instructors' toolkit, instructors interested in designing their own tasks can certainly be creative and incorporate various communicative procedures into their learning tasks that target the features in the genres or part-genres in question.

How to Create in Genre Analysis Tasks a Socio-Rhetorical Situation Suitable for a Multidisciplinary Group of Learners

Swales (1990) emphasizes the fact that the multidisciplinary mix of students in research writing classes means that instructors should construct a socio-rhetorical situation surrounding a task in a certain way so that students can differentially contribute to the task even though their engagement with the task may be more or less temporary. Simply put, the multidisciplinary mix of course participants should be able to find a task relevant and should be able to participate in it regardless of their disciplines and despite the fact that the research writing classroom is only an emerging and temporary community that they may exit near the end of a class session to return to their own disciplinary discourse community.

Let's consider a task in *Abstracts and the Writing of Abstracts* (Swales & Feak, 2009), where students are asked to consider what the situation is like in their respective disciplines when they analyze a sample abstract in political science. The authors use questions to create a community of learning where students are emerged in the socio-rhetorical situation of exploring research genres. After that, they present four sample RA abstracts in Task Three (pp. 6–8), from psychology, education, mechanical engineering and food service, and art history, and ask their readers to choose the one closest to their individual area to analyze.

Another way to create an emerging socio-rhetorical situation in a task to engage learners in a multidisciplinary research writing class is to choose sample texts relatively accessible to the whole class, such as the example in Swales and Lindemann (2002). Here a series of abstracts on the relatively accessible topic of engineering education were used so that everyone could contribute to the discussion and to engage in the task (see Swales, 2009c, for the backstory behind this task).

Another example of using texts accessible to the whole class to create a socio-rhetorical situation unique to the class can be seen in their use of the concept of discourse community in a series of tasks in *Telling a Research Story* (Feak & Swales, 2009). They use the concept to illustrate how one can organize a variety of studies in a literature review through using different criteria. The concept is supposedly relevant and accessible to most of the course participants in advanced academic writing classes. It is relevant because Feak and Swales create the context of a research project on the academic writing challenges of L2 writers in which the concept is used. Since most of the course participants are very likely L2 writers, they may find the topic as well as the role of the concept of discourse community in it relevant. It is accessible because Feak and Swales define it very broadly as encompassing "forms of communication that are created by, directed at, and used by a particular group such as scholars in a research area," and most of the course participants, given their status as research students, may find themselves in such a group—among other groups (Feak & Swales, 2009, p. 12).

In fact, most, if not all the sample texts used in the Swales and Feak series of textbooks seem accessible to an educated reader and learner of graduate-level research writing; such a choice may reflect their attention to this criterion of designing and using genre analysis tasks to create an emerging socio-rhetorical situation for a multidisciplinary mix of learners. Units Seven and Eight in *AWG* exemplify this criterion (Swales & Feak, 2012a). In these two units, examples are on this diverse set of topics: the occurrence of a species of bird in an area in the United States, consumer behaviors in buying stolen goods, identifying genuine and counterfeit currency, divided attention and pedestrians' safety, children's postsurgical pains, group work and the effects of criticisms, a certain nineteenth century artist, highway bridges, university-community collaboration, harvesting energy from ocean waves, and biostatisticians' perception of fraud in medical research. These topics, as seen from the excerpts in the two chapters, are accessible for creating a socio-rhetorical situation in class for the analysis of the rhetorical context, organization, and lexico-grammatical features in the samples. As a result, students will be able to contribute to the analysis to varying degrees.

The primary goal of my discussion here is to understand "the care and thought that Swales and Feak have given to the construction of tasks" (Belcher, 1995, p. 177) and to familiarize novice instructors with the criteria behind effective genre analysis tasks that are tailored to selected genre samples. Toward this end, Table 4.1 summarizes the criteria, with definitions and examples, that Swales (1990) suggests as especially applicable to the design of tasks for analyzing research genres and part-genres, tasks that are especially amenable to in-class guided inductive analysis of genre samples.

Students' Discovery-Based Analysis of Genre Samples

Another activity that could form part of the methodology of a genre-oriented research writing class is to ask students to conduct genre analysis out of class. As noted by Tardy (2009), students' "written reflection or analysis [of multiple instances of a genre] can push students to locate connections, patterns, and differences that are meaningful to them" (p. 284). In fact, after reflecting on the not-so-effective in-class genre analysis tasks in a graduate-level writing class she observed, Tardy (2009) wonders whether the genre analysis in that course may "have been more successful if the writers had been required to carry out a written genre analysis, collecting and analyzing a small corpus of sample texts" (p. 129). Given the limited

Table 4.1: Criteria, Definitions, and Examples of Genre Analysis Tasks

Criterion	Definition	Example
To create a series of goal-oriented activities	A genre analysis task is linked to other tasks to form a series of activities that aim to achieve a particular goal.	Four related tasks to help students understand the academic request letter genre (Swales, 1990)
To sequence genre analysis tasks carefully	A task can progress from one to the next by moving among the three dimensions of genre analysis: rhetorical context, rhetorical organizational patterns, and lexico-grammatical features.	Moving from rhetorical context to lexico-grammatical features and, finally, to rhetorical organizational patterns in a series of questions that analyze RA abstracts (Swales & Feak, 2009)
To build various cognitive and communicative procedures into genre analysis tasks	Tasks should involve various communicative procedures (writing, considering rhetorical effects, filling out questionnaires, using an imaginary or constructed rhetorical situation, guided writing).	Using specific analysis questions, filling out a Likert-type questionnaire, constructing a dialogue between a tutor and a writer, and other communicative procedures when learning about academic support genres (Swales & Feak, 2011), etc.
To create in genre analysis tasks an emerging sociorhetorical situation suitable for a multidisciplinary mix of students	Construct a sociorhetorical situation surrounding a task in a way that individual participants can differentially contribute to the task even though their engagement with the task may be more or less temporary.	Using concepts, topics, and samples accessible and relevant to the multidisciplinary mix of students in research writing classes, such as those topics/samples on engineering education, discourse community, L2 academic writing, highway bridges, etc. (Feak & Swales, 2009; Swales & Feak, 2012a; Swales & Lindemann, 2002)

time in each class session in a typical course, I would further the argument by suggesting that such a written genre analysis preferably be conducted out of class.

How to Guide Students to Analyze Genre Out of Class

Let us now turn our attention to how students could be guided to analyze their collected genre samples out of class (see my relatively brief description of such an assignment in Cheng, 2006a, 2007b, 2008a, 2008b, 2011a, 2015a). Previous sections of my research courses and workshops have focused on the JA genre (see similar practices in Gustafsson, Eriksson, & Karlsson, 2016; Huang, 2014; and others). In-class discussions of genre exemplars, often through a guided inductive approach with a set of general questions to uncover the rhetorical organization, the lexico-grammatical features, and the rhetorical contexts in the selected sample presented and discussed in class, often constituted the main in-class activity, as pointed out in a previous section in this chapter (see Figures 4.1 to 4.5).

Eight out-of-class genre analysis tasks often complemented such in-class explicit discussions of genre-specific features. In these tasks, students independently analyzed the Introduction, Methods, Findings, Discussion, and other sections in their collected JAs. They copied and pasted various parts of the JAs and used the edit and comment functions (coloring, italicizing, and boldfacing, among others) in Microsoft Word to analyze the texts. Figure 4.6 contains a sample assignment sheet for guiding such out-of-class tasks.

Some Perspectives on How to Assign Students to Conduct Out-of-Class Genre Analysis

The purpose section in the assignment sheet shows that at least two interrelated purposes have been incorporated into this assignment. The first purpose is for students to use the tasks to discover the genre-specific features that will be useful

Figure 4.6: Sample Assignment Sheet for Out-of-Class Genre Analysis

---

"Journal Article (JA) Analysis Tasks" Assignment Sheet
(Tasks 1–8)

Why?

These tasks aim to help you understand the context, organization, and linguistic features in the JAs in your collection. I hope that your analysis can help you write your own JAs, thesis/dissertation, and other research documents in this class and in the future. At the same time, I hope that the tasks will help you form the habit of paying close attention to *how* JAs and possibly other research genres in your field are written, rather than just *what* is written in these genres. Through these tasks and the related classroom discussions, I hope that you will learn an approach to analyzing familiar and unfamiliar genres in your field in and beyond this class. You can then use this approach to continue to teach yourself to write. You may even be able to use this approach to teach your students/advisees how to read and write research writing in the future.

How?

From the five JAs in your collection, choose several paragraphs from two different JAs to analyze in each task. The sections from which you will choose your paragraphs will be different in each task. For example, for Task 1 this week, choose several paragraphs each from the Introduction sections of two different JAs to analyze. Next time, the paragraphs could be from the Method sections in two journal articles. A list of the schedule and the focuses in each task is near the end of this assignment sheet.

Read these paragraphs carefully. Comment on some contextual, organizational, or linguistic features in them. These features could be anything that you consider to be important, relevant, useful, problematic, or just noteworthy to you as a current or future writer of research writing. Explain why these features are important, relevant, useful, problematic, or just noteworthy to you. Provide some details about what the features are and why they are noteworthy.

Limit your analysis to five features/points in each task.

If you are not sure about how to do your analysis, you could refer to the list of questions below. Note that these are the questions we use in class regularly to analyze the samples I selected from your collections:

Figure 4.6. (Continued)

[The questions omitted here; see Figure 4.1.]

Some special notes about your analysis:

1. You do not have to answer these questions one by one in your own analysis. They form the framework that you can fall back on in case you are not sure about how to start or what to look for in the samples. Instead, focus on the features that really speak to you as a current or future research writer.

2. If you notice anything similar to, or different from, what we have discussed in class, you could comment on them. However, do not use these genre analysis tasks to just confirm what we have discussed in class. Instead, use these tasks to help you uncover aspects of the samples that you consider to be important/useful/problematic/noteworthy to you.

3. Copy and paste the relevant parts of the JAs and use the edit and comment functions (coloring, italicizing, and boldfacing, among others) in Microsoft Word to analyze the texts. Some previous students have found the format of a two-column table with the left column as the original text and the right column with the analysis very useful.

4. After reading a particular JA analysis task by you, I may raise one or two questions mainly to ask you to clarify some points in your analysis. In your subsequent JA analysis task, address these questions, if any. For example, your JA analysis Task 2 will consist of two parts: Part One is your analysis of two new sections, each consisting of a sample you will be analyzing, and Part Two is your answers to my questions on your JA Task 1. If I see anything interesting in the text samples, I may also point them out to you.

Due dates and focuses

There are eight RA analysis assignments throughout the semester. The suggested focus in each task is listed below and the due dates are listed in the weekly schedule.

Task 1: the opening paragraph of a JA; claiming centrality

Task 2: reviewing the literature

Task 3: opening a research gap

Task 4: research purpose, research questions, significance of topic, roadmap, ...

Task 5: methods

Task 6: results or findings

Task 7: discussion

Task 8: conclusion

to them as current and future writers of academic and research texts (see awareness of genres as described in Chapter 2). The second, and arguably the more important, is to develop their awareness of genre analysis as an approach or a tool so that they can use it to analyze any new genre exemplars that they will need to write in this class and beyond (see the goal of developing genre awareness described in Chapter 2).

The assignment sheet also shows that students are encouraged to highlight any organizational, lexico-grammatical, contextual, or other features in their selected JAs that they may consider to be useful, problematic, or just noteworthy to them as current or future writers of JAs. Keeping the task discovery-based is consistent with the kind of learner-driven approach to explicit discussions of genre exemplars that I prefer. Because some students may not know how to start or what to look for, especially at the beginning of the course, I include the same guiding questions used for the in-class analysis of genre exemplars (see Figure 4.1) in the assignment sheet. These questions draw students' attention to the rhetorical organizational, the lexico-grammatical, and the contextual features in various genre samples. Apart from serving as a possible framework for those who may not know how to carry out their own analysis independently, these guiding questions aim to continue to educate students about how to use the genre-focused approach to teach research writing to themselves. They can even use the framework to teach writing to others after they graduate and become advisors themselves.

Another emphasis in this assignment is to constantly remind students that they are not supposed to merely display in these out-of-class genre analysis tasks what they have learned in class. Instead, they are supposed to use the tasks as a self-directed learning tool to discover what may be important, useful, problematic, or just noteworthy to them and to develop their genre awareness and their autonomy as learners of research writing. To achieve this purpose, they are reminded in the assignment sheet to highlight and focus on any features in the samples that speak to them as research writers—features that they feel are useful, important, relevant, interesting, problematic, or just features that attract their attention for any reason, especially when they keep their current or future writing needs in mind.

I also limit the features that they are asked to analyze to five, including any comments on the texts. When I first assigned this series of tasks, I encouraged students to comment on everything they noticed as important or noteworthy, but I learned very quickly that quality sometimes matters more than quantity does, and less is often more. Although I encouraged limiting their comments to only five features, a lot of the course participants often pointed out and commented on more than five features, something I secretly relished because the features analyzed often revealed a lot about how they may be learning research genres (e.g., Cheng, 2011b, 2015a).

The suggested focus of each task depends on what an instructor would like to emphasize in a particular class. In fact, when I started to assign this task many years ago, the foci in different tasks were quite different from what is presented here. For example, when I used this task in the first few iterations of a graduate-level writing course, the tasks were not so neatly anchored to the different sections in a JA. Instead, I included a task where the students were asked to focus on academic style (corresponding to Swales and Feak [2012a]) and then included another task where students were asked to just practice identifying a move and its steps in any section of an JA. I then progressed to a task where the students were asked to focus on the whole Introduction of a JA before moving to the gap statement and the section about the research purpose (e.g., Cheng, 2007b). After trying these tasks out in multiple sections of quite a few courses, I finally settled on these standard sections in a JA, as students very likely need to learn to write these sections in their first published JA and in their dissertation. I can certainly see other instructors focusing on another genre, such as grant proposals (L. Flowerdew, 2016), if they assign these out-of-class genre analysis tasks in their courses or workshops.

Two Cases to Show the Effects of Students' Out-of-Class Genre Analysis Tasks on Their Learning

How have the students in some of my previous writing courses conducted their out-of-class genre analysis tasks? I have reported on this topic in some previous publications (Cheng, 2006a, 2007b, 2008a, 2008b, 2011b, 2015a, 2015b); two cases will be explored here.

Ling's Case

Ling, an L2 graduate student from China, was in her third semester as a doctoral student in finance and business studies. Ling's out-of-class genre analysis tasks showed her effort to balance what she may have learned through the in-class discussions with what she discovered on her own in her reference JAs (Cheng, 2008b).

Specifically, Ling's analysis seemed to indicate that she was familiar with the overall JA rhetorical organization, at least in the introduction of JAs in her field and was able to analyze the move pattern clearly and accurately. For example, her analysis of the rhetorical organization in her JA samples showed a clear and consistent pattern from her genre analysis Task 2. When analyzing a segment in the introduction of an JA in her reference collection, for instance, she labeled the move and reconstructed the purpose of the move (e.g., *claiming the centrality* and *to persuade the readers that this area is very important,* see Cheng, 2008b, p. 395). Her ability to recognize and analyze the JA move pattern in her collection was also driven by her knowledge of the JA genre from some previous writing workshops and a thesis writing course she took when she was an MA student.

So, what did Ling learn in class? I noticed that her out-of-class analysis of the genre samples was characterized by her intensive focus on the differences between what had been discussed in class and what she perceived to be unique to her field; thus, the analysis tasks gave her the space to expand on some features she perceived to be unique to her field, a mode of learning highly consistent with the instructional goals in this case (awareness of genres as described in Chapter 2). She also highlighted these perceived disciplinarily unique lexico-grammatical features through referencing what she saw as the discrepancies between in-class discussions of genre samples and what she noticed in her own samples. We can see this mode of engaging with genre in her out-of-class genre analysis tasks in Table 4.2.

Ling's analysis of a literature review shown in Table 4.2 reveals her effort to connect class discussions with her own discovery of the genre-specific features in her field. I had previously discussed with the class how an JA writer can impose some order on the various studies he or she reviews "in order to demonstrate that there is an organizing mind at work" (Swales & Feak, 2000, p. 119), so it is especially noteworthy that, in [1], Ling took that on. She first acknowledged the lack of connections among the reviewed studies as a potential problem, but she was quick to defer to the implicit knowledge of the readers in the research community that would enable a reader to "figure out the internal logic." Meanwhile, she noticed that some researchers do use "transitional phrases to build up the strong logical relation" among various studies they review. The observation she generated from these perspectives as seen in the text sample she analyzed was that one should "never under-do it" nor "overdo it." Her analysis here suggests a rhetorically engaged analysis of this highly complex issue that had been discussed in class.

In other places in her analysis, she referred to textual practices in her reference collection that seemed "a little odd" to her (see [2] in Table 4.2), such as the lack of the gap-identifying move, when such a move had been emphasized in previous in-class discussions of other genre samples. Similarly, she brought up what she perceived to be a difference in the sample she looked at from what was "taught in class" (see [3] in Table 4.2). Specifically, she noticed "a common practice in the field of finance to briefly discuss the main results in the introduction, especially in empirical studies" (see [3] in Table 4.2). She also brought up a case of "breaking the rules introduced in class" (see [4] in Table 4.2). Specifically, "the secondary goal rather than the primary goal is elaborated" near the end of the

Table 4.2: Excerpts from Ling's Genre Analysis Tasks Connecting In-Class and Out-of-Class Genre Analysis

Features Ling Commented On	Excerpts from Ling's Comments
The logical connections between moves	[1] In some papers, the internal logical relationship among the specific studies is not obvious. I guess in this case, the authors assume that the research community can figure out the internal logic although sometimes it may not be an easy job for some starters like me. Yet in other papers, the authors use transitional phrases to build up the strong logical relation among those studies. The bottom line is that we should never under-do it nor should we overdo it. —Ling's Analysis Task 5, p. 6 (see Cheng, 2008b, p. 397)
The absence of the gap-identifying move	[2] In paragraph 6, the authors seemed to fill a research gap by laying out the principal goal of the study using a standard sentence like "the principal goal of this study is to. . ." <u>What sounds a little bit odd to me</u>, however, is that they didn't open a research gap at all .... Maybe the authors should have briefly reviewed what have been done in views of this idea and pointed out the research gap DIRECTLY. .... But unfortunately, the authors failed to do that for some reasons. —Ling's Analysis Task 3, p. 4; my emphasis (see Cheng, 2008b, p. 398)
The presence of the result move	[3] <u>It is taught in class</u> that the Result section should not appear in the Introduction. But to my knowledge, it is a common practice in the field of finance to briefly discuss the main results in the Introduction, especially in empirical studies.... —Ling's Analysis Task 3, p. 5, my emphasis (see Cheng, 2008b, p. 399)

Table 4.2 (Continued)

Features Ling Commented On	Excerpts from Ling's Comments
The emphasis on secondary research objective	[4] This move consists of three sub-moves: 1. Announcing the primary goal. 2. Announcing the secondary goal. 3. Elaborating on the secondary goal. Here it seems to be another case of breaking the rules introduced in class: the secondary goal rather than the primary goal is elaborated. I guess it is because, in this specific research, the primary goal is very obvious and easy to understand while the secondary goal is abstruse and thus needs more explanation. —Ling's Analysis Task 4, p. 2, my emphasis (see Cheng, 2008b, p. 400)
Certain unique centrality-claiming techniques	[5] The authors mainly claim the importance of this area by appealing to practitioners' view. My observation is that it is a common technique to refer to a practitioners' journal (e.g., *Wall Street Journal* and *New York Times*) when claiming centrality in my field. —Ling's Analysis Task 4, p. 4 (see Cheng, 2008b, p. 400)
Some unique citation practices	[6] The papers are usually grouped chronologically.... There is no "and" in front of last item when the citations are put at the end of a sentence....We rarely use "et al." even if there are 3 or more than 3 authors.... When original words are quoted, quotation marks are used.... Sometimes we use the initials of authors' last names (e.g., ABDL) to represent the papers with more than 3 authors.... —Ling's Analysis Task 5, p. 6 (see also Cheng, 2008b, p. 401)

Introduction of the JA she analyzed. Other instances of disciplinarily unique textual practices she highlighted included "appealing to practitioners' view," as opposed to referring to other research studies as pointed out in class, when JA authors claim the importance of a research area in her field (see [5] in Table 4.2). She also brought up some actual occurrences in her field regarding citation practices that may be different from what had been pointed out in class (see [6] in Table 4.2).

In short, Ling's out-of-class genre analysis tasks show that she seemed to be familiar with the basic move structure in JA introductions as well as with the overall framework of genre analysis consistent with the genre-focused approach to research writing. Such presumed familiarity seemed to have led to her focused attention to how certain features played out in the JAs in her field that she may have only been implicitly aware of in the past. Her out-of-class genre analysis tasks demonstrate her meaningful remediation of her existing genre knowledge and the resulting new understanding of the genre samples. Her effort to connect in-class discussions of the genre samples with her own discovery of genre-specific features (see [2], [3], and [4]), her heightened awareness of features that she perceived to be unique to her field (see [5] and [6]), and her finer appreciation of certain textual features as a result of her rhetorically engaged analysis of an issue brought up in class previously (see [1]) all signal a form of learning consistent with the discovery-based approach to genre analysis and with the goals of genre-focused learning. (Readers interested in reading more about Ling's genre analysis tasks can refer to Cheng, 2008b, where I present more than 18 excerpts from her work as well as contextualize her case in detail to document her learning in her out-of-class analysis.)

Varnesh's Case

Varnesh was a doctoral student in chemistry from a Southeast Asian country and was in the second semester of his degree study. Although still not very widely read in his field, Varnesh seemed to respond to a JA from his reference collection that he chose to analyze quite thoughtfully (see Cheng, 2011b, for more details).

When, for example, Varnesh conducted an out-of-class genre analysis tasks that focused on the Methods section in a JA in his reference collection, he highlighted a prepositional phrase *by applying the single-point method, 10b similar Ka values (ca. 2300 M-1) were calculated for the ...* in the Methods section in the JA he analyzed. He referred to this phrase as an example of a "fast method," as seen in this excerpt in one of his genre analysis tasks:

> In the next two sentences also written in past passive voice. Author has use "By applying the single-point method" it seems to be author used fast method. There in no justification why he used that method. In my point of view its better to explain why he used that method out of hundreds of methods. (see Cheng, 2011b, pp. 76–77, for Varnesh's genre-analysis Task 5)

The notion of "speed" to get at "the variability in method descriptions" was introduced in class prior to this genre-analysis task based on my presentation to the class of some examples from Swales and Feak (2000, p. 206) where the prototypical sentence pattern for indicating a fast method included "gapping," such as in *the samples were microtomed, placed in solution, centrifuged, and stored* or *occurrences were noted, scanned into the computer, and sorted into frequency categories* (Swales & Feak, 2000, p. 206). A method description can also be "fast" if it relies on citations or previously used standard methods, as pointed out to the class during in-class genre analysis.

Therefore, the prepositional phrase highlighted by Varnesh was not typically related to what was conventionally perceived to be a lexico-grammatical feature for a "fast" method description; in fact, it looks more like an example of another prototypical feature in the Methods section called "left dislocation." Swales and Feak (2000) have pointed out that left dislocations occur when material is placed to the left of the grammatical subject.

It might have been possible to dismiss Varnesh's comment as a misguided version of what he was supposed to have learned in class. When I looked at his comment closely, however, I found something quite noteworthy. Specifically, I noticed that Varnesh first identified the prepositional phrase *by applying the single-point method* as facilitating a fast method when a prepositional phrase like that was not prototypically related to fast method description. He then, quite interestingly, went on to criticize the use of this prepositional phrase as the authors' attempt to unjustifiably rush the description of the method. We can see his criticism in this comment: *There in [sic] no justification why he used that method. In my point of view its [sic] better to explain why he used that method out of hundreds of methods.* In other words, he argued that the use of the prepositional phrase *by applying the single-point method,* which he incorrectly considered to be a device for describing a fast method, had led to the omission of the proper justification for choosing this single-point method (*there in* [sic] *no justification why he used that method*). The omission had, in turn, resulted in the method being perceived by him as too fast (*in my point of view its* [sic] *better to explain why he used the method out of hundreds of methods*).

Justifying the method adopted in a study carefully was a point emphasized when we discussed the Methods section in class. Varnesh seemed to have picked up on this point because he made this comment on how the authors justified the use of a particular solvent elsewhere earlier in the same task:

> By looking at the scheme first question comes to my mind is why CHCl3? Why not other solvent. (There are hundreds of solvents can be used in chemical reactions). Then he justify why he used the particular solvent. It's like communicating with the reader. This is good way of writing according to because it's easy to understand the subject matter for beginners. (see Cheng, 2011b, pp. 76–77, Varnesh's genre-analysis Task 5)

Compared with his comment on how the authors have justified a previously described method *adequately*, his critique of the authors' use of the '*by applying. . .*' prepositional phrase as justifying the use of the single-point method *inadequately* was not just attending to this language feature on its own; rather, his comments seemed to be part of his overall effort to evaluate whether the method in the JA had been described carefully, which was an important rhetorical dimension specific to the Methods section in a research article. He also seemed to be using this feature as the lens to look at how the authors of journal articles he analyzed may or may not be connecting with the readers successfully ("It's like communicating with the reader. This is a good way of writing...because it is easy to understand the subject matter for the beginners"). Seen in this light, a seemingly misguided application of what he may have learned in class actually pointed to his engagement with the rhetorical contextual issues in his out-of-class analysis.

Like Ling's case, Varnesh's example shows us how the out-of-class genre analysis tasks have given course participants a meaningful space to explore discipline-specific textual features, to make meaningful connections between what they learned in class and what they discovered on their own, and to practice genre analysis as a conceptual framework—all of which are consistent with the instructional goals of genre-focused research writing classes.

Questions for Reflection and Discussion

1. Study the questions in Figure 4.1 carefully. Do you feel that these questions have captured what a thoughtful analysis of genre should be? Why or why not? Are there any questions that you would like to add to or delete from the list? Are you familiar with any other frameworks of genre analysis? If so, explain what these other frameworks of genre analysis usually cover. Compare them with the framework in Figure 4.1. What may be the strengths and weaknesses of each of these frameworks in terms of their suitability for analyzing graduate-level research genres?

2. This chapter shows two examples of how to use findings from existing genre analysis studies or pedagogical materials to develop teaching points to guide students' inductive, discovery-based analysis of genre in class. Are you familiar with any genre analysis studies? Find one of these studies and look at the findings (Yang and Allison, 2003, on results and conclusions, for example). Can the findings be translated into teaching points? If yes, what would be the teaching points? If not, what may be the reasons that prevent the findings from being turned directly into pedagogical points?

3. Read Figures 4.2, 4.3, 4.4, and 4.5 again. Can you think of any additional teaching points based on your reading of the two sample texts (see Figures 4.2 and 4.4) that could be added to Figures 4.3 and 4.5? Are there any teaching points in Figures 4.3 and 4.5 that you consider to be not so significant and would like to remove from the list? Why or why not?

4. This chapter looks at the criteria for designing genre analysis tasks based on Swales' work. Among the criteria described in this chapter, which one stands out to you as the most important one for guiding you to design effective genre analysis tasks? Why?

5. If you have taught graduate-level writing before, have you ever assigned students to collect and analyze genre samples out of class? If yes, what did you ask your students to do? How are your out-of-class genre analysis tasks similar to, or different from, those described in Figure 4.6 in this chapter? What may be the reasons behind some of the similarities and differences? If you have never assigned students to collect and analyze genre samples out of class, what may be the reasons for not doing so (not familiar with this type of assignment, too time consuming, etc.)? Has the description in this chapter convinced you to assign these out-of-class genre analysis tasks in the future? Why or why not?

6. Follow the instructions in Figure 4.6 and try one of these out-of-class genre analysis tasks yourself (try Task 3 in Figure 4.6, for example). Reflect on the process. Is the task logistically challenging? How much time did you spend on this task? Which aspects of the genre samples did your five comments focus on? Do you feel that your comments have deepened your understanding of the genre or part-genre in question in any way? After your reflections, would you still assign such a task to your students in the future? If not, why not? If yes, would you modify this task in any way? Why or why not?

Chapter 5

Writing Tasks and Evaluating Students' Discipline-Specific Writing

A natural extension of the topics addressed in Chapters 2–4 would be how writing tasks are often assigned in the graduate-level research writing classroom and how to evaluate discipline-specific student writing.

The Four Dimensions of Writing Tasks in the Graduate-Level Research Writing Classroom

Requiring Students to Write on Discipline-Specific Topics

Writing tasks, broadly speaking, are those that require students to produce writing. They have been assigned in a variety of ways and settings. The pedagogical reality of a multidisciplinary classroom has led instructors, naturally, to assign discipline-related writing. As examples, Cargill, Cadman, and McGowan (2011) asked their students to analyze successful departmental models and then to develop a topic specific to their areas of study, compose a related research question, and write a short paragraph about the topic and the question, while Lynne Flowerdew (2016) asked students to write a grant proposal abstract based on a project in their fields. Swales and Feak also often ask users of their books to perform discipline-related writing tasks. In *AWG*, for example, they ask their students to "write a short reaction to a paper in your field or to an oral presentation you have attended" (Swales & Feak, 2012a, p. 275) or to "write (or rewrite) your Methods section for some of your own research" (p. 305). There are additional examples of requesting students to write on discipline-specific topics in *Creating Contexts: Writing Introductions across Genres* (Feak & Swales, 2011, p. 98) and in *Abstracts and the Writing of Abstracts* (Swales & Feak, 2009, p. 24).

Requiring Students to Writing for Different Audiences

In their textbooks, Swales and Feak often ask their readers to practice writing for different audiences: In *AWG*, they point out how "your understanding of your audience will affect the content of your writing" (2012a, p. 4) and then ask readers to analyze two texts on the same topic. Drawing readers' attention to the different vocabulary items, details, and target publication venues that have supposedly been driven by the needs of different audiences in the two texts, they then assign readers to "write a short definition of a term in your field for two different audiences," one consisting of "graduate students in a totally unrelated field" and the other "could be students in your own graduate program" (p. 6).

In *Creating Contexts: Writing Introductions across Genres*, Feak and Swales (2011) first analyze a range of features specific to the genre of book reviews, including the kinds of information suitable for inclusion in book reviews and the *as* clauses often used to open a book review (*as the potential reader may suspect..., the author...*) (p. 29). The readers are, then, asked to write two short introductions to a review of the very book the readers are reading—*Creating Contexts: Writing Introductions across Genres*—"for two different audiences: (1) readers of a journal in your field and (2) your instructor or students at your institution" (p. 31). Other examples of requiring students to write for different audiences include Cargill, Cadman, and McGowan (2001) where their students from across the disciplines were asked to "write a brief explanation of your research topic for the TESOL lecturer, who is a nonexpert in your field" (p. 95). The students were, then, required to write another version for a different audience, such as an engineering student writing to a group of engineering students and faculty members, presumably based on the same research topic.

Requiring students to address the needs of different audiences is consistent with the goal of the genre-focused approach to graduate-level research writing instruction—raising students' rhetorical consciousness—because understanding and targeting the needs of different audiences constitute part of one's rhetorical consciousness.

Asking Students to First Analyze, and then Write

Apart from requiring or encouraging students to write on discipline-specific topics or content materials and to write for different audiences, graduate-level research writing instructors and scholars have also designed or assigned writing tasks that have been carefully scaffolded by preceding genre analysis tasks (see Chapter 4). For example, L. Flowerdew's (2016) workshop attendees were asked to work on proposals based on their own discipline-specific topics after the proposal genre had been analyzed extensively.

Swales and Feak's discipline- and audience-based tasks also often follow their careful analysis of the rhetorical organizational patterns and the lexico-grammatical features they hope their students will apply in the writing tasks. In fact, most, if not all, of the writing tasks in Swales and Feak's series of textbooks have been carefully guided by their detailed analysis of the target genre or part-genre to be practiced in the writing task (see Task Seven, for example, in *AWG;* Task Eight in *Abstracts;* and Task Three in *Creating Contexts*).

Engaging Students in the Writing Process

Some instructors of graduate-level research writing have engaged students in the writing processes, such as brainstorming for ideas or writing as a group or in pairs. An interesting example of this comes from Paltridge (1997) in his course on thesis proposals. First, he provided students with the abstract and key tables and figures from the Methods section of a research project relevant to the interests of a specific group of students and then asked the students to plan, in pairs or as a group, the writing of a proposal based on that particular piece of research. That done, Paltridge asked about the areas that needed to be addressed in each section of the proposal, and his students wrote a rough draft of the proposal. After the students presented these draft proposals to the rest of the class and invited comments and suggestions on how they might develop their proposals further, the outlines and the notes they had taken throughout the course were used to develop proposals for their own individual theses (p. 67).

Gustafsson, Eriksson, and Karlsson (2016) have built peer response—a part of the writing process—into their course focusing on traditional JAs. The peer response activities not only provide additional formative feedback that the instructors cannot provide but have instilled in their students a writing habit or culture that emphasizes social interactions (see also Starfield, 2003, 2016). Gustafsson, Eriksson, and Karlsson (2016) noticed that the peer response activities make explicit and destabilize PhD students' deeply entrenched assumptions of the disciplines they are a part of and lead them to notice the consequences and effects of their textual options. They noticed that their students "appreciate the resulting opportunity to re-evaluate" their written work (p. 266). As one student put it, "It has really been an eye-opener to realize that sentences and entire texts that make complete sense to the writer, i.e., me, can be perceived as almost incomprehensible to another reader" (p. 266). See also Cargill, Cadman, and McGowan (2001) and Douglas (2015) for other examples of writing tasks that engage students in the writing process in their graduate-level research writing classes.

Incorporating the Four Dimensions into the Same Writing Task: An Example

Although novice instructors of research writing could learn to incorporate these and other related dimensions into the writing tasks assigned in the graduate-level research writing classroom, it seems to me that the descriptions in these cases still lack adequate details about how the tasks have been developed or assigned, and there is little information as to how the writing was evaluated. Consequently, some important answers are still needed. A question that readers may have is related to the rationales behind some of the dimensions in the writing assignments, such as asking students to write for different audiences. In addition, how do the different dimensions (writing for different audiences, but on the same discipline-specific topic, for example) work together in an actual writing assignment, especially when students are to write a longer piece that may span multiple moves in a part-genre or in a genre? How can we build a stronger connection between the analysis and the writing of genres or part-genres, given that some of the writing tasks reported in the literature often use genre analysis to scaffold writing tasks? What should instructors look for in a piece of writing as indicators of students' learning and development? How can instructors read and evaluate students' discipline-specific or discipline-related writing samples that often contain unfamiliar topics, logics, styles of argument, organizations, and lexico-grammatical features?

In trying to address some of these issues, I will describe one of the discipline-related writing tasks I have previously assigned (see Figure 5.1).

An additional writing assignment that I have typically assigned is comparable to this, but requires students to write a section other than the Introduction (e.g., Methods, Findings, Discussion, or Conclusion). In other words, "introductory" or "introduction" are switched out from the sample assignment sheet in Figure 5.1 and replaced with "Discussion," "Methods," or the name of another part-genre. The same parameters described in Figure 5.1 still apply.

How Have the Four Dimensions of Writing Tasks Been Built into This Example?

I expand on the four dimensions that have been built into this sample assignment here.

Figure 5.1: Sample Assignment Sheet for Introductions

Writing Three Introductions

<u>Purpose</u>

To practice using the genre-specific features we have learned to write the introductory sections of three research genres or the same introduction part-genre for three different rhetorical contexts.

<u>Procedures</u>

Step 1

Write an introduction section similar to that in a standard data-based JA in your field. Your introduction can be based on a current or a future research project. If you have completed a project but have not written it up, use this opportunity to write it up.

Before writing, reflect on the features in the JA introductory sections we have been discussing and will continue to discuss in class. Look at your analysis of the JA introductory sections in your reference collection. Think about the following questions:

- What moves can I incorporate into my introduction? Why? What are the rhetorical contexts (readers' needs, my purpose, ...) that make these moves and not other moves suitable for my introduction?

- What linguistic features can I use in my introduction? Specifically, what are the typical words or sentences often used in the moves in the introduction in my field? What are the sentence patterns? What rhetorical purposes can these linguistic features help to achieve, and how would the readers react to them?

Do not write separate, unrelated moves. Instead, write a coherent and well-structured introduction where one move flows naturally and coherently to the next.

Figure 5.1 (Continued)

Do not try to write an introduction that you think I may like or one that is exactly the same as those analyzed in class. Instead, write one that you feel would meet the expectations of research peers in your field. Think about who your readers are, what they may or may not know, and what they may need from you. Consider carefully the purpose of each move and the purpose for the whole introduction as well.

Step 2

After you have written the introduction of a standard JA in your field (see Step 1 above), write two additional versions of introductions for two different rhetorical contexts. Base these two additional versions of your introductions on the same research project that you used for your standard JA introduction in Step 1 above. For example, you can write the introduction of a grant proposal or that of your thesis proposal. You could also write the introductory sections of a journal article, but this time for a different audience (write it for the practitioners in your field as opposed to for fellow researchers, for example).

If you choose genres other than JA, you may need to analyze the introductory sections in your target genres before your writing. If you choose to stay with the JA genre but would write for different audiences, think about the needs of these audiences carefully. Talk with me if you are not sure about how to write these two additional versions.

Step 3

After you have written the three versions, analyze your own writing as if you were analyzing others' writing in your genre analysis tasks. Do not list everything you have done in your writing. Instead, point out about five features and explain why they are noteworthy. How have these features helped you achieve your purposes in your text? How have they helped you meet the needs of your readers? In other words, view this step as your chance to explain to me how you have used certainly noteworthy features to achieve your rhetorical purposes and meet your readers' needs. You could point out more than five features, but the quality of your analysis is more important than the quantity is.

Similar to how you have carried out the genre analysis tasks, you can use the editing and comment functions in Microsoft Word for this step.

Step 4

After you have submitted your writing and your analysis of it to me, schedule a conference with me for us to talk about your writing.

Writing on Discipline-Specific or-Related Topics or Content Materials

As shown in Figure 5.1, the course participants were asked to practice writing a JA introduction based on a current, future, or a recently completed research project (and an additional section in a subsequent assignment). This aspect of the assignment adheres to a basic requirement for designing classroom-based writing tasks—validity (White, 1994). Because I emphasize exploring genre-specific features of discipline-specific writing, and students are required to extensively analyze genre exemplars from their fields (see Chapter 4), asking students to produce discipline-specific writing helps ensure construct validity—the consistency between what is required, what is learned, and what is being evaluated (Hamp-Lyons, 2003; Hyland, 2003). In fact, asking students to write something related to their research projects is quite common in graduate-level research writing courses, as we have seen in my review of others' writing tasks and in Freeman (2016), Starfield and Mort (2016), and Tierney (2016).

Writing for Different Audiences, for Different Rhetorical Contexts, or in Different Genres

Instead of writing only one introduction, course participants were asked to write three introductions based on the same research project or the same content material but to tailor their introductions to three rhetorical contexts that may fit their current or future needs (see Step 2 in Figure 5.1). The rhetorical contexts could be different in the target genres (a journal article, a proposal, and a thesis, for example) or in the audience's needs (to write for an audience consisting of practitioners, a non-specialist expert audience in a parallel field, and a specialist audience in one's own area of research).

The assignments discussed in Cargill, Cadman, and McGowan (2001) and Swales & Feak (2009, 2011, 2012a) mainly requested students to write for different audiences. However, I have allowed for the possibility of writing the introductory sections in different genres—that is, although only JA introductions had been discussed extensively in class up to this writing task, I encouraged the students to use their rhetorical consciousness developed through analyzing the JA introductory sections to analyze and then write the introductory sections of related research genres, such as those in a grant proposal or in a thesis. Instead of asking students to write different versions at the same time, students were asked to work on the JA introduction first as the presumed baseline version (see Step 1 in Figure 5.1) before experimenting with the different rhetorical parameters in the other versions. Doing so can help make this task more manageable, especially to the less confident research writers, than asking them to handle three versions simultaneously.

This aspect of the assignment adheres to another basic requirements for designing classroom-based writing tasks—interest (White, 1994). The interest level can be seen in my observation of students in previous courses who were intrigued by the challenge of showcasing three different ways to perform a step in a move, such as claiming centrality. They realized that they had to reexamine their previous analyses of the genre exemplars to ascertain how variations in the rhetorical organizations and lexico-grammatical features could be related to the rhetorical purposes in a particular step or move. As one student put it, "It's almost like trying to solve an engineering problem!" Another student mentioned that her research group had recently submitted two research papers to two different journals based on two different angles that arose from the same research project, so she understood the relevance of this requirement.

Incidentally, years after I first required students to write for different audiences or in different genres, I noticed that two behavioral ecologists (Hailman & Strier, 2006) describe the "desirability of spreading over different readerships separate but related papers on a given topic" (p. 96). They point out that this consideration frequently applies to publishing papers based on a doctoral dissertation, where an author may want to "alert workers in several different fields" to one's research. They give the example of three different chapters of a thesis on birdsong going variously to an ornithological journal, a behavioral journal, and a journal devoted to bioacoustics (p. 96). Their description certainly lends support to this dimension of the assignment.

Analyzing One's Own Writing

One dimension of writing tasks in the graduate-level research writing classroom is to task students with analyzing the valued genres before writing, as noted in a previous section in this chapter. In my assignment, students also need to analyze genre samples before they write (see Chapter 4). I have also incorporated another type of analysis that has not been reported in the literature—students are asked to analyze, or annotate, the three versions of their own writing by commenting on some noteworthy features (see Step 3 in Figure 5.1). Their analysis helps me and themselves understand how certain rhetorical organizational or lexico-grammatical features were intentionally used to address the needs of different audiences or to achieve diverse rhetorical purposes in different genres. In addition, comparing students' writing tasks with their self-annotations as well as with their genre analysis tasks helps me determine whether students have developed any rhetorical consciousness of how genre is influencing their writing (the learning objective about developing genre awareness as described in Chapter 2) and whether any genre-specific features learned through in-class discussions and out-of-class genre-analysis tasks may or may not have been integrated into the concrete organizational patterns or the lexico-grammatical features (the learning objective about the awareness of genres as seen in Chapter 2).

Conferencing as Part of the Writing Process

As noted in a previous section in this chapter, engaging students in the writing process is a dimension of writing tasks in the graduate-level research writing classroom. In my case, engaging students in the process of writing takes the form of conferencing, as seen in Step 4 in Figure 5.1. I typically let students know that I would provide some comments and questions related to the rhetorical organizations and the lexico-grammatical features on their first drafts before returning them. Then, we would have a writing conference—a form of discourse- or writing-based semi-structured interview—that would be driven by questions such as

- Your version 2 is much shorter than Version 1. Why?
- You don't explain this term here in Version 3. Why not?

In other words, the questions are based on what may have appeared to me as intriguing, problematic, puzzling, or just noteworthy in their first drafts. I aim to use these and other similar questions to gauge whether the students are able to verbalize any rhetorical considerations behind their texts. Questions and comments can then lead to suggestions on improving their papers such as:

- You criticize the Smith study as *inadequate*. Do you feel you need to explain more here to support your claim? Why or why not?
- You say here that this study is *crazy*. Is *crazy* a word that researchers in your field often use to criticize others' works? What would be a more common word for that purpose? Why do you think it is more suitable than *crazy*?

Others have mentioned the importance of conducting conferences with graduate student writers, but the goal seems to be to understand students' content area better (e.g., Frodesen, 1995; Tierney, 2016). For example, when describing how to offer individual consultations to graduate student writers, Tauber (2016) emphasizes the importance for writing specialists to "act as a kind of thought partner—reflecting and amplifying clients' ideas in order to help them clarify their concepts and arguments" and to serve as "an immediate audience where clients can work through a text until they are ready to show it to their advisor" (p. 649). In a similar vein, others have pointed out that writing specialists should help students to "ask their [disciplinary] supervisors better questions" so as to help students to "use their supervisor's time more efficiently" when working with graduate students' writing in individual conferences (Freeman, 2016, p. 224). In my case, the conferences certainly constituted a unique opportunity for me to understand and occasionally to help students reflect on and to amplify the ideas and content materials in students' discipline-specific writing, a point suggested by Tauber (2016). However, the more important goal was to use the conference as part of the writing process and as an opportunity to gauge students' development of rhetorical consciousness, if any, through focusing on the genre-specific features in their writing, a goal consistent with the learning objectives in research writing classes (see Chapter 2).

How Do the Four Dimensions Assist in Understanding and Evaluating Students' Discipline-Specific Writing?

To what extent can the four dimensions of the writing task work in conjunction and how can they help instructors understand and evaluate students' discipline-specific writing? To answer these questions, I present the case of a former student with the pseudonym of Fengchen, who was a PhD student in electrical engineering from China in a previous graduate-level research writing course (Cheng, 2006a, 2007b, 2008a). My analysis focuses more on my reflections of what I have learned as an instructor. It is worth noting here that, because of the focus on student learning (as opposed to teacher learning) that was part of my previously published research (Cheng, 2006a, 2007b, 2008a), many of the reflections on writing tasks and on teacher learning that constitute the focus of my discussion here have not been published. Since the student's writing serves more as the conduit for me to discuss writing tasks and to reflect on teacher learning, I will not present any excerpts from those studies although I will describe the student's writing in the relevant places. Interested readers should refer to Cheng (2006a, 2007b, 2008a) for more focused discussions on student learning.

How can the four dimensions of writing tasks that have been built into the sample writing assignment sheet in Figure 5.1 help us understand and evaluate students' discipline-related writing? First, the four dimensions in the writing assignment can help us understand students' developing sense of audience and rhetorical context. For example, at the required writing conference (see Step 4 in Figure 5.1), Fengchen explained that he wrote three versions of introductions for three different journal articles based mainly on what he perceived to be the differences in the three projected audiences. In his required annotations of the three versions (see Step 3 in Figure 5.1), he explained that the first version was written for a general audience in the broad field of "communications." Because the field of communications may include researchers from electrical engineering to those from "information technology," he stated that the readers of this first version may read it as a general-interest article and may need more background information on the topic (Fengchen's annotation of Version 1). He pointed out that, by contrast, the second and the third versions both targeted specialist audiences who might be more familiar with his specific topic than the general audience of the first version may be. Between the two specialist audiences of the second and the third version, he perceived the audience of the third version to be the "experts" who may be more invested in and, consequently, may be more critical of his research—the "finding-fault group"—in his words (The writing conference transcript).

We can see how the annotations and the writing conference helped me to tap into how the student had rhetorically constructed the three audiences for the three introductions. In fact, I learned a lot from his explanations in his annotations and from him during the writing conference. When we met, I was able to describe to him a parallel situation in which an ESP researcher may target three possible audiences with different aspects of a genre analysis study: the general audience of researchers in applied linguistics (the first version), the more specialized audience of researchers in second language writing and EAP (the second version), and the third audience of researchers whose research focuses on ESP genre analysis (the third version). We then had an interesting conversation about the similarities between these parallel situations. I asked him whether the third audience was necessarily more critical or more prone to "finding fault," as he had claimed in his self-annotations, than the first or the second audience may be. Maybe the third audience would view it as a mission to nurture the research in the highly specialized area so that the area would gain more visibility among researchers in the broader field? Although we were not able to reach a consensus about this point, I found the student's projection of the three audiences, as I came to understand it through his annotations and the discussion at the writing conference, very useful. With his permission, I have since shared this way of projecting the different audiences for one's writing with students in later courses and workshops, and some students have thus been able to construct their audiences in a similar way.

The discussions with Fengchen and with other students have also helped draw my attention to how established scholars in different fields may view the relationships between academic journals and audiences. For example, I noticed how two scholars in physical geography perceive the audiences of different journals in a way slightly different from how Fengchen or I did. Specifically, Parsons and Knight (2015) present the example of the journal *Permafrost and Periglacial Processes* as "a must" for specialists working on periglacial geomorphology. However, apart from such a specialist journal, researchers working in this field may want to communicate to a wider audience if they have something to report that has wider significance: "The journal *Nature* doesn't have many articles on periglacial geomorphology, but any that it does have will probably be very important" (p. 45). Reporting to a more general audience would seem more significant in this case, and the prestige of the journal *Nature* may be a variable as described by Parsons and Knight (2015), something Fengchen or I may not have taken into full account when we considered the different audiences based on his writing.

Second, the four dimensions in the writing assignment can help us understand the genre-specific features in students' writing. More important, they can give us a better sense of how these genre-specific features may or may not have been used with clear rhetorical considerations in mind. This point becomes clear if we look at how Fengchen reviewed the literature in the three versions.

Specifically, in his literature reviews in the three versions, Fengchen reviewed three Media Access Control (MAC) protocols for distributing bandwidth resources that were all protocols of the wireless access system. These resources are Packet Reservation Multiple Access (PRMA), Idle Sense Multiple Access (ISMA), and Distributed-Queuing Request Update Multiple Access (DQRUMA). For ease of reference, we will call these three protocols Protocol A (PRMA), Protocol B (ISMA), and Protocol C (DORUMA), respectively. (Readers interested in reading Fengchen's writing could look at Cheng, 2007b, where I present three excerpts from his three introductions in which he reviewed the three protocols.)

It is not important to understand what these protocols actually were here although the relationship among them will become clearer, especially when we look at the student's explanations in his annotations and at the writing conference later. In Version 1, which was for a supposedly general-interest audience of a broad-based academic journal, Fengchen presented the functions and inner systems of each protocol before he evaluated it, including pointing out its problems. Specifically, he followed this organization in his review of the three protocols: Protocol A -> Protocol B -> Protocol C. For example, he presented Protocol A this way:

> One of the earliest MAC protocol is [Protocol A] proposed by Goodman in [1]. In [Protocol A], the time axis is divided into two types of time slots: the idle slot and the reserved slot. If a slot is used by a data packet, it returns to the idle state; while if the slot is occupied by a voice packet, it remains at the reserved state until the whole voice frame is over.

He then critiqued this protocol this way: "However, due to the frame construction in [Protocol A], the system displays inefficiency when the bit rate of the services is low" (Fengchen's writing sample).

His annotations of this version allowed me to understand the rhetorical considerations behind this particular rhetorical organization—he was aware of at least two rhetorical purposes for reviewing the protocols. These were to (1) show the readers the advantages and disadvantages of each protocol and to (2) imply that his specific project that he was to present subsequent to the literature review was "a refinement of other person's work" (Fengchen's annotation of his writing). More important, his annotations showed me how he was aware of the way these two purposes had been shaped by the needs of the readers of this particular version—specifically, a better understanding of all three of these protocols and in that particular order could prepare the readers relatively unfamiliar with this research area to understand the rationale for his specific project better.

I also noticed from his annotations how he felt that the rhetorical pattern adopted in this version had helped him coordinate these rhetorical considerations effectively. In his annotations, he pointed out that the item-by-item, review-critique pattern adopted in this version was a "normal way to review the previous research" (Fengchen's annotation of Version 2). In other words, to him, this pattern represented a baseline one that RA authors would often use to review existing studies, including the protocols he was reviewing. It, thus, only seemed logical that the least specialized or sophisticated audience be presented with the baseline pattern first. In the writing conference, he explained that this "item-by-item" pattern could ease his comparatively generalist target audience into the topic because this intended audience may not be very familiar with his specific research topic. "There is no need to mix them [the protocols] all," he explained in the writing conference, because "they [the projected generalist readers of this version] may become confused because they are not ready" (The writing conference transcript).

I noticed that, in Version 2 of his Introduction, Fengchen adopted a pattern of reviewing the literature that was different from that in Version 1. Specifically, he presented both Protocol A and Protocol B and then critiqued them together. After that, he described Protocol C and critiqued it. It seems that the main difference between Version 1 and Version 2 is that he reviewed Protocol A and Protocol B separately in Version 1 but combined them as a unit to review together in Version 2. His annotations, again, helped me notice his awareness of the rhetorical purposes driving this rhetorical (re)organization. According to him, he intended to use "both of these two researches ([Protocol A] and [Protocol B])" as "negative examples to contrast with [Protocol C]" (Fengchen's annotation of Version 2). He reviewed Protocol C separately because he felt that it was, in his view, more "efficient" than the first two protocols. As a result, Protocol C, though with its own faults, was the one he intended to "confirm and make an improvement on" (Fengchen's annotation of Version 2). He pointed out in his annotations that, since the overall purposes of "these three paragraphs are not only the literature review but also serve the function of establishing the research gap and show the road for further study," the new rhetorical (re)organization may, in his view, be more effective.

I learned from the discussion at the writing conference how his awareness of the rhetorical purposes might have, again, interacted with his awareness of his readers' needs. He mentioned that, since the readers of Version 2 represented a more specialist audience than that of Version 1, they might be more familiar with this special topic. Therefore, "mixing the protocols" a bit, meaning combining Protocols A and B in his review, in the second version could actually help clarify and even highlight the advantage of Protocol C over the first two without the risk of confusing the readers (The writing conference transcript). In a word, his writing, his annotations, and the discussions at the writing conference helped me realize how Versions 1 and 2 were equally motivated by his rhetorical considerations, such as his awareness of the rhetorical purposes of these two versions, of the background knowledge of the two projected audiences, and of the resulting needs and reactions of the audiences. From this case, we can see how asking students to write multiple versions can afford instructors of research writing a unique opportunity to understand and evaluate not just learners' use of genre-specific organizational and linguistic features, but also their rhetorical knowledge (or the lack thereof), defined as the ability to consider "the specific audience for and purpose of a particular text, and how best to communicate rhetorically in that instance" (Beaufort, 2004, p.140). After all, the ability to turn genre-specific features one knows into the resources for meeting the needs of multiple audiences points to a very sophisticated level of writing skills for any writer, graduate-level research writers included.

Third, the four dimensions in the assignment sheet can offer instructors a valuable opportunity to understand learners' writing performance through looking at the intentionality in students' writing. Specifically, Fengchen's annotations of his own writing have helped me understand whether the use of certain features was accidental or purposeful, thus giving me a sense of any intentionality or agency behind his writing. They have also helped me notice the rhetorical knowledge driving any intentional use of the genre-specific features. This point becomes evident if we look at Fengchen's comments on the distinctions between Version 1 and Version 3 in which he switched the order of the two protocols. Specifically, I noticed that the rhetorical pattern in Version 3 was different from those in Version 1 and Version 2. In Version 3, Fengchen returned to the "item-by-item" pattern adopted in Version 1 where each item was reviewed and critiqued separately. However, in contrast to Version 1 where he first reviewed Protocol A before he reviewed Protocol B, in Version 3, he first reviewed Protocol B before he reviewed Protocol A. When I first read Version 3, I thought he was just shuffling the three protocols aimlessly as a trick to complete the potentially challenging task of producing three introductions based on the same material. After reading his writing, examining his self-annotations, and discussing with him at the writing conference, however, I started to realize that the way he switched the order in which Protocol A and Protocol B were reviewed in Versions 1 and 3 was, again, underpinned by his rhetorical considerations, and the switch was purposeful, rather than accidental.

For example, in his self-annotations, Fengchen explained that the inner logic of Version 3 was "like a struggle from wired to wireless." Invoking his disciplinary knowledge, he explained that Protocol B had become a "primitive theory in wireless field" because it was based on wired, as opposed to wireless, cable communication. Placing Protocol B at the beginning, therefore, allowed him to follow the disciplinary insider's logic of moving from a *wired* (presumably primitive) protocol to a *wireless* (supposedly sophisticated and advanced) protocol in his review of the three protocols. The question, then, becomes why he did not do the same for Version 1. Interestingly, he commented in the writing conference that such an organization may have been wasted on the readers of Version 1 because they may not be aware of, and may not need to be burdened with, the insider "logic of this special area." He believed that a chronological order of moving from Protocols A to C, as he followed in Version 1, would suit the needs of that generalist, broad-based audience better. By contrast, he felt that the pattern adopted in Version 3 was a better way to not only review the three protocols to meet the needs of the highly specialist audience of Version 3, but also to show these potentially skeptical "advanced readers" (meaning the more skeptical expert reader) his awareness of the "logic," or the implicit disciplinary narrative, that gave rise to his specific research topic (The writing conference transcript).

Finally, the multiple versions targeting different audiences, together with self-annotations and writing conferences, can help us tackle the issue of discipline specificity in student writing to some extent. Such a specific pedagogical reality presents a special challenge for assessing students' writing performance in my case and a possible hurdle faced by many other teachers of advanced academic writing: What do we do with the discipline-specific writing samples our students produce in research writing courses? If we are not sure we can fully understand the content of this writing, how can we evaluate it?

Swales and Lindemann (2002) have pointed out that "no instructor, however polymathic and experienced, can ever hope to unlock the huge door" of the entire academic universe of discourse of students from various disciplines (p. 118). Although such an argument can certainly ease our minds regarding these questions, some have pointed out that instructors of graduate-level writing may not want to "distance ourselves from the content domains in which graduate researchers are seeking to master academic writing in English" (Allison et al., 1998, p. 211). As a result, instructors may still be interested in knowing how these questions could be addressed.

Fengchen's case shows how encouraging and guiding students to write for different audiences based on the same research project or content, coupled with students' self-analysis and explanations of their writing through writing conferences, can help instructors assess students' discipline-specific writing to a certain extent. To be honest, after reading the three versions, I did not feel that I had fully understood what Protocol A, Protocol B, or Protocol C were (I still don't). But that may be beside the point; I am not an electrical engineer and never will be. However, as a writing instructor, I was able to learn from the strategic (re)organization of the three protocols and, more important, from the student's annotations and explanations during the writing conference what the "vital problems" and the "contributions" of each of these protocols, at least as articulated by the student, were. In addition, by reading his texts and his annotations closely and by posing various questions during the writing conference, I was able to understand how he articulated the internal logic linking the three protocols—the logic that propelled him to adopt, in his words, a "stepping-forward" style of argument in which "the later ... [one] viewed the article [protocol], the more consent (meaning his positive attitude) ... [one shares] about the research." His explanation allowed me to see how he was attempting to follow what he perceived to be the disciplinary insider's logic (The writing conference transcript).

Being able to guide students to articulate their discipline-related way of arguments and understanding such arguments through students' articulation may be more productive than feeling overly anxious about or being fixated on the technical details. I believe that writing instructors who remain intellectually curious can figure out the discipline-based arguments that the students make in their writing, especially if they are willing to talk with their students and are patient enough to listen to and help their students articulate their rhetorical and disciplinary reasoning behind their texts (see Allison et al., 1998, for a similar argument). Although instructors may still not be able to judge whether the arguments or logic articulated by their students are technically accurate, that may never be the point, as long as instructors keep in mind the goal of teaching graduate-level research writing, which is to help students raise their rhetorical consciousness. As an instructor, I would be perfectly happy if Fengchen or other students are able to articulate the logics and arguments in their writing to their disciplinary professors, even if such logics or arguments may not be perfectly in sync with that perceived by their disciplinary professors. As noted by others, it would be the responsibility of the disciplinary professors to help students with content issues, but such a job would certainly be made a lot easier if their students have become a lot more rhetorically aware through graduate-level research writing instruction (Freeman, 2016; Sundstrom, 2016; Tauber, 2016).

In sum, the case of Fengchen has shown how incorporating the four dimensions into a writing assignment in graduate-level research writing instruction can offer instructors unique opportunities to understand and evaluate students' writing, including discipline-based writing. I hope that reflecting on these and other related dimensions could help others develop writing assignments that will meet the needs in their own pedagogical contexts.

Rubrics for Evaluating Discipline-Specific Writing

In a report of how an international graduate student became a successful writer, Phillips (2014) noticed that the student benefitted very little from a cross-disciplinary graduate-level writing course for multilingual writers. The student received little positive feedback from his teacher. Phillips observed that the instructor identified problems like "lang. is non-idiomatic" and "sentence structure" but rarely offered the student alternative language or any particularly constructive comments towards revision or future writing projects (p. 78). A case like this points to the importance of providing written comments on students' work and to having a set of criteria on which to base that feedback.

The literature has included some reports of grading rubrics targeting discipline-specific academic writing. Stoller and her colleagues, for example, discuss how they developed and validated a set of grading criteria to measure learning outcomes in their *Write Like a Chemist* project funded by the National Science Foundation in the United States (Stoller, Horn, Grabe, & Robinson, 2005). Their final grading criteria encompassed both those unique to chemistry writing (e.g., "properly formatted tables, schemes, figures"), those typically required by English faculty (e.g., "free of surface errors"), and those deemed as important by both parties (e.g., "correct grammar, tense, ... and scientific abbreviation, superscripting, and subscripting, etc.") (p. 97). Their grading standards and analytic scale were sensitive to their context of a large-scale, grant-supported project in which undergraduate students' chemistry research papers would be graded consistently by faculty members in multiple institution across the United States. Although Stoller et al.'s rubric (2005) was designed for undergraduate students in chemistry, the practice of encompassing discipline-specific criteria as well as criteria by English instructors can be adopted and adapted for graduate-level research writing classes.

Elsewhere, other instructors have developed rubrics specific for evaluating graduate students' writing (e.g., Hyland, 2004b; Paltridge, 2001). As early as 1998, Allison et al. (1998) developed a set of criteria that forms the diagnostic assessment profile for graduate student writers. Although these criteria were based on their perceptions of graduate students' writing problems at the University of Hong Kong rather than on any specific writing assignment, the four major criteria (communicative success, substantiation, discourse elements, and editing) can serve as the basis for grading rubrics for evaluating graduate students writing.

In terms of my writing assignments, I used a set of grading criteria like those in Figure 5.2. Readers may notice that the criteria consist of a set of questions. Some of them speak to the overall rhetorical organization and the moves/steps in it (Questions 1 and 2). One question aims to draw students' attention to the lexico-grammatical features specific to their fields that they were supposed to practice using in their writing (Question 3). Other questions point to some of the general writing quality, such as coherence and cohesion (Questions 4 and 5) and surface errors (Question 6). For their annotations, I included two rather general questions to draw their attention to what they should be doing in their annotations (Questions 7 and 8).

I included these questions because they reflected what I emphasized in students' writing, and I intentionally kept these questions general so that I could have room to expand on these questions when commenting on their work orally or in writing. I usually wrote down some substantive comments based on each of the criteria after reading their drafts.

Readers planning to adopt an assignment similar to that in Figure 5.1 can adopt and adapt the rubric in Figure 5.2.

An additional source of information for developing rubrics to suit one's needs is the "guide for authors" of academic journals. These guides often describe the requirements for each section of the journal article, and some of these requirements could be used as grading criteria. Instructors could look at multiple guides and choose common requirements as rubric criteria. For

Figure 5.2: Sample Grading Criteria for the Tasks Described in Figure 5.1

Your paper:

1. Are the three versions sufficiently different? (x points)

2. Do they include the moves and steps that that are often used in the genre or genres that you target with the three versions? (x points)

3. Have you used some of the linguistic features that people often use in the genre or genres that you target with the three versions? (x points)

4. Have you used clear topic sentences and transitions between paragraphs? (x points)

5. Have you maintained strong logical connections among the sentences in each paragraph? (x points)

6. Have you carefully edited your paper for grammatical, mechanical, document design, and citation errors (pay special attention to the requirements in your field)? (x points)

Your annotations:

7. Have you explained clearly why and how the three versions are different (audiences, journals, genres, and others)? (x points)

8. Have you pointed out at least five noteworthy features that you have used in your writing and explain why you have used them that way? (x points)

example, I have noticed that many journals from which my students selected their journal articles for analysis (see Chapter 4) often guide authors to offer sufficient details in the Methods and Material section of their papers so that the work can be reproduced. At the same time, authors are told to include only a reference if they adopted a method that had already been published, and only changes to the previously published methods should be described. This requirement could then become a grading criterion. If instructors assign students to collect journal articles to analyze (see Chapter 3) or encourage students to target specific journals in their field with their writing (see this chapter), the guides for authors in these journals nominated by students will be very useful for rubrics development.

Questions for Reflection and Discussion

1. This chapter introduces four dimensions researchers and practitioners have incorporated into their writing tasks in the graduate-level research writing classroom. Among the four dimensions, which one stands out to you as the most important—a dimension that you feel compelled to incorporate into the writing tasks in the graduate-level research writing classes you teach or will teach in the future? Why?

2. Think of a writing task you have assigned in your own graduate-level writing class or one that you have been asked to write when you were in a graduate-level research writing class. What was the task like? What did you, as the instructor, ask your students to write, or what were you, as the student, asked to write? Does the task include any of the four dimensions described in this chapter? Does it include any other dimensions that have not been described in this chapter? What may be the reasons behind the additional dimension or dimensions?

3. This chapter describes a writing assignment with all four dimensions incorporated into it. What do you think of this assignment? In your view, what are its strengths, if any? Would you modify this assignment in any way if you assigned it in a future writing class? What would you change, and why? For example, would you be able to achieve the same pedagogical purpose if you asked your students to write only two versions instead of three? Why or why not?

4. Have you used any rubrics to grade graduate-level research writing, or, if you have not taught before, have others used grading rubrics to grade your graduate-level research writing? Describe the rubrics. What criteria do they include? What are the strengths and weaknesses of these rubrics compared with the one in Figure 5.2?

Chapter 6
Building and Updating the Knowledge Base for Effective Research Writing Instruction

What should practitioners of research writing instruction incorporate into their knowledge base to work effectively in and out of the genre-focused research writing classroom? This chapter addresses this and other related issues.

Become Familiar with L2 and EAP Instructional Approaches and Issues

Many practitioners of graduate-level writing instruction often, if not mostly, work with L2 student writers or L2 novice academics (e.g., Gustafsson, Eriksson, & Karlsson, 2016). To become familiar with L2 writing and EAP writing instructional approaches and issues in general would, therefore, be important. Books that focus on L2 writing and EAP writing are useful for updating one's knowledge in these areas (e.g., Charles & Pecorari, 2016; Ferris, 2009; Ferris & Hedgcock, 2014; Hyland, 2015b; Paltridge et al., 2009). These and other valuable resources have, for example, expanded on the unique characteristics of L2 writers and the different L2 student populations (e.g., international visa students, resident immigrant students, EFL students, and Generation 1.5 students, as opposed to graduate students). They have informed teachers of the different theoretical and pedagogical traditions in L2 composition instruction, such as the product-oriented traditions, the process movement, and the post-process era, among others, and, thus, can help one determine whether, and to what extent, these approaches are related to the genre-focused approach discussed in this book. For example, the examination of the shifts in pedagogical focus in L2 writing instruction, from focusing on texts, to creative expression, to disciplinary content, to discourse community, and to social political issues (e.g., Ferris & Hedgcock, 2014; Hyland, 2015b) can help practitioners reflect on where graduate-level writing instruction may fit into these existing or shifting paradigms. The ways these and other books specify the various approaches to syllabus design and lesson planning applicable to L2 writing and academic writing classes, such as process-driven vs. genre-driven courses or course sessions, can also be very useful. The various ways of developing tasks and using technologies in L2 writing class as well as the methods of responding to and assessing L2 student writing described in detail in these books and resources can also contribute to one's knowledge base and help one reflect on what is especially unique to graduate-level academic writing instruction.

In sum, although teachers of research writing often deal with a unique student population—graduate students and junior scholars—that may be different from those often targeted by these books that discuss L2 writing instruction in general, understanding how similar or related topics and concepts have been understood in the broader context of L2 writing and EAP writing instruction would be beneficial and should be part of building and updating one's knowledge of graduate-level research writing, especially for those who work primarily or exclusively with L2 graduate students. Indeed, as Casanave (2017) points out, writing teachers, "in all cases," benefit from the knowledge about the theoretical foundations of L2 writing instruction (p. viii).

Compared with the previously mentioned resource books that provide a comprehensive view of what L2 writing or EAP writing instruction usually entails (e.g., Charles & Pecorari, 2016; Paltridge et al., 2009), other books that provide comparatively more in-depth perspectives on working with multilingual writers can also be a valuable source of building and updating one's knowledge of graduate-level research writing. For example, in a volume on controversies in L2 writing in the series co-edited by Diane Belcher and Jun Liu and published by the University of Michigan Press, Casanave (2017) looks at the conflicting opinions about intercultural rhetoric, paths to improvement, assessment, the dilemma of plagiarism, and writing in the digital era in L2 writing instruction. She hopes that a deeper understanding of these key issues can help teachers decide for themselves what to do in their classes when confronted with these issues. Some of the key issues highlighted by Casanave (2017), such as the different paths to improvement, what counts as plagiarism vs. textual borrowing, and the distinctions between the pragmatist as opposed to the critical approach to teaching academic writing, are directly applicable to the research writing classroom. In fact, since these topics have not been covered in detail in the present book, readers of this book should definitely refer to Casanave (2017) as a source to build their knowledge of these highly relevant and applicable topics.

Joe Bloch's (2008) focus on technologies in the L2 composition classroom in the same series could also be useful for building and updating instructors' knowledge for effective graduate-level research writing instruction. As noted in the previous chapters, technologies are increasingly used in research writing classes. For example, Kuteeva (2013) as well as Paltridge and Woodrow (2012) used blogs in their writing classes to help their graduate students develop genre awareness or reflect on research writing practices. Lee and Swales (2006), Charles (2007, 2012), and others used corpus tools for their students to learn both the rhetorical organizational patterns and the lexico-grammatical features in research genres. Therefore, developing a deeper understanding of the debates about technologically enhanced writing and writing instruction and becoming familiar with the technologies often used in L2 writing and academic writing, such as blogging and concordancing, which are all topics covered in Bloch's book, can be an important component in the knowledge base of practitioners of graduate-level research writing instruction. New technologies related to collaborative writing, such as Google Drive and wiki, some of which have been discussed in Bloch (2008), could be directly applied in the research writing classroom to enhance students' analysis of genre exemplars (see Chapter 4 of this book) and help students annotate their writing (see Chapter 5) in an interactive manner with instructors and fellow students enabled to respond to some of the analyses or annotations conveniently online. Seen in this light, these and other technologies related to writing instruction in general, as covered by Bloch, should be incorporated into research writing instructors' toolbox and knowledge base.

The previous chapters talk about conducting teacher-led discussions of genre exemplars through sample-neutral questions or sample-specific tasks (Chapter 4), providing written responses on students' writing (Chapter 5), and carrying out instructor-student conferences to discuss students' discipline-specific writing (Chapter 5). The understanding of these topics can definitely be enriched by the discussion of the various topics in *Connecting Speaking & Writing in Second Language Writing Instruction* by Weissberg (2006). Having a clear understanding of how the connections between speaking and writing play out in writing tasks, peer-review work, group writing and reviewing activities, conferencing, dialogue journals, and teacher written feedback as discussed in great lengths in Weissberg can certainly contribute to the knowledge base of instructors and enable them to use these activities in their research writing classroom.

A final example of an in-depth look at L2 writing issues especially applicable to the teaching of graduate-level research writing is Hirvela's second edition of *Connecting Reading & Writing in Second Language Writing Instruction* (2016). Hirvela discusses the integration of reading and writing instruction thoroughly with his careful survey of the related theory, research, and pedagogy. Understanding the relationship between reading and writing should form part of the knowledge base of instructors of research writing. The previous chapters have looked at how instructors of graduate-level writing classes can guide students to analyze genre exemplars and gauge students' development of rhetorical awareness through looking at students' abilities to read as a writer and to write as a reader. Two of the three major frameworks presented in Hirvela—reader response theory and reading for writing—have definitely helped put the discussions in the present book into the larger theoretical context about reading-writing connections and can, thus, contribute to the knowledge of practitioners who work with graduate-level research writers.

Experiment with the Pedagogical Initiatives Targeting L1 Graduate-Level Research Writers

Apart from becoming familiar with the approaches to teaching L2 writing and EAP, learning about the challenges facing L1 graduate-level research writers and the pedagogical initiatives targeting this population should become part of the knowledge base of instructors of graduate-level writing classes regardless of which group of students instructors work with. As pointed out in Chapter 1, difficulties in producing graduate-level research writing is not strictly a problem with L2 writers. In fact, some instructors of graduate-level research writing have found themselves working with both L2 and L1 students (e.g., Freeman, 2016; Paltridge, 2016; Simpson, 2016a; Starfield, 2016; Starfield & Mort, 2016; Sundstrom, 2016; Tierney, 2016). Even instructors working primarily with L2 learners can benefit from their knowledge of the initiatives or innovations related to working with L1 graduate students and from learning, in general, "how much graduate writing pedagogy shares across a plethora of contexts" (Sundstrom, 2016, p. 201; see also Simpson, 2016a, 2016b; Simpson et al., 2016).

For example, using writing groups, writing camps, or writing retreats to support L1 research students' writing development has attracted the attention of academic supervisors and doctoral researchers in the United Kingdom (e.g., Murray, 2015), the United States (e.g., Busl, Donnelly, & Capdevielle, 2015), and Australia (e.g., Aitchison & Guerin, 2014; Paltridge, 2016).

In the United States, for instance, Busl, Donnelly, and Capdevielle (2015) describe what they called a "significant innovation" in meeting the unique challenges facing graduate students: the writing camp. According to Busl, Donnelly, and Capdevielle, the writing camp is a full-week immersion experience modeled on the Dissertation Boot Camp that began at the University of Pennsylvania in 2005 (Lee & Golde, 2013). They note that many writing camps have often been run by partnerships of graduate schools, writing centers, libraries, and other support units in many U.S. universities.

Using Lee and Golde's (2013) categories, Busl, Donnelly, and Capdevielle (2015) draw our attention to two kinds of writing camps: the Just Write camps and the Writing Process camps. The Just Write camps are based on the assumption that graduate students already possess the necessary skills and behaviors to write successfully, and they simply need a dedicated, distraction-free time and a physical space to get down to writing (see Casanave, 2017, for her comment on how difficult it is for graduate students to find the time and energy for concentrated writing). The location is usually quiet with adequate table space and sufficient power outlets for students to use laptops and other electronic devices. Students are provided with set hours, such as from 8 AM to 4 PM every day for a week, to use the space. Refreshments, such as breakfast and coffee in the morning and snacks in the afternoon and, occasionally, even lunch may be provided, depending on available funding. Just Write camps often do not have specific instruction on writing or on the writing process. A slightly different version, which is often not institutionally organized, is called Shut Up and Write! (See Mewburn, Osborne, & Caldwell, 2014, and see http://thesiswhisperer.com/shut-up-and-write/ for the history and the principles behind it.)

The Writing Process camps, by contrast, often encourage conversations about writing in addition to providing the time and space for writing. They operate on the assumption that the attendees may lack the skills and behaviors necessary to complete a dissertation or other complex research writing projects. Consequently, these camps offer focused instruction on writing processes such as maintaining a dissertation log or brainstorming or other strategies to help overcome writer's block. Writing consultants or tutors may also be available. Some writing retreats or camps have also focused on topics related to the process of writing for publications, such as the reasons for writing for publication, the strategies for choosing one's target journals, writing article abstracts, and responding to reviewers' reports (Paltridge, 2016).

Busl, Donnelly, and Capdevielle (2015) provide some examples of writing camps offered at a mid-sized private research university in the midwestern region of the United States. They used pre-and post-camp surveys and daily logs kept by participants to look at the participants' development of self-efficacy and motivations as research writers after taking part in these writing camps. They noticed that the camps positively affected the beliefs and behaviors of the graduate student attendees. They suggest that writing camps should include programming that emphasizes discussion, collaboration, and process-improving behaviors in order to improve attendee's self-efficacy, motivation, and their control of the writing process.

Compared with the writing camps that emphasize Just Write or knowing about and controlling one's writing process as described by Busl, Donnelly, and Capdevielle (2015), the writing groups organized at some universities in Australia seem to have incorporated a lot of discussion, collaboration, as well as the development of skills beyond just those related to the writing process. In fact, researchers and practitioners in Australia seem to have contributed the most to the theory and practice behind writing groups as pedagogy for graduate students (e.g., Aitchison & Guerin, 2014; Aitchison & Lee, 2006; Maher, Seaton, McMullen, Fitzgerald, Otsuji, & Lee, 2008). Aitchison and Lee (2006), for example, describe the thesis writing circles (TWCs) started by the Learning Skills Unit at the University of Western Sydney (UWS). They describe these TWCs as typically meeting weekly. The three-hour meetings were often guided by agenda items, which often included critiquing new written work, discussing a particular aspect of writing or the genre-specific aspects of the thesis, and reviewing revised writing. Different from the Just Write or Writing Process camps, these TWCs also had various linguistic or genre-specific focuses determined ahead of time so that participants could coordinate their writing with the aspect under review in a particular week. These focuses included examining thesis structures, learning to write research questions, learning to use evidence in argument development, addressing specific concerns such as the researcher's voice, and tackling micro-level questions about style and grammar. Similarly, the off-campus writing retreats organized by the Faculty of Education and Social Works at the University of Sydney have incorporated a session where the rhetorical organization of journal article abstracts was discussed explicitly with the retreat participants. Sample responses to reviewers' comments have also been shown and analyzed in the retreats (Paltridge, 2016).

Participants in writing groups similar to those described by Aitchison and Lee (2006) have reported in the literature about the positive effects of these groups. Maher et al (2008), who were former doctoral students and participants of a writing group similar to the one described in Aitchison and Lee (2006), elaborate on the writing and reading skills and techniques that they noticed that they had developed through participating in the writing group. For example, they felt that the writing group had helped them develop skills to engage directly and systematically with each other's writing. As a result, they had become better at critically evaluating other students' writing as well as their own writing. The process of engaging in sustained reviews and critiques of their own and one another's drafts, they noticed, had allowed them to develop a more refined understanding of the dialogic practices of research writing, to shape their scholarly identities, and to form strong social and emotional bonds as fellow research writers (see the description of a similar effect of peer interactions, but in an L2 classroom setting, in Gustafsson, Eriksson, & Karlsson, 2016).

More interestingly, Maher et al. (2008) felt that they had learned how to work actively within the structure of a dissertation. Through the writing group, they were able to conceptualize the whole dissertation at a 'macro' level, deal with the text down to the sentence or micro level, and understand the relations between these levels. Specifically, they noticed that "through working with our own and one another's evolving [dissertation] structures, we began to grasp the work of attending explicitly to the conceptual and structural work of determining and articulating the relationships among the different parts and of parts to the whole" (p. 270). Such an understanding is not just limited to "building conceptual linkage and coherence," but also down to the textual level as well, as seen in the reflections of the participants (p. 270).

Other than the writing group or writing retreat pedagogy described, other initiatives and innovations that can promote graduate students' learning of research literacy include the Three Minute Thesis (3MT®) competition at many university campuses. The 3MT® was first started at the University of Queensland in Australia in 2008 (http://threeminutethesis.org). It is a research communication activity to help students develop academic and research communication skills for presenting their research to a non-specialist, but educated, public audience in an understandable and concise manner. Students have only three minutes and one static slide to convey to their audience what they do in their graduate-level research projects and the importance of their projects. Since its inception, enthusiasm for the 3MT® concept has grown with the 3MT® adopted by over 170 universities across more than 18 countries worldwide. My current institution first held a 3MT® competition in 2013, and some of the winners went on to compete against 3MT® winners from other universities in the Conference of Southern Graduate Schools (CSGS) regional 3MT® competition. I noticed that both L1 and L2 speakers were among the finalists and winners in the last few years. Even though 3MT® is a speaking activity, instructors of writing classes can certainly explore its relevance to their writing classes. For example, writing instructors could turn some of the 3MT® presentations into part of the genre analysis tasks so that our students can develop a more acute sense of audience for one's writing. Instructors can ask students to develop a written version of 3MT®—a pamphlet, maybe, or an author summary of a thesis or journal article that targets an educated lay audience (see Breeze, 2016, for her study of a new genre called author summary that is similar to 3MT® in the need to address a lay audience). Students can be guided to pay special attention to how such a pamphlet or author summary may be different from an article abstract for an expert, specialist audience. Questions like these and the possible resulting pedagogical practices can certainly help broaden the pedagogical horizons of many instructors of graduate-level writing courses and can have a positive impact on their professional practices.

Apart from writing groups and 3MTs®, a recent notable proposal reported in the L1 writing literature urges writing scholars to offer independent consulting as a viable way to share their expertise with graduate-level research writers and with advisors and programs working with graduate students (Tauber, 2016). Tauber, an L1 composition specialist, believes that writing specialists could play a wide variety of independent consulting roles. These include helping graduate programs plan writing instruction and support, offering consulting to graduate-level writers, and delivering workshops and writing groups targeting graduate students and their advisors, among others. For example, writing specialists as independent consultants could work with graduate students directly. Such consulting work could involve helping students to clarify conceptual issues in their discipline-specific projects, to revise and edit their work, to develop an effective writing process, to navigate academic culture and build scholarly identity, to overcome the feelings of isolation that plague many graduate student writers working on their theses and dissertations, among others.

Writing specialists' independent consulting with graduate-level research writers, according to Tauber (2016), could also involve working between graduate student writers and their advisors. She reports that she often has to help her graduate student clients understand and operationalize feedback from disciplinary faculty because a significant percentage of them could not understand what some of the feedback from disciplinary faculty actually means and would often ask for help in working effectively with their advisors and committees. In fact, she suggests that writing specialists working as independent consultants present to the disciplinary faculty the option of the writing specialist serving as a "transparent, nonvoting" part of students' thesis teams where the faculty member and the independent writing consultant can see each other's feedback and consult with each other when necessary (p. 652). She reports that the faculty members she has worked with in this role have "expressed trust in [her] capacities and perspectives on students' work, have felt respected and supported by [her] approach to working with them and with their students, and have even expressed relief at being able to triangulate their own perceptions of student work through a third party" (p. 652). Along the same line of argument, she urges writing specialists to play an active role in supporting graduate faculty as well as educating graduate faculty about issues related to graduate-level research writing by, for example, giving workshops to faculty thesis advisors (see a similar argument in Paltridge & Starfield, 2007).

Tauber describes these possibilities for working with graduate-level writers and their advisors and programs in the context of her larger argument for academics to work as "an extra-institutional consultant" (p. 643) and as "alternative academics" (p. 653) who choose not to follow or who may not have the opportunity to follow the traditional career path of a tenure-track, full-time writing faculty. Such a context may or may not be applicable to the target audience of this book. However, many of her thoughtful suggestions for working effectively with graduate-level research writers and their advisors through individual consultations could become part of the professional development and expanded skills of instructors working with graduate-level research writers. These suggestions include developing the ability to listen to disciplinary faculty in order to perceive and propose new roles one can play in helping graduate-level writers; to learn to become effective participants in a wide range of institutional and departmental cultures; to build credibility through posing the right questions and active listening; and to combine many roles that may include those of a writing coach who helps students focus on writing process and project management, an editor, and a thought-partner who helps students reflect on and amplify their own concepts and arguments, among many others (see Burgess & Cargill, 2013, for a similar, but less expanded argument about working with multilingual students at the graduate level through individual consultations).

In sum, I have looked at multiple examples of pedagogies or practices supporting graduate-level research writing that emanate from or mainly originate from the scholarly communities that work with L1 graduate-level research writers. I hope that the description has given the readers of this book a clearer idea about these pedagogies as well as any additional resources if they plan to take up some of these initiatives or pedagogies. At the same time, I hope that it has become evident now that I am not arguing that instructors of research writing should hustle to start organizing writing groups or writing camps, 3MT® competitions, or working as independent consultants. In fact, some of these pedagogies or practices require institutional resources (Paltridge, 2016), some of which may not be available to instructors of graduate-level writing. Instead, I hope to use these examples to illustrate how researchers and practitioners of graduate-level research writing instruction, especially those working within the ESP genre-focused framework, could benefit from learning about and reflecting on the research writing instructional initiatives, pedagogies, and practices in other disciplinary and geographical areas (e.g., Brooks-Gillies et al., 2015; Simpson et al., 2016; Zawacki & Cox, 2014), regardless of the linguistic backgrounds of their students. Journals such as *Studies in Higher Education, Teaching in Higher Education, Higher Education Research and Development, WAC Journal,* and *Across the Disciplines* include many articles that often focus on issues and pedagogies related to L1 graduate students' research writing. Online resources, including blogs such as *Patter* (http://patthomson.net/), *The Thesis Whisperer* (http://thesiswhisperer.com/), or *The Explorations of Style* (http://explorationsofstyle.com/) and online professional communities such as the Consortium on Graduate Communication (CGC) (https://www.gradconsortium.org/) are also very useful resources to learn about issues related to L1 graduate-level research writing instruction that could benefit those interested in the genre-focused approach to graduate-level writing instruction.

Understand Students' Learning or Practices of Research Writing in Non-Classroom Settings

The chapters in this book have mainly covered learning and teaching graduate-level writing in classroom or classroom-related settings. What happens to graduate students' research writing practices and their learning of research genres outside the classroom, especially when the boundary between classroom- and non-classroom-based learning of research writing may not be clear cut? Tardy (2009), for example, reminds us of how graduate students may come "to classrooms with writing tasks that they are completing in their content courses, at work, or in their independent research" and "they leave the writing classroom and go directly to their lab, to a study group, or even to a research conference" (p. 9; see a similar observation in Tauber, 2016). Given such an observation, how do graduate students learn and practice research writing outside of the writing class, if such a writing class is available to begin with? How do they learn to participate in their own communities of practice (Lave & Wenger, 1991) through their research writing practices? How do they interact with their disciplinary advisors or supervisors surrounding their research writing activities? Do they link what they have learned in the writing classroom with their discipline-specific writing practices out of class? Understanding these and other issues, either through close reading of the literature on learning and practicing research writing in non-classroom settings or through one's own research in such settings, should probably become an integral part of building and updating one's knowledge of research writing instruction.

Many studies have looked at the important and challenging questions listed in the previous paragraph (e.g., Casanave, 2002, 2014, 2016; Casanave & Li, 2008; Paltridge, Starfield, & Tardy, 2016; Prior, 1998). These studies have documented graduate students' out-of-class learning of research writing through the framework of community of practice, legitimate peripheral participation, or situated learning (Lave & Wenger, 1991). Such a framework often defines learning as about "the relations between newcomers and old-timers," about "activities, identities, artifacts, and communities of knowledge and practice," and about "the process by which newcomers become ... a full participant in a sociocultural practice" (p. 29). The theory of legitimate peripheral participation rests on the belief that involvement in the communities of knowledge and practice is synonymous with learning.

These studies are also often informed by the theoretical frame of "academic literacies," which views writing as a sociocultural practice occurring within a complex social system that incorporates issues of epistemology, power, and identity in students' process of meaning-making as burgeoning or active participants in the academy (Lea, 2004, p. 742). This theoretical frame often invokes the concepts of voice and identity to interpret the different perspectives of those who play the game of academic writing (e.g., Aitchison et al., 2012; Casanave, 2002; Turner, 2012).

Studies that adopted one or both of these two frameworks can offer unique analytical tools that directs one's attention to learners' participation in sociocultural communities and to the "tough love and tears" of learning academic writing either independent of, during, or beyond the research writing classroom (Aitchison et al., 2012, p. 435). Some of the accounts of graduate students playing the "serious, identity-transforming academic identity games" in the academic enculturation process, with all the struggles and conflicts (e.g., Casanave, 2002, p. 141; see also Blakeslee, 1997; Prior, 1998), are engrossing. When such a process goes awry or almost awry, as in the case study of Virginia by Casanave (2002) or as in Fujioka's narrative (2008), the accounts are poignant and thought provoking. As a result, they can offer instructors interested in the genre-focused learning and teaching of research writing insights and resources to reflect on their own and their students' research writing practices and on their teaching of research writing.

Among the illuminating studies in this tradition, studies that either originated from a graduate-level research writing course (e.g., Belcher, 1994; Wang & Yang, 2012) or were a continuation of a writing course (e.g., Tardy, 2009) may be especially important for building and updating one's knowledge of research writing instruction. Since these studies often make direct or implicit connections to writing instruction, they could be useful conduits for understanding one's course participants, for reflecting on one's pedagogical practices, and for deepening one's overall knowledge of research writing instruction.

For example, in a study that originated from a dissertation writing class she taught at a large university in the United States, Belcher (1994) looked at how three course participants interacted with their mentors/advisors in their home programs of Chinese literature, applied mathematics, and human nutrition. During the class, Belcher started to notice the possible effects of the advisor-student relationship on the students' socialization into their disciplinary communities of practice. With this growing realization, Belcher contacted her students' advisors for a mid-term hour-long interview to seek the advisors' perspectives on their advisees' dissertation projects and progress, on these advisee' strengths and shortcomings as novice professionals and writers in their disciplines, and on the advisors' own perceived influences on the students. Approximately one year after her dissertation class ended, Belcher interviewed the advisors again to hear their final assessment of their students as professionals.

Belcher then discusses the three cases in detail in her journal article. In the first case, Belcher noticed that a Chinese student in Chinese literature with the pseudonym Li suffered from one problem in his writing: Almost every sentence in his dissertation drafts seemed to be filled with gratuitous literary allusions or references to literary critics. Through interviewing Li's advisor, Belcher learned of Li's advisor's perception of Li as a "bibliomaniac" who was more fascinated by citing the critical theorists he read than by critiquing these theorists. When commenting on Li's dissertation proposal drafts, the advisor attempted to model the desirable critical thinking process through extensive critical commentary. Such an attempt was received by Li unenthusiastically. According to Belcher, Li read his advisor's extensive comments and the criticism of his numerous references to contemporary Western critical theory as a flat rejection of such a theory. He did not see it as his advisor's effort to push him toward a more critically analytical stance in his research writing.

Belcher then presents two additional cases that are equally fascinating: a not-so-successful student called Ko in applied mathematics and a highly successful student called Keoungmee in human nutritional studies. Ko seemed to be overly interested in showcasing his novel solutions to engineering problems in his writing, but his advisor felt that engineers, the intended audience of research papers in applied mathematics, might not be interested in or able to appreciate the processes that led to those solutions that Ko was so keen on displaying (see my discussion of the importance of guiding students to recognize the differences in and, consequently, to write for, different audiences in Chapter 5). Ko's advisor even invited an engineer to work on a collaborative project so as to show Ko the needs of his target audience, at least a target audience as perceived by Ko's advisor. Ko, however, believed that the engineer lacked the ability to completely understand Ko's mathematics. Even his advisor, Ko felt, was not always able to follow his mathematical reasoning, which, in Ko's view, was his audience's problem, not his.

In the case of the successful student called Keoungmee, a student from Korea, the relationship between her advisor and her was relatively untroubled. Keoungmee encountered challenges in her research, but she never doubted that her research would make a major contribution to her field and to humanity and that her dissertation would find a ready audience. Her advisor assumed the roles of Keoungmee's co-learner in her project and proved to be a major source of moral as well as academic support for Keoungmee in her endeavors.

In another study, Tardy (2009) looked at how a student in computer science from China with the pseudonym Paul learned to write his master's thesis through the help of Dr. Xu, Paul's advisor. Different from the cases of Li and Ko in Belcher's study, Paul's relationship with his advisor Dr. Xu was not fraught with various identity crises. Tardy noticed that the multiple levels of feedback from Dr. Xu influenced Paul's understanding and writing of the thesis genre profoundly. For example, at the initial stage of Paul's thesis writing process, Dr. Xu suggested to Paul an area that, in Dr. Xu's opinion, was more practical and manageable than the work Paul would have had to do if Paul had planned to continue for a PhD, which Dr. Xu knew Paul would not. When Paul became frustrated with his progress later in the research process, Dr. Xu encouraged Paul to continue with what Dr. Xu perceived as a valuable line of research.

Dr. Xu also provided detailed comments on Paul's drafts. For example, Dr. Xu changed the subject or agent within a clause or altered the logical connection among clausal or phrasal elements in quite a few places in Paul's third draft of his thesis. He also changed some passive constructions to active voice and added the pronoun *we* as the agent in these sentences. In addition, he broke some longer sentences into one or more shorter sentences even when Paul's original sentences were already very short. Dr. Xu also provided extensive comments on the rhetorical organization of Paul's master's thesis. For example, he advised Paul to reorganize the thesis by integrating some of the background details into the experimental results rather than outlining them all in the beginning of the thesis. He stressed the importance of showing the work's significance in the Introduction. Such comments prompted Paul to revise his Introduction thoroughly.

Belcher and Tardy use these cases to discuss issues such as the different teaching styles of the students' advisors—cooperative, collaborative, or self-replicative, among others—on these students' research literacy development. They also use these cases to illuminate issues such as the discourse communities that students may feel comfortable in, as opposed to the discourse communities they are supposed to participate in. These case studies also have a lot to say about power and authority in students' learning of research writing in non-classroom settings. For example, Tardy noticed how Paul's understanding of the master's thesis genre had grown "from just a vague sense of length to a fully rhetorical understanding of presenting research effectively to his readers" (2009, p. 222), possibly due to his deference to, and willingness to learn from, Dr. Xu as an expert with knowledge and expertise in the area. As a result, Paul nearly always followed Dr. Xu's available advice, contrary to Li and Ko as seen in Belcher's study.

These insights are, admittedly, all very important for understanding the possible connections between classroom-based vs. out-of-class learning of research writing. What I find even more illuminating in cases like these is how they could potentially help instructors interested in the genre-focused approach to learning and teaching research writing to reflect on classroom pedagogical practices, especially due to what these researchers have pointed out to be the direct relevance of these cases to classroom learning. For example, given the struggles the students went through when they did not have a successful mentor/mentee relationship, Belcher (1994) asks how instructors of research writing can help students learn to establish constructive mentoring relationships with faculty in their fields of study that would enable students to achieve their goals. Very interestingly, Belcher suggests that teachers of research writing, who regularly hold conferences with their students, may have already modeled a type of interaction that not only encourages students' pride in the ownership of their ideas and texts, but also sharpens their sensitivity to readers' responses (see my discussion in Chapter 5 as well as the arguments by Freeman, 2016, and Tauber, 2016, about writing teachers playing the role of a literacy broker who helps students understand disciplinary faculty members' feedback on their writing). She believes that these elements may usefully transfer to other contexts. This is an angle that many teachers may not be aware of even when they hold writing conferences regularly with their students and may be something they need to attend to carefully in their conferences as part of building and updating their knowledge of research writing instruction.

Similarly, even though Paul had already left the academic writing course when Tardy studied his thesis writing process, Tardy's special focus on the course and what happened after the course in her analysis of Dr. Xu's feedback to Paul could be a valuable source for reflections. For example, Tardy (2009) points out how Paul mainly perceived language style as an issue of formality. He even perceived formal language use as "the most useful content of the [graduate-level writing] course" that Tardy observed (p. 208). Tardy concludes that the concrete changes suggested by Dr. Xu have "provided Paul with guidance in formal conventions" (p. 212) as well as helped extend "Paul's understanding of stylistic form beyond the issue of formality" (p. 213). The advice from Dr. Xu to Paul about changing the rhetorical organization to highlight the significance of his study, Tardy notes, has increased Paul's understanding of the rhetorical goals in his master's thesis. Observations like these can certainly help instructors reflect on and validate their genre-focused research writing instructional practices.

Even places where the connections between classroom-based and nonclassroom–based learning may not be clear, at least not clearly pointed out in the studies reviewed, provide sources of reflections. For example, Tardy (2009) notices that certain factors may explain why Paul almost never resisted Dr. Xu's advice, different from Li and Ko in Belcher's study. Paul's lack of interest in academic research and his preference for concrete work with practical applications were in conflict with the type of research writing required in his master's thesis. Tardy wonders whether Paul would have questioned more of Dr. Xu's advice and suggestions had he intended to become an academic researcher. It seems that there is little that instructors of research writing can do when a student has lost interest in academic research or in the kind of standard data-based research paper that we often emphasize in our writing courses (e.g., Burgess & Cargill, 2013). Similarly, Li and Ko in Belcher's study seemed a little too headstrong and not receptive enough to their advisors' feedback. These seems to be issues related to students' life trajectories and personality traits that teachers of research writing can do very little about.

Or maybe teachers of research writing can do something about these issues? For example, if we, as writing instructors, learned of Paul's loss of interest in academic research, maybe we could encourage him to carry out genre analysis of practitioner-based articles or theses, instead of the standard research articles that target research peers (see Fengchen's case in Chapter 5 where he made the distinctions between the two). Similarly, if we noticed a problem like Li's, maybe we could ask the advisor to suggest some well-written journal articles where a critically analytical voice or stance is projected very strongly as exemplary samples for Li to analyze. If we knew that Ko was not convinced of the importance of relegating complicated mathematical formulas to the footnotes, as his advisor suggested that he should do in order to meet the needs of his engineering audience, maybe we could ask Ko's advisor for some good samples and analyze these with Ko in our writing classes or during our office hours/conferences?

These suggestions are, by no means, criticisms of Belcher's pedagogical practices or the practices of the teacher Tardy (2009) observed. Instead, I use them as examples to show how studies of learners in nonacademic settings could be valuable resources for teachers to reflect on issues directly related to their classroom-based practices, and the reflections could help enhance their knowledge of research writing instruction.

Learn about the Discipline-Specific Nature of Research Writing

Instructors working with, or planning to work with, students on discipline-specific or discipline-related writing may have asked these questions: How can I be sure that I have correctly read the rhetorical organizational patterns and the lexico-

grammatical features in the discipline-specific samples collected by students, if I can even make sense of them at all to
begin with (see Chapter 4)? Relatedly, how can I be sure that
I have read and understood a sample of my students' writing
correctly, given the intimidating discipline-specific topics
as well as the unfamiliar organizational patterns and lexico-
grammatical features in it (see Chapter 5)? My answer to these
questions is that one probably can never be sure. However, this
feeling of uncertainty should enhance an instructor's commitment to learning as much about discipline-specific textual and
writing practices as possible because of the multidisciplinary
mix of students typically found in research writing courses
and students' wish to learn to write in a way consistent with
the expectations and the textual features in their fields (see
Chapter 1). Increasing one's knowledge of discipline-specific
writing and writing practices, therefore, should be a coherent
part of building and updating one's knowledge as a practitioner
of research writing instruction.

One way to increase our knowledge of disciplinary specificity in research writing is to interact with researchers/faculty
members in various disciplines (e.g., Swales, 1998). Johns
(1997) has developed a series of questions that undergraduate
students can use to interview their faculty or experienced students who have been in the discourse community for a while in
various fields about discipline-specific writing practices. These
questions include the faculty or expert students' motivation
to study their respective selected subjects, their educational
backgrounds, and the important research or teaching topics in
their disciplines, among other questions. More important, she
presents a series of questions that students can use to probe
into text-as-artifacts in a particular discipline through interacting with faculty or expert students. Although these questions
are developed with the undergraduate students Johns often
works with in mind, they can be easily modified if practitioners of graduate-level research writing instruction would like
to interview discipline-specific faculty or expert students.
For example, the text-as-artifacts questions in Johns are all
related to why a certain textbook has been adopted and how

it is used in an undergraduate subject-matter class. Instructors of graduate-level research writing classes could adopt and adapt these questions to ask disciplinary specialists about the communicative purposes, the rhetorical organizational patterns, and the lexico-grammatical features in the genres often read or written by the disciplinary experts. Since many of the students in research writing courses are already "expert students" themselves who have had some sense of the expectations in their respective discourse communities, teachers of research writing can use these questions to interview their own students in order to learn as much about the disciplinary practices in students' fields as possible (e.g., Buell & Park, 2008).

More recently, Rogers, Zawacki, and Baker (2016) describe a series of questions they used to interview faculty members about dissertation writing. These questions include the faculty members' experience in writing their own dissertation, the shape of and conventions for the dissertation in the faculty's respective fields and how students learn these conventions, the role of the dissertation in one's professional careers, the most challenging areas of dissertation writing, and their experience in working with multilingual dissertation writers. Although these questions were developed for data-collection purposes in a research project, they could serve as the questions for instructors to interview their students' faculty advisors as part of an effort to understand the discipline-specific nature of research writing.

We have seen the value of talking with students and their disciplinary advisors in earlier discussions. The advisors in the cases in Belcher (1994), for instance, articulated to her the target audiences of writing in applied mathematics and the importance of adopting a critical stance in literary studies. Tardy (2009) was able to detect from Dr. Xu's feedback on Paul's thesis drafts Dr. Xu's preference for short sentences as well as for stating the agent of actions clearly. As described in Chapter 5, the opportunity to talk with Fengchen and other students has taught me a lot about the discipline-specific textual practices in these students' fields.

Of course, interacting with faculty and expert students in various fields intensively through interviews and observations, as suggested by Johns (1997) and as practiced by Belcher (1994), Rogers, Zawacki, and Baker (2016), and Swales (1998), may not be practical either because instructors of graduate-level research writing may not have easy or steady access to faculty members in various fields or because the interviews or observations may be too time consuming to both parties. Johns (1997) suggests that engagement with discipline-specific faculty and expert students should, ideally, be "contextualized" as well as "prolonged and repetitive" (p. 108). To develop this level of engagement may not be practical for instructors of research writing whose classes often consist of students from ten or more disciplines in each section (see Chapter 1) and whose often low institutional status as graduate students themselves or as contingency faculty may not grant them steady access to disciplinary specialists (see the descriptions of graduate-level research writing courses staffed by contract faculty or part-time instructors in Freeman, 2016; Phillips, 2016; and Starfield, 2016). For example, when I first taught a graduate-level academic writing class years ago, I was myself still a graduate student, a not-so-uncommon situation (e.g., Min, 2016; Norris & Tardy, 2006; Prior & Min, 2008). My attempts to contact some faculty members to learn about the writing of their students in my class were not exactly met with great enthusiasm. Even when status differences may not be an issue, writing specialists may lack the "bandwidth to engage in ... cross-disciplinary work" (Tauber, 2016, p. 643; see a similar observation by Anthony, 2011). Even where there is "political will" for cross-disciplinary work, "institutional politics and funding silos" can make it difficult to arrange any partnerships between writing specialists and disciplinary faculty (p. 632; see a successful example of such prolonged engagement with faculty members in another discipline in Swales, 1998).

Given such a situation, other methods can potentially help teachers of research writing learn as much as possible about discipline-specific writing practices in different fields. For example, one could read the studies of discipline-specific genres carefully to increase one's knowledge of these genres (e.g., Hyland, 2000). Numerous of such studies have appeared in *English for Specific Purposes, Journal of English for Academic Purposes, Written Communication,* and other journals. Chapter 1 provided a brief overview of how some of these genre analysis studies have examined various aspects of research genres. The wide range of contextual, organizational, and linguistic features examined in these studies can certainly help those interested in working with graduate-level research writers to increase their knowledge of research genres in various fields and their awareness of disciplinary specificity in research writing.

In Chapter 2, I pointed out that the widely available studies on various genres and part-genres is one of the three reasons that the ESP approach to genre analysis is especially applicable to the teaching of graduate-level research writing. In fact, the literature includes examples of practitioners of graduate-level writing instruction who have incorporated the findings from some of these studies into their pedagogical practices. For example, Swales has introduced, reviewed, and incorporated the findings from many of these studies in his monographs (1990, 2004) and in his textbook series with Feak (e.g., 2012a).

In Chapter 4, I explained, with two examples, one on the literature review part-genre (see Figure 4.3) and the other on the discussion part-genre (see Figure 4.5), how existing studies could help instructors develop teaching points that engage students in discussions of genre samples through sample-neutral questions. To a large extent, I am assuming that instructors of graduate-level research writing are already in the habit of reading existing studies on research genres across the disciplines to increase their knowledge of discipline-specific writing and to enhance their teaching. Therefore, I will not delve into any further details about this well-acknowledged source of increasing one's knowledge about research writing instruction here.

Instead, I will focus on an additional source for learning about discipline-specific research writing, which involves reading discipline-specific guidebooks on research writing.

I have always enjoyed reading various guidebooks on discipline-specific research methodologies and research writing, especially those authored by disciplinary specialists for a discipline-specific audience (biologists describing research writing and textual practices to fellow researchers, advanced undergraduate, or graduate students in biology, for example). I am keenly aware of writing scholars' criticisms of some of these guidebooks. Swales and Najjar (1987), for example, point out the distinct mismatches between the prescriptions offered in published guides and handbooks on article introductions and actual practices. They found the descriptions of research genres in these handbooks and guides to be too general with many of them not based on any examination of actual texts. Similarly, after looking at nine thesis writing guidebooks, Paltridge (2002) points out that these guidebooks covered many important aspects of the research process, such as the steps involved in selecting a topic or planning and researching for a proposal. These guidebooks, however, did not give detailed advice on the structure or the content of individual chapters or the complete range of available thesis options.

Although Swales and Najjar (1987) and Paltridge (2002) seem to be talking more about discipline-general guidebooks, I find these observations to be consistent with what I have often noticed when I read discipline-specific research writing guidebooks. Therefore, when reading these discipline-specific guidebooks, I would often keep these caveats in mind and would pay close attention to what could be useful to me as a disciplinary outsider, ignoring what may be too general or too trite to be educative. For example, I would pay special attention to what new genres may be discussed in these books or how established genres may be discussed in an insightful manner based on the discipline in question. I would also pay particular attention to any insights on disciplinary cultures and discipline-specific ways of knowledge construction and argument making offered by these disciplinary insiders that may be new to me.

For instance, a book that I recently read is by Gladon, Graves, and Kelly called *Getting Published in the Life Sciences* (2011), which is based on a course they taught at Iowa State University called Publishing in Biological Sciences Journals and on what they believe to be the successful outcomes achieved by the students in that course. The three authors teach or used to teach in the areas of horticulture and natural resource ecology and management. Their status as disciplinary insiders makes me particularly interested in what they may have to say about writing in the life sciences.

Assuming the position of an armchair anthropologist of research writing, I have learned quite a few things about writing in the life sciences, to say the least. For example, I learned that authors in the life sciences "must use *Systeme Internationale* for all aspects of manuscript preparation" (p. 14), which sent me to do an internet search of what *Systeme Internationale* entails and how it is often used in journal articles in the life sciences. I also learned from their discussion that scientists nowadays have adopted the principles of reducing the size of a journal article to that of a 'least publishable unit' to increase their research productivity when two to five of such units would have made up the content of a paper in the past (see my discussion of the different, but somewhat related, practice of guiding students to use the same or related content materials to write for different audiences in Chapter 5). Such a comment in the book led me to the Vancouver Document, which is described in their book as a common set of instructions entitled *the Uniform Requirements for Manuscripts Submitted to Biomedical Journals* that govern the practice of about 3500 biomedical journals. I was a little surprised to find that, according to the authors, the regular research reports in most biochemical journals average about three to five printed pages and that enzymatic analysis is a common subsection in the Materials and Methods section where the enzymatic preparation and enzymatic analysis steps should be separated, as emphasized in their book. Another topic I find illuminating in their book is about co-authorship in research in other areas. I have always found the discussion about how to use one's name for academic purposes in Swales and Feak (2000) very interesting, but the lengthy discussion of how to assign authorship and the careful description of the various point systems for allocating authorship in Gladon, Graves, and Kelly (2011) would certainly give any instructors a lot to talk about when working with students in the life sciences!

Note that Chapter 3 of this book talks about guiding students to collect authentic examples of journal articles from different fields to form their reference collections. Many of these guidebooks provide great details about the journals in the respective fields. For example, a handbook on writing in geography lists both *Progress in Physical Geography* and *Progress in Human Geography* as journals regularly carrying review articles and progress reports, while those deciding to work on periglacial geomorphology should read the journal *Permafrost and Periglacial Processes* (Parsons & Knight, 2015). Another book on research writing in construction lists sixteen journals read by scholars in the field, including five published by the American Society of Civil Engineers (Naoum, 2012). Comments and lists like these can certainly help instructors increase their knowledge of discipline-specific writing and help guide their pedagogical practices in the graduate-level research writing classroom, a point I have made in Chapter 3.

Apart from these anthropologically interesting as well as pedagogically applicable details, I have also learned something quite useful about what these disciplinary insiders perceived to be the effective writing process, as in the case of the book on publishing journal articles in the life sciences (Gladon, Graves, & Kelly, 2011). Although they acknowledge the importance of the IMRaD sequence of sections, they warn readers sternly about not using this sequence of sections for developing a manuscript. Note that Swales and Feak (2012a) present the journal article in the order of Methods-Introduction-Discussion because the Methods section is what authors of journal articles tend to write first. Swales and Luebs (2002) also taught a course to graduate students in social psychology that was structured around the parts of an empirical journal article arranged according to what they presumed to be the order of increasing writing difficulty: Methods, Abstracts, Results, Introductions, and Discussions. Burgess and Cargill (2013), by contrast, start their course on research writing with the Results section because they believe it is the section and the section alone that other researchers read as well as the section where one must highlight the importance of one's findings, something novice researchers are often not able to do, according to Burgess and Cargill (2013). Gladon, Graves, and Kelly (2011), different from the practitioners of research writing instruction mentioned above, suggest that their readers follow this particular order for preparing a manuscript: develop a take-home message, develop a provisional title, Results, References, Materials and Methods, Introduction, Discussion, Abstract, and title/by-line/keywords/authorship footnotes.

The supposed effectiveness of this particular order is, quite unsurprisingly, based more on the authors' experience of writing journal articles than on any empirical data on life science research writers' effective composing processes. They do, however, justify the order by offering some details. For example, they suggest that the Results section be finished before much of the Materials and Methods section because "too much revision of the materials and methods section may need to be done when the result section has not yet been solidified" (p. 15). The rationale for ordering other sections are not clearly stated, but I can figure out why they made the suggestion. For example, the Results and Methods sections, once completed, may help one decide which items from the literature to include or to exclude in the Introduction based on the results and methods, and the Discussion section follows the Introduction section because the literature items discussed in the Introduction may need to be re-analyzed or re-examined in the Discussion section in light of the results. I am not very sure why the references should be prepared between writing the Results and the Methods sections, as suggested by the authors. Maybe that is something that could serve as a conversation starter if one has the chance to talk with a professor or an expert student in the life sciences.

Another point that I learned from the author is the importance of constructing a take-home message before working on any section. The take-home messages, according to Gladon, Graves, and Kelly (2011), are "the central messages or ideas you want the reader, every reader, to grasp at the time they have finished reading the article" (p. 76) and should "hit the readers between the eyes" (p. 75). They give examples of take-home messages such as *"ethylene must be present within tomato fruit tissue for the tomato to turn red during ripening"* or *"holding germinated olding impatiens seeds in 1 to 2% oxygen, balance 99 or 98% nitrogen, for 12 to 14 hours reduces radicle growth to less than 1 mm, but the radicle and shoot will resume normal growth when the germinated seed is returned to air"* (p. 77). Such take-home messages, in their view, should be stated clearly in the Discussion section, but they should be written down before the writing process begins so that every section would be guided by, and would build up, the consistent take-home message.

I find such a suggestion to be interesting because it helps me reflect on both my own teaching and on what I have read in the literature on research writing instruction. Regarding teaching, I have noticed the problem of not having any take-home message in my own students' writing. In other words, the articles or dissertations do not answer the "so what" question clearly or cogently enough. However, I had thought that having some strong take-home messages was more relevant to writing in the social sciences or was more applicable to the Discussion section. It is, thus, interesting to see that this idea not only applies in the life sciences but can also serve as the centerpiece that guides every section.

Regarding the literature, I noticed that Cargill and O'Connor (2012), Cargill, O'Connor, and Li (2012), and Burgess and Cargill (2013) have identified not being able to package information to present and discuss the most important and novel findings of research to the chosen audience as a major problem and one of the three key areas that they covered in their workshops for novice research writers in the sciences. However, they seem to have viewed this challenge as pertaining mainly to writing the Discussion section of a journal article. In fact, one of their writing exercises is to ask their workshop participants to practice writing the discussion, but highlighting the most relevant information. Similarly, Rogers, Zawacki, and Baker

(2016) interviewed dissertation advisors from various fields and found that one challenge facing dissertation writers, as identified by the advisors they interviewed, was the difficulty in "conceptualizing the main argument of the dissertation and why it matters" (p. 61). The advisors pointed out the difficulties in "seeing the big picture," "understanding the spin," "explaining the meaning of all these things [the data sets]," "articulating the so-what," seeing what the facts [one has gathered] "really tell you," and "moving from the concrete to larger concepts" as the struggles their advisees faced (p. 61). Similar to Cargill, O'Connor, and Li (2012), these advisors seem to be connecting this unique challenge to mainly or merely the writing of the findings or Discussion chapter or section. Gladon, Graves, and Kelly (2011), by contrast, seem to have used the notion of a "take-home" message as the key concept to discuss the writing of every part of the journal article genre, rather than just the Results section, even emphasizing the role of such a take-home message in the pre-writing stages of brainstorming and outlining.

Since instructors of graduate-level research writing often have to deal with various research genres, many disciplinary insiders' views on genres in their field are always sources for enriching writing instructors' knowledge, especially when these authors invoke their disciplinary knowledge to describe the genres specific to their fields. For example, in a book on graduate-level writing in music, Boyle, Fiese, and Zavac (2004) present different types of written documents that graduate students in music can write to capture the culminating experience of a graduate music degree. According to the authors (the first and second authors are faculty members in music), these written documents are "variously called project papers, recital papers, theses, essays, or dissertation" depending on factors such as "the nature of the academic program, the nature of the culminating experience, the extent, breadth, and/or depth of the program requirements for the culminating experience" and tradition (p. 90). They then describe these papers in detail. For example, they talk about how a recital paper about the works of unfamiliar composers should be written differently from that of a paper about well-known composers. They also point out what a "theoretical analysis" means in graduate-level music paper and how a theoretical analysis should be set against the discussions of performance issues. Such fine-grained analysis of genres could certainly enhance the knowledge of graduate-level instructors, showing them how the same genre, such as graduate thesis/dissertation, could play out differently in different fields or subfields.

Instructors of graduate-level writing could also benefit from how disciplinary insiders invoke their understanding of the communicative purposes as understood by them to describe some fine-grained differences within a genre. For example, in the book on graduate-level writing in music, Boyle, Fiese, and Zavac (2004) point out that the faculty members in the classical performance program at their institution require their graduate students to write and defend the recital papers at least one semester before the recital. The jazz faculty members, by contrast, require their graduate students to submit and defend the recital paper *after* the recital. According to Boyle, Fiese, and Zavac (2004), the variation is due to the differently perceived communicative purposes of the recital paper. They point out that the faculty members in the classical performance programs perceive the communicative purpose of the recital paper as mainly to help "the student recitalist gain an in-depth understanding of the historical, analytical, and performance aspects of the music" (p. 33). Therefore, defending the recital paper prior to the recital would serve such a communicative purpose and would facilitate students' learning and under-standing of the recital repertoire as well as their preparation of the recital. By contrast, the jazz faculty members view the communicative purpose of the master's recital papers dif-ferently as "a retrospective description and analysis of the performance," including descriptions of original composi-tions and the improvisational aspects of the performance (p. 90). We may remember that the communicative purpose of a genre often defines what the genre is (Swales, 1990; see also a detailed discussion of the role of communicative purposes in defining and analyzing genres in Chapter 2 of this book). Since rhetorical purposes driving a particular genre are often impervious to disciplinary outsiders, including writing instructors working with students across the disciplines, seeing how these books not only describe the subcategories of certain familiar genres but also do so through laying out the communicative purposes could be useful for developing writing instructors' knowledge of research genres as well as their understanding of disciplinary specificity in research genres.

In sum, as noted earlier, many graduate-level research writing classes often consist of students across disciplines (see Chapter 1), and these classes are often taught by novice instructors, many of whom may be graduate students themselves (see Chapter 1). These novice instructors often feel unprepared or underprepared and often make problematic assumptions about writing in the disciplines (Min, 2016). This pedagogical reality points to the importance for research writing instructors to learn about discipline-specific writing and writing practices, which is the focus of this subsection. Different paths could lead to instructors' development of knowledge about discipline-specific writing, including interacting with faculty and expert students in the disciplines and reading closely genre analysis studies on research genres in different disciplines. Using the examples here, I hope to show how discipline-specific guidebooks could be an additional possible resource for increasing instructors' knowledge of discipline-specific writing, especially when novice instructors may not have steady access to faculty members or expert students in various disciplines for time-intensive interviews or observations. As noted from my brief analysis, these guidebooks could be a window into the discipline-specific perspectives on the research and writing processes as well as into the communicative purposes behind discipline-specific genres. These perspectives on discipline-specific writing and textual practices help foreground some of the disciplinarily sanctioned or preferred ways of knowledge making and research writing and could, thus, be a possible additional source for developing instructors' knowledge of research writing in different fields.

Conduct Action Research of the Research Writing Classroom

Sundstrom (2016) points out that "a, if not *the*, primary challenge to academic structures for graduate writing is that faculty [in other areas] see [graduate-level] writing support as remedial and separate from research" (p. 201, original emphasis). Given such an observation, an additional area of developing one's knowledge for effective instruction in the genre-focused research writing classroom may involve learning to conduct research. Because many instructors of graduate-level research writing offer classes or workshops in many formats and even coordinate various programs for supporting graduate writing (Simpson et al., 2016), action research could be an especially valuable form of research. Learning to conduct action research, among other forms of research such as pedagogically driven or informed genre analysis studies (e.g., Feak & Swales, 2010), could, therefore, be an integral part of the knowledge base of those working with graduate-level writers. Action research involves adopting a self-reflective approach to subjecting one's own teaching contexts to questioning or problematizing and, as a result, to developing new ideas and alternatives. Such alternatives or improvements are based on action researchers' systematic collection of data in their own classes or in their broader teaching contexts (Burns, 2010).

The genre-centered approach to graduate-level research writing instruction described in the previous chapters can offer teachers many opportunities to carry out action research projects that focus on the course participants (Chapter 1), the texts they analyze and learn to write (Chapter 4 and Chapter 5), or the course itself. For example, I have carried out various case studies of graduate students in previous sections of my classes. Through these studies, I have developed a better understanding of students who analyzed genre exemplars in their fields to develop a rhetorical and an evaluative understanding of research texts (Cheng, 2008b), to make sense of how academic criticisms work in one's field (Cheng, 2006a), to link one's analysis of genre samples to one's existing genre knowledge and disciplinary knowledge (Cheng, 2008a), to recontextualize the knowledge gained through one's genre analysis in one's writing tasks (Cheng, 2007b), and to develop rhetorical awareness through focusing on genre-specific lexico-grammatical features (Cheng, 2011b, 2015b).

These studies have helped me understand how students can be introduced to the genre analysis framework in instructional settings and can apply the framework to their own analysis of discipline-specific research texts. Looking at my own students has allowed me to test how genre analysis can serve as an instructional framework for facilitating learners' noticing and learning of genre-specific features and the underpinning rhetorical reasoning, among other things they can learn in the research writing classroom. Next, I examine the case of a student in my class to illustrate how I have benefitted from the process of conducting action research. I will reanalyze some published data with a focus on how a pedagogically driven research project could help one to build and update one's knowledge of research writing instruction (Cheng, 2015a).

In one section of a graduate-level research writing course that focused on the journal article (JA) genre, I noticed some interesting examples from the genre analysis tasks of a graduate student with the pseudonym of Patricia (see Chapter 4 about the details related to assigning the genre analysis tasks). Patricia was from a Latin American country and was a third-semester doctoral student in veterinary medicine with a special focus on food technology when she took the course. In one of her genre analysis tasks, she analyzed the introductory section of a JA published in the *Journal of Food Protection* (Younts-Dahl, Galyean, Loneragan, Elam, & Brashears, 2004), a journal she often read for her content courses.

Consistent with the the goals and principles in genre-focused learning of research writing (see Chapter 3), she described what she saw as the rhetorical purposes in each subsection that she analyzed. For example, she explained that the first three sentences that begin with "*escherichia coli* O157 has become a public health concern" in the original article she analyzed showed that "… the author is creating centrality showing why it is important study the bacteria and its prevalence in cattles" (Patricia's genre analysis Task 2). She also highlighted what she perceived to be the noteworthy lexico-grammatical features that performed the rhetorical moves in these subsections. For example, she pointed out that the phrase "has become a public health concern" in the JA was, to her, "useful to create centrality in this area." Similarly, the phrase "have focused on" in the sentence "epidemiological studies have focused on gaining an understanding of the distribution, prevalence, and potential risk factor" was, in her words, the authors' efforts to show "the objectives of previous studies" (Patricia's genre analysis Task 2). These are only some of the examples that show how she analyzed the JA. Readers interested in the details in her genre analysis tasks can revisit Chapter 4 about how I typically assigned students to analyze genre exemplars as well as read the multiple excerpts from Patricia's genre analysis work in Cheng (2015a).

Patricia's analysis of one subsection in the introduction of that JA caught my attention. In a nutshell, she characterized that subsection as about the JA authors' effort to create "controversy" so as to create "a gap of study." The sentence that Patricia highlighted as performing this rhetorical purpose is "the increase [of *E. coli* o157] in reported prevalence may be a result of improvements in methodologies used to isolate the pathogen from feces and the environment" (Younts-Dahl et al., 2004, p. 1). We may remember that the introduction to an JA often includes three moves—establishing a research territory, establishing a research niche, and presenting the present work—as seen in the framework described by Swales (1990, 2004) and as seen in my description of the pedagogical materials in Chapter 3 (e.g., Swales & Feak, 2012a; see Appendix C). Indicating a research gap, as possibly pointed out by Patricia here, is a step in Move 2—establishing a research niche.

When I looked closely at the article analyzed by Patricia, I noticed that that subsection and the sentence I included in the previous paragraph that she analyzed did not seem to contain any lexico-grammatical features to indicate that it was part of the authors' effort to criticize previous work in order to "create controversy" or to create "a gap of study," despite Patricia's claim. I asked her to explain in a subsequent genre analysis task what she meant by "creat[ing] a controversy" or "creating a gap of study" in that subsection in the JA she had analyzed. Her analysis prompted me to suspect that she may be projecting certain rhetorical motives probably unintended by the authors of the article.

Unsure of her claims, I analyzed the original JA (Younts-Dahl et al, 2004) very closely myself. I noticed that the authors were not really criticizing previous publications that reported on the increasing prevalence of *E. coli* o157 in order to open a research gap for their own study, contrary to what Patricia claimed in her analysis. They were not trying to show that their own project could rectify the problem of the reported false increase in the previous studies, again, contrary to Patricia's analysis that she included in a subsequent genre analysis task. Instead, the study reported in the JA Patricia analyzed seemed to be a continuation of the authors' previous research efforts to continue to test various strategies to decrease *E. coli* o157.

In other words, my analysis of the JA prompted me to think that Patricia may have interpreted a rather ordinary statement as, in her words, fulfilling the rhetorical purpose of "creat[ing] controversy" and as what she perceived to be the authors' effort to create a gap for their study. She seemed to have projected "creating a research gap" as the rhetorical purpose when my own analysis revealed very little evidence that such a purpose was intended. In theory, a study that is the continuation of a previous study may not be very explicit about any gap in previous studies the authors reviewed because they may just be conducting a study to add additional dimensions to the authors' or others' previous studies. If this is the case, why did the "opening a research gap" move figure prominently in Patricia's analysis, even when she was analyzing, in my view, a supposedly gap non-salient study?

This episode prompted me to reflect on my own genre knowledge, my knowledge of discipline-specific writing, and my teaching based on such knowledge. When I reexamined the teaching materials I used in Patricia's section and in other similar sections, I noticed that all the samples I used to discuss the Swales' CaRS framework for writing article introductions seemed to have highlighted Step 1B ("Indicating a gap") in Move 2 ("Establishing a niche") (Swales, 1990, 2004; see also Appendix C). These materials all contained quite explicit gap statements with gap-enacting lexico-grammatical features similar to those described in Swales (1990). For example, they included sample sentences such as "however, explicit quantitative analyses of the extent to which vapor and liquid phases conductances change in parallel during plant development are lacking" or "there is little or no insight into the relative importance of the different dimensions of market knowledge as drivers of product innovation performance" in which adversative sentence connectors such as *however* or negative or quasi-negative quantifiers such as *little or no* are used to highlight a gap to be filled later. Readers interested in how samples were typically used in my classes to discuss genre-specific features could revisit Chapter 4.

The chapter in Swales and Feak's textbook (2012a) that I used to introduce the CaRS framework to the class presented two forms of "establishing a niche": by "indicating a research gap in the previous research" and "by extending previous knowledge in some way" (p. 331). The first form received four and a half pages of coverage with extensive examples of several language patterns useful for carrying out this form of "mini-critique" (Swales & Feak, 2012a, p. 348). By contrast, "extending previous knowledge in some way" as a form of "establishing a niche" is introduced by Swales and Feak as an "alternative type" of establishing a niche often used in term papers or short communications (2004, p. 260) with only one paragraph of coverage and three one-sentence examples and an even briefer treatment in Swales and Feak (2012a).

Therefore, is it possible that the "critique -> opening a gap" connection had been highlighted as a privileged form of "establishing a niche" in the pedagogical resources that I drew upon and in the pedagogical materials that Patricia was exposed to? Had I been attaching great importance to the "critique -> opening a gap" connection in my own genre knowledge and, as a result, overemphasized the status of "opening a research gap" in establishing a research niche in my own teaching, possibly influenced by the way the CaRS framework was described in the literature and in the existing pedagogical materials? Is it likely that, due to my teaching, Patricia was able to notice that a niche was being created, but, possibly due to the lack of focused attention to "extending previous knowledge in some way" as a form of creating a research niche in my teaching, Patricia may have overreached in her analysis to find a gap or controversy that was not really there?

We can see how an action research project driven by what I noticed as a potential "error" or "incidence" in one of my students' genre analysis tasks has helped me to reflect on a problem in my own genre knowledge as well as the possible impact of such a problem on my teaching. After further reflections on this issue, I found myself starting to seek out additional examples of this "alternative type" of establishing a research niche in JAs to read in order to enrich my genre knowledge and my knowledge of discipline-specific writing for possible pedagogical applications. I have also learned to compare students' analysis of JAs with my own analysis as well as with what I have read in published genre analysis studies more carefully.

I have previously argued that EAP researchers and teachers need to examine closely how participants in research writing courses learn (Cheng, 2006b). Indeed, Patricia's "incident," as understood through an action research project that emphasizes teachers' reflections like this, draws our attention to the continuous relevance of this research direction. Researching one's own classes and one's own students can further our understanding of how students deepen their awareness of the relations between rhetorical organization, lexico-grammatical features, and, most important, the underpinning rhetorical context in their genre-focused learning of research writing. Numerous books and resources are available on the specific procedures one could adopt in action research projects to study one's own classes or program (e.g., Burns, 2010). Therefore, I will not elaborate on these procedures here. Instead, I hope to show through my own study of Patricia's case that action research that emphasizes deep reflections as well as systematic collection of data can potentially help develop more alert and better informed instructors of research writing, instructors who can continue to develop and reorganize their own knowledge of research genres and their knowledge and practice of guiding their students to analyze discipline-specific genres.

This chapter elaborates on five areas that I believe are useful for helping instructors build or update their knowledge of genre-focused research writing instruction. These five areas, by no means, represent a comprehensive list of areas that are adequate for building and updating one's knowledge for effective research writing instruction. Instead, I hope that they can serve as examples to encourage instructors to continue to engage the literature, to reflect on their own and on others' practices, and to embark on their own paths of professional self-development as effective and confident practitioners of graduate-level research writing instruction.

Questions for Reflection and Discussion

1. Citing Casanave (2017), I point out in this chapter that writing teachers, "in all cases," benefit from the knowledge about the theoretical foundations of L2 writing instruction (Casanave, 2017, p. viii). To what extent are you familiar with the theoretical foundations of L2 writing instruction? For example, are you familiar with the different approaches to L2 writing instruction (product-oriented, process-oriented, post-process, text-oriented, writer-oriented, or reader-oriented, among different categories of approaches)? Which approach or approaches would the genre-focused approach to graduate-level research writing instruction described in this book fit into? Why?

2. Have you, either as a graduate student or as a writing instructor working on your own research writing, participated in any graduate-level research writing camps, groups, or retreats? What types of camps, groups, or retreats were these? Who were the participants? What were their disciplinary back-

grounds? Have these camps, groups, or retreats affected your beliefs about research writing or changed your behaviors as a writer in any way? For example, have they changed your self-efficacy as a writer, your motivation, or your control of your writing process, among other possible influences? Why or why not? If you have never attended any research writing camps, groups, or retreats, what may be the reasons for not having done so?

3. Have you organized any writing camps, groups, or retreats for graduate-level research writers? If yes, what resources were you able to draw upon to make these camps, groups, or retreats happen (internal or external funding, institutional requirement or support, or students and colleagues' enthusiasm for such camps or groups, for example)? What types of camps, groups, or retreats were these? Who were the participants? What were their disciplinary backgrounds? Have these camps, groups, or retreats affected the participants' beliefs about research writing or changed their behaviors as a writer in any way? For example, have they affected the participants' self-efficacy as a writer, their motivational levels, or their control of their writing process? Why or why not? If you have never organized any research writing camps, groups, or retreats before, what may be the reasons for not having done so? Has the discussion in this chapter persuaded you as well as provided you with the details and references for you to start organizing these camps, groups, or retreats at your own institution? Why or why not?

4. Apart from the initiatives or pedagogies targeting L1 graduate-level research writers discussed in this chapter, what other initiatives or pedagogies targeting this student population are you familiar with? These could be very specific to your own institution or anything that you have learned about through reading. Do you feel that other writing instructors working with graduate-level research writing should become familiar with these additional initiatives or pedagogies as well? Why or why not? Alternatively, if you are not familiar with any additional initiatives or pedagogies targeting L1 research writers, pick one from those discussed in this chapter and explain why you may or may not want to incorporate it into your future pedagogical practices.

5. This chapter argues for the importance of understanding students' learning or practices of research writing in *non*-classroom settings. My emphasis, however, is on how knowing about students' learning outside of class can have direct implications for classroom-based learning and teaching. If you have taught graduate-level research writing before, did you make any conscious efforts to know about your students' learning of research writing or their literacy practices outside of class? Why or why not? If you have tried to learn about your students' literacy practices outside of class, has such knowledge affected your classroom-based practices? Why or why not? If you have not tried to learn about your students' research literacy practices outside of your class or if you have not taught research writing before, has the discussion in this chapter, especially the cases in Belcher (1994) or Tardy (2009), changed your perceptions of the relationship between non-classroom- and classroom-based learning of research writing in any way? Why or why not?

6. This chapter argues for the importance of knowing as much about discipline-specific writing as possible as well as offers different approaches to increasing one's knowledge in this area. Do you agree that instructors of research writing should know as much as possible about discipline-specific writing? Why or why not? Among the various approaches to learning about discipline-specific writing, which one is the most effective, in your opinion? Which one is the most practical? How so? Can you think of any additional ways to know about discipline-specific texts or writing practices?

7. Have you conducted any research projects to understand your own graduate-level research writing classes better? If so, what were the projects like? Do you feel that the projects have helped you understand your students, your classroom practices, or your own development as a teacher of research writing better? Why or why not? If you have never taught research writing before or have never collected any data in your own classes, has the case discussed in this chapter persuaded you to conduct such a project in the future? Why or why not? Overall, do you feel that learning to study one's classroom systematically should be part of the knowledge base of a research writing instructor? Why or why not?

Appendixes

Appendix A

We assume that you will be using a typical organizational pattern for your paper—in other words, the IMRD format or some variant of it. Fortunately, many of the units deal with topics that are relevant for this purpose, as shown in this list.

Research Paper Parts	Relevant Topics Covered
Title	Unit Eight: Titles
Abstract	Unit Five: Summary writing Unit Eight: Abstracts
Introduction	Unit Two: General-specific Unit Three: Problem-solution Unit Six: Critiques
Methods	Unit Three: Process descriptions
Results	Unit Four: Location statements Unit Four: Highlighting statements Unit Four: Qualifications
Discussion	Unit Four: Explanations Unit Five: Summaries
Acknowledgments	Unit Eight: Acknowledgments
References	(not dealt with in this book)

(Swales & Feak, 2012a, p. 286)

Appendix B

As the RP in English has developed over the last hundred years or so, the four different sections have become identified with four different purposes.	
Introduction (I)	The main purpose of the Introduction is to provide the rationale for the paper, moving from a general discussion of the topic to the particular question, issue, or hypothesis being investigated. A secondary purpose is to attract interest in the topic—and hence readers.
Methods (M)	The Methods section describes, in various degrees of detail, methodology, materials (or subjects), and procedures. This is the narrowest part of the RP.
Results (R)	In the Results section, the findings are described, accompanied by variable amounts of commentary.
Discussion (D)	The Discussion section gives meaning to and interprets the results in a variety of ways. Authors make a series of "points," at least some of which refer to statements made in the Introduction.

(Swales & Feak, 2012a, p. 285)

Appendix C

Creating a Research Space

The Introductions of RPs typically follow the pattern in Figure 16 in response to two kinds of competition: competition for readers and competition for research space. This rhetorical pattern has become known as the create-a-research-space (or CARS) model (Swales, 1990).

Figure 16. Moves in Research Paper Introductions

Move 1—Establishing a research territory
   a. by showing that the general research area is important, central, interesting, problematic, or relevant in some way (optional)
   b. by introducing and reviewing items of previous research in the area (obligatory)

Move 2—Establishing a niche**
   by indicating a gap in the previous research or by extending previous knowledge in some way (obligatory)

Move 3—Occupying the niche
   a. by outlining purposes or stating the nature of the present research (obligatory)
   b. by listing research questions or hypotheses (PISF***)
   c. by announcing principal findings (PISF)
   d. by stating the value of the present research (PISF)
   e. by indicating the structure of the RP (PISF)

The one exception to this occurs in certain RPs that deal with "real world" problems, as in Engineering. In some cases, Move 1 deals with these problems without a literature review and the previous research on attempted solutions is postponed to Move 2 (see the text on pages 335–336).

**In ecology, a niche is a particular microenvironment where a particular organism can thrive. In our case, a niche is a context where a specific piece of research makes particularly good sense.

***PISF = probable in some fields, but rare in others.

(Swales & Feak, 2012a, p. 331)

Appendix D

The Structure of Discussion Sections

Move 1—Background information   optional,
(research purposes, theory, methodology)   but PISF

↓

Move 2—Summarizing and reporting key   obligatory
results

↓

Move 3—Commenting on the key results   obligatory
(making claims, explaining the results,
comparing the new work with the
previous studies, offering alternative
explanations)

↓

Move 4—Stating the limitations of the   optional,
study   but PISF

↓

Move 5—Making recommendations for   optional
future implementation and/or for future
research

PISF = probable in some fields

(Swales & Feak, 2012a, p. 368)

Appendix E

Here are some potential areas for inclusion in the introduction that have been proposed by several researchers. Consider whether or not these are typical or likely in your field. Mark those that are likely with a ✓+, those that are unlikely with a ✓–, those that may optionally be used with a ✓, and those about which you are unsure with a question mark (?).

____1. A discussion of examples to illustrate the topic (Anthony, 1999; Árvay and Tankó, 2004)

____2. Definitions of important terms (Anthony, 1999; Duszak, 1997)

____3. An evaluation of the research presented (Anthony, 1999).

____4. A description of data analysis procedures (Li and Ge, 2009)

____5. A description of the methodology (Ayers, 2008)

____6. Asserting your right to fill the gap as in "As the recipient of an Arts and Humanities Grant, for a project entitled 'Translators as Cultural Agents in the Global Information Age,' I have addressed this question . . . " (Corbett, 2007)

____7. A discussion of a theoretical framework (Árvay and Tankó, 2004)

____8. Signaling the newsworthiness or the new contribution of the research as in "Our main claim here is that . . . " (Dahl, 2009)

If any of these were to be included in an RA introduction in your field, in which part of the introduction should they go?

(Feak & Swales, 2011, p. 57)

References

Aitchison, C., Catterall, J., Ross, P., & Burgin, S. (2012). 'Tough love and tears': Learning doctoral writing in the sciences. *Higher Education Research & Development, 31*, 435–447.

Aitchison, C., & Guerin, C. (Eds.) (2014). *Writing groups for doctoral education and beyond: Innovations in practice and theory.* New York: Routledge.

Aitchison, C., & Lee, A. (2006). Research writing: Problems and pedagogies. *Teaching in Higher Education, 11*, 265–278.

Allison, D., Cooley, L., Lewkowicz, J., & Nunan, D. (1998). Dissertation writing in action: The development of a dissertation writing support program for ESL graduate research students. *English for Specific Purposes, 17*, 199–217.

Anthony, L. (2011). Products, processes and practitioners: A critical look at the importance of specificity in ESP. *Taiwan International ESP Journal, 3*(2), 1–18.

Badenhorst, C., Moloney, C., Rosales, J., Dyer, J., & Ru, L. (2015). Beyond deficit: Graduate student research-writing pedagogies. *Teaching in Higher Education, 20*, 1–11.

Basturkmen, H. (2009). Commenting on results in published research articles and masters dissertations in language teaching. *Journal of English for Academic Purposes, 8*, 241–251.

Basturkmen, H. (2010). *Developing courses in English for specific purposes.* New York: Palgrave Macmillan.

Basturkmen, H., East, M., & Bitchener, J. (2014). Supervisors' on-script feedback comments on drafts of dissertations: Socializing students into the academic discourse community. *Teaching in Higher Education, 19*, 432–445.

Bawarshi, A. S. (2003). *Genre and the invention of the writer: Reconsidering the place of invention in composition.* Logan: Utah State University Press.

Bawarshi, A. S., & Reiff, M. J. (2010). *Genre: An introduction to history, theory, research, and pedagogy.* West Lafayette, IN: Parlor Press.

Beaufort, A. (2004). Developmental gains of a history major: A case for building a theory of disciplinary writing expertise. *Research in the Teaching of English, 39*, 136–185.

Belcher, D. (1994). The apprenticeship approach to advanced academic literacy: Graduate students and their mentors. *English for Specific Purposes, 13*, 23–34.

Belcher, D. (1995). [Review of the books *Academic writing for graduate students: A course for nonnative speakers of English* and *Academic writing for graduate students: Commentary,* by J. M. Swales & C. B. Feak]. *English for Specific Purposes, 14*, 175–186.

Belcher, D. (1997). An argument for nonadversarial argumentation: On the relevance of the feminist critique of academic discourse to L2 writing pedagogy. *Journal of Second Language Writing, 6*, 1–21.

Belcher, D. (2006). English for specific purposes: Teaching to perceived needs and imagined futures in worlds of work, study, and everyday life. *TESOL Quarterly, 40*, 133–156.

Belcher, D. D. (2009). How research space is created in a diverse research world. *Journal of Second Language Writing, 18*, 221–234.

Belcher, D. (2012). Considering what we know and need to know about second language writing. *Applied Linguistics Review, 3*, 131–150.

Belcher, D., & Braine, G. (1995). *Academic writing in a second language: Essays on research and pedagogy.* Norwood, NJ: Ablex.

Berkenkotter, C., & Huckin, T. (1995). *Genre knowledge in disciplinary communication: Cognition/culture/power.* Mahwah, NJ: Lawrence Erlbaum.

Bitchener, J. (2010). *Writing an applied linguistics thesis or dissertation: A guide to presenting empirical research.* New York: Palgrave Macmillan.

Blakeslee, A. M. (1997). Activity, context, interaction, and authority: Learning to write scientific papers in situs. *Journal of Business and Technical Communication, 11*, 125–169.

Bloch, J. (2008). *Technologies in the second language composition classroom.* Ann Arbor: University of Michigan Press.

Boyle, J. D., Fiese, R. K., & Zavac, N. (2004). *A handbook for preparing graduate papers in music* (2nd ed.). Houston, TX: Halcyon Press, Ltd.

Breeze, R. (2016). Tracing the development of an emergent part-genre: The author summary. *English for Specific Purposes, 42*, 50–65.

Brooks-Gillies, M., Garcia, E. G., Kim, S. H., Manthey, K., & Smith, T. (2015). Graduate writing across the disciplines, introduction. *Across the Disciplines, 12*(3). Retrieved from http://wac.colostate.edu/atd/graduate_wac/intro.cfm

Buell, M. Z., & Park, S. J. (2008). Positioning expertise: The shared journey of a South Korean and a North American doctoral student. In C. P. Casanave & X. Li (Eds.), *Learning the literacy practices of graduate school: Insiders' reflections on academic enculturation* (pp. 201–217). Ann Arbor: University of Michigan Press.

Bunton, D. (2005). The structure of PhD conclusion chapters. *Journal of English for Academic Purposes, 4*, 207–224.

Burgess, S. (2017). Accept or contest: A life-history study of humanities scholars' responses to research evaluation policies in Spain. In M. Cargill, & S. Burgess (Eds.), *Publishing research in English as an additional language* (pp. 13–31). Adelaide, Australia: University of Adelaide Press.

Burgess, S., & Cargill, M. (2013). Using genre analysis and corpus linguistics to teach research article writing. In V. Matarese (Ed.), *Supporting research writing: Roles and challenges in multilingual settings* (pp. 55–72). Oxford, England: Chandos Publishing.

Burns, A. (2010). *Doing action research in English language teaching: A guide for practitioners*. New York: Routledge.

Burrough-Boenisch, J. (2003). Shapers of published NNS research articles. *Journal of Second Language Writing. 12*, 223–243.

Busl, G., Donnelly, K. L., & Capdevielle, M. (2015). Camping in the disciplines: Assessing the effect of writing camps on graduate student writers. *Across the Disciplines, 12*(3). Retrieved from http://wac.colostate.edu/atd/graduate_wac/busletal2015.cfm

Cargill, M., & Burgess, S. (2017). Introduction: Unpacking English for research publication purposes [ERPP] and the intersecting roles of those who research, teach and edit it. In M. Cargill, & S. Burgess (Eds.), *Publishing research in English as an additional language* (pp. 1–11). Adelaide, Australia: University of Adelaide Press.

Cargill, M., Cadman, K., & McGowan, U. (2001). Postgraduate writing: Using intersecting genres in a collaborative, content-based program. In I. Leki (Ed.), *Academic writing programs* (pp. 85–96). Alexandria, VA: TESOL.

Cargill, M., & O'Connor, P. (2012). Identifying and addressing challenges to international publication success for EFL science researchers: Implementing an integrated training package in China. In R. Tang (Ed.), *Academic writing in a second or foreign language: Issues and challenges facing ESL/EFL academic writers in higher education contexts* (pp. 21–44). New York: Bloomsbury.

Cargill, M., O'Connor, P., & Li, Y. (2012). Educating Chinese scientists to write for international journals: Addressing the divide between science and technology education and English language teaching. *English for Specific Purposes, 31*, 60–69.

Cargill, M., O'Connor, P., Ruffiudin, R., Sukarno, N., Juliandi, B., & Rusmana, I. (2017). Scientists publishing research in English from Indonesia: Analyzing outcomes of a training intervention to inform institutional action. In M. Cargill, & S. Burgess (Eds.), *Publishing research in English as an additional language* (pp. 169–186). Adelaide, Australia: University of Adelaide Press.

Casanave, C. P. (2002). *Writing games: Multicultural case studies of academic literacy practices in higher education.* Mahwah, NJ: Lawrence Erlbaum.

Casanave, C. P. (2014). *Before the dissertation: A textual mentor for doctoral students at early stages of a research project.* Ann Arbor: University of Michigan Press.

Casanave, C. P. (2016). What advisors need to know about the invisible "real-life" struggles of doctoral dissertation writers. In S. Simpson, N. A. Caplan, M. Cox, & T. Phillips (Eds.), *Supporting graduate student writers: Research, curriculum, & program design* (pp. 97–116). Ann Arbor: University of Michigan Press.

Casanave, C. P. (2017). *Controversies in second language writing: Dilemmas and decisions in research and instruction* (2nd ed.). Ann Arbor: University of Michigan Press.

Casanave, C. P., & Li, X. (Eds.) (2008). *Learning the literacy practices of graduate school: Insiders' reflections on academic enculturation.* Ann Arbor: University of Michigan Press.

Charles, M. (2007). Reconciling top-down and bottom-up approaches to graduate writing: Using a corpus to teach rhetorical functions. *Journal of English for Academic Purposes, 6*, 289–302.

Charles, M. (2012). 'Proper vocabulary and juicy collocations': EAP students evaluate do-it-yourself corpus-building. *English for Specific Purposes, 31*, 93–102.

Charles, M. (2014). Getting the corpus habit: EAP students' long-term use of personal corpora. *English for Specific Purposes, 35*, 30–40.

Charles, M., & Pecorari, D. (2016). *Introducing English for academic purposes*. New York: Routledge.

Cheng, A. (2006a). Analyzing and enacting academic criticism: The case of an L2 graduate learner of academic writing. *Journal of Second Language Writing, 15*, 279–306.

Cheng, A. (2006b). Understanding learners and learning in ESP genre-based writing instruction. *English for Specific Purposes, 25*, 76–89.

Cheng, A. (2007a). Simulation-based L2 writing instruction: Enhancement through genre analysis. *Simulation and Gaming, 38*, 67–82

Cheng, A. (2007b). Transferring generic features and recontextualizing genre awareness: Understanding writing performance in the ESP genre-based literacy framework. *English for Specific Purposes, 26*, 287–307.

Cheng, A. (2008a). Analyzing genre exemplars in preparation for writing: The case of an L2 graduate student in the ESP genre-based instructional framework of academic literacy. *Applied Linguistics, 29*, 50–71.

Cheng, A. (2008b). Individualized engagement with genre in academic literacy tasks. *English for Specific Purposes, 27*, 387–411.

Cheng, A. (2011a). ESP classroom research: Basic considerations and future research questions. In D. Belcher, A. M. Johns, & B. Paltridge (Eds.), *New directions in English for specific purposes research* (pp. 44–72). Ann Arbor: University of Michigan Press.

Cheng, A. (2011b). Language features as the pathways to genre: Students' attention to non-prototypical features and its implications. *Journal of Second Language Writing, 20*, 69–82.

Cheng, A. (2015a). Genre analysis as a pre-instructional, instructional, and teacher development framework. *Journal of English for Academic Purposes, 19*, 125–136.

Cheng, A. (2015b). Rethinking the paths toward developing ESP practitioners' specialized knowledge through the lens of genre analysis. *English as a Global Language Education, 1*, 23–45.

Cho, D. W. (2009). Science journal paper writing in an EFL context: The case of Korea. *English for Specific Purposes, 28*, 230–239.

Cortes, V. (2007). Genre and corpora in the English for academic writing class. *ORTESOL Journal, 25*, 9–16.

Cortes, V. (2011). Genre analysis in the academic writing class: With or without corpora? *Quaderns de Filologia: Estudis Lingüistics, 16*, 65–80.

Cortes, V. (2013). The purpose of this study is to: Connecting lexical bundles and moves in research article introductions. *Journal of English for Academic Purposes, 12*, 33–43.

Cortina, L. M., Magley, V. J., Williams, J. H., & Langhout, R. D. (2001). Incivility in the workplace: Incidence and impact. *Journal of Occupational Health Psychology, 6*, 64–80.

Cotos, E., Link, S., & Huffman, S. (2016). Studying disciplinary corpora to teach the craft of discussion. *Writing & Pedagogy, 8*, 33–64.

Curry, M. J. (2016). More than language: Graduate student writing as "disciplinary becoming." In S. Simpson, N. A. Caplan, M. Cox, & T. Phillips (Eds.), *Supporting graduate student writers: Research, curriculum, & program design* (pp. 78–96). Ann Arbor: University of Michigan Press.

Curry, M. J., & Lillis, T. (2017a). Foreword. In M. Cargill, & S. Burgess (Eds.), *Publishing research in English as an additional language* (pp. xv–xviii). Adelaide, Australia: University of Adelaide Press.

Curry, M. J., & Lillis, T. (Eds.). (2017b). *Global academic publishing: Policies, perspectives and pedagogies.* Bristol, England: Multilingual Matters.

Devitt, A. J. (2004). *Writing genres.* Carbondale: Southern Illinois University Press.

Devitt, A. J., Reiff, M. J., & Bawarshi, A. S. (2004). *Scenes of writing: Strategies for composing with genres.* New York: Pearson/Longman.

Douglas, J. (2015). Developing an English for academic purposes course for L2 graduate students in the sciences. *Across the Disciplines, 12*(3). Retrieved from http://wac.colostate.edu/atd/graduate_wac/douglas2015.cfm

Dudley-Evans, T., & St John, M. J. (1998). *Developments in English for specific purposes: A multidisciplinary approach.* Cambridge, England: Cambridge University Press.

Duszak, A., & Lewkowicz, J. (2008). Publishing academic texts in English: A Polish perspective. *Journal of English for Academic Purposes, 7*, 108–120.

Englander, K. (2014). *Writing and publishing science research papers in English: A global perspective.* New York: Springer.

Eriksson, A. (2012). Pedagogical perspectives on bundles: Teaching bundles to doctoral students of chemistry. In J. E. Thomas, & A. Boulton. (Eds.). *Input, process and product: Developments in teaching and learning corpora* (pp. 195–211). Brno, Czech Republic: Masarya University Press.

Fairbanks, K., & Dias, S. (2016). Going beyond L2 graduate writing: Redesigning an ESL program to meet the needs of both L2 and L1 graduate students. In S. Simpson, N. A. Caplan, M. Cox, & T. Phillips (Eds.), *Supporting graduate student writers: Research, curriculum, & program design* (pp. 139–158). Ann Arbor: University of Michigan Press.

Feak, C. B. (2016). EAP support for post-graduate students. In K. Hyland, & P. Shaw (Eds.), *The Routledge handbook of English for academic purposes* (pp. 489–501). New York: Routledge.

Feak, C. B., & Swales, J. M. (2009). *Telling a research story: Writing a literature review.* Ann Arbor: University of Michigan Press.

Feak, C. B., & Swales, J. M. (2010). Writing for publication: Corpus-informed materials for postdoctoral fellows in perinatology. In N. Harwood (Ed.). *English language teaching materials: Theory and practice* (pp. 279–300). Cambridge, England: Cambridge University Press.

Feak, C. B., & Swales, J. M. (2011). *Creating contexts: Writing introductions across genres.* Ann Arbor: University of Michigan Press.

Feak, C. B., & Swales, J. M. (2014). Tensions between the old and the new in EAP textbook revision: A tale of two projects. In N. Harwood (Ed.), *English language teaching textbooks: Content, consumption, and production* (pp. 299–319). New York: Palgrave Macmillan.

Feng, H., & Shi, L. (2004). Genre analysis of research grant proposals. *LSP & Professional Communication, 4*, 8–32.

Ferris, D. R. (2009). *Teaching college writing to diverse student populations.* Ann Arbor: University of Michigan Press.

Ferris, D. R, & Hedgcock, J. S. (2014). *Teaching L2 composition: Purpose, process, and practice* (3rd ed.). New York: Routledge.

Flowerdew, J. (1993). An educational, or process, approach to the teaching of professional genres. *ELT Journal, 47*, 305–316.

Flowerdew, J. (2011). Reconciling contrasting approaches to genre analysis: The whole can equal more than the sum of the parts. In D. Belcher, A. M. Johns, & B. Paltridge (Eds.), *New directions in English for specific purposes research* (pp. 119–144). Ann Arbor: University of Michigan Press.

Flowerdew, J. (2015). Some thoughts on English for research publication purposes (ERPP) and related issues. *Language Teaching, 48*, 250–262.

Flowerdew, J. (2016). English for specific academic purposes (ESAP) writing: Making the case. *Writing & Pedagogy, 8*, 5–32.

Flowerdew, J., & Forest, R. W. (2015). *Signalling nouns in English: A corpus-based discourse approach.* New York: Cambridge University Press.

Flowerdew, J., & Li, Y. (2009). The globalization of scholarship: Studying Chinese scholars writing for international publication. In R. M. Manchón (Ed.), *Writing in foreign language contexts: Learning, teaching, and research* (pp. 156–182). Bristol, England: Multilingual Matters.

Flowerdew, L. (2015). Using corpus-based research and online academic corpora to inform writing of the discussion section of a thesis. *Journal of English for Academic Purposes, 20,* 58–68.

Flowerdew, L. (2016). A genre-inspired and lexico-grammatical approach for helping postgraduate students craft research grant proposals. *English for Specific Purposes, 42,* 1–12.

Fredericksen, E., & Mangelsdorf, K. (2014). Graduate writing workshops: Crossing languages and disciplines. In T. M. Zawacki & M. Cox (Eds.), *WAC and second language writers: Research towards linguistically and culturally inclusive programs and practices* (pp. 347–367). Anderson, SC: Parlor Press.

Freedman, A. (1994). "Do as I said": The relationship between teaching and learning new genres. In A. Freedman & P. Medway (Eds.), *Genre and the new rhetoric* (pp. 191–210). London: Taylor & Francis.

Freeman, J. (2016). Designing and building a graduate communication program at the University of Toronto. In S. Simpson, N. A. Caplan, M. Cox, & T. Phillips (Eds.), *Supporting graduate student writers: Research, curriculum, & program design* (pp. 222–238). Ann Arbor: University of Michigan Press.

Frodesen, J. (1995). Negotiating the syllabus: A learning-centered, interactive approach to ESL graduate writing course design. In D. Belcher & G. Braine (Eds.), *Academic writing in a second language: Essays on research and pedagogy* (pp. 331–350). Norwood, NJ: Ablex.

Fujioka, M. (2008). Dissertation writing and the (re)positioning of self in a "community of practice." In C. P. Casanave & X. Li (Eds.), *Learning the literacy practices of graduate school: Insiders' reflections on academic enculturation* (pp. 74–89). Ann Arbor: University of Michigan Press.

Gladon, R. J., Graves, W. R., & Kelly, J. M. (2011). *Getting published in the life sciences.* Hoboken, NJ: Wiley & Sons, Inc.

Gosden, H. (1995). Success in research article writing and revision: A social-constructionist perspective. *English for Specific Purposes, 14,* 37–57.

Gustafsson, M., Eriksson, A., & Karlsson, A. (2016). Facilitating writing in the tension between the quasi-generic and the multidisciplinary: Chalmers University of Technology. In S. Simpson, N. A. Caplan, M. Cox, & T. Phillips (Eds.), *Supporting graduate student writers: Research, curriculum, & program design* (pp. 255–271). Ann Arbor: University of Michigan Press.

Haggerty, K. D., & Doyle, A. (2015). *57 ways to screw up in grad school: Perverse professional lessons for graduate students.* Chicago: University of Chicago Press.

Hailman, J. P., & Strier, K. B. (2006). *Planning, proposing, and presenting science effectively: A guide for graduate students and researchers in the behavioral sciences and biology* (2nd ed.). New York: Cambridge University Press.

Halliday, M. A. K. (1995). *An introduction to functional grammar* (2nd ed.). London: Edward Arnold.

Hamp-Lyons, L. (2003). Writing teachers as assessors of writing. In B. Kroll (Ed.), *Exploring the dynamics of second language writing* (pp. 162–194). Cambridge England: Cambridge University Press.

Harwood, N. (2007). Political scientists on the functions of personal pronouns in their writing: An interview-based study of "I" and "we." *Text & Talk, 27*, 27–54.

Harwood, N. (2009). An interview-based study of the functions of citations in academic writing across two disciplines. *Journal of Pragmatics, 41*, 497–518.

Hirvela, A. (1997). "Disciplinary portfolios" and EAP writing instruction. *English for Specific Purposes, 16*, 83–100.

Hirvela, A. R. (2016). *Connecting reading & writing in second language writing instruction* (2nd ed.). Ann Arbor: University of Michigan Press.

Holbrook, A., Bourke, S., Lovat, T., & Dally, K. (2004). Investigating PhD thesis examination reports. *International Journal of Education Research, 41*, 98–120.

Hopkins, A., & Dudley-Evans, T. (1988). A genre-based investigation of the discussion sections in articles and dissertations. *English for Specific Purposes, 7*, 113–121.

Huang, J. C. (2010). Publishing and learning writing for publication in English: Perspectives of NNES PhD students in science. *Journal of English for Academic Purposes, 9*, 33–44.

Huang, J. C. (2014). Learning to write for publication in English through genre-based pedagogy: A case in Taiwan. *System, 45*, 175–186.

Hutchinson, T., & Waters, A. (1987). *English for specific purposes: A learning-centered approach*. Cambridge, England: Cambridge University Press.

Hyland, K. (1998). Boosting, hedging and the negotiation of academic knowledge. *TEXT, 18*, 349–382.

Hyland, K. (1999). Academic attribution: Citation and the construction of disciplinary knowledge. *Applied Linguistics, 20*, 341–367.

Hyland, K. (2000). *Disciplinary discourses: Social interactions in academic writing*. Harlow, England: Longman.

Hyland, K. (2002). Specificity revisited: How far should we go now? *English for Specific Purposes, 21*, 385–395.

Hyland, K. (2003). Genre-based pedagogies: A social response to process. *Journal of Second Language Writing, 12*, 17–29.

Hyland, K. (2004a). Disciplinary interactions: Metadiscourse in L2 postgraduate writing. *Journal of Second Language Writing, 13*, 133–151.

Hyland, K. (2004b). *Genre and second language writing*. Ann Arbor: University of Michigan Press.

Hyland, K. (2015a). *Academic publishing: Issues and challenges in the construction of knowledge*. New York: Oxford University Press.

Hyland, K. (2015b). Teaching and researching writing (3rd ed.). New York: Routledge.

Hyland, K. (2016). Academic publishing and the myth of linguistic injustice. *Journal of Second Language Writing, 31*, 58–69.

Hyland, K., & Tse, P. (2004a). "I would like to thank my supervisor": Acknowledgements in graduate dissertations. *International Journal of Applied Linguistics, 14*, 259–275.

Hyland, K., & Tse, P. (2004b). Metadiscourse in academic writing: A reappraisal. *Applied Linguistics, 25*, 156–177.

Hyon, S. (1996). Genre in three traditions: Implications for ESL. *TESOL Quarterly, 30*, 693–722.

Johns, A. M. (1997). *Text, role, and context: Developing academic literacies*. New York: Cambridge University Press.

Johns, A. M. (Ed.) (2002). *Genre in the classroom: Multiple perspectives*. Mahwah, NJ: Lawrence Erlbaum. .

Johns, A. M. (2003). Genre and ESL/EFL composition instruction. In B. Kroll (Ed.), *Exploring the dynamics of second language writing* (pp. 195–217). New York: Cambridge University Press.

Johns, A. M. (2008). Genre awareness for the novice academic student: An ongoing quest. *Language Teaching, 41*, 237–252.

Kanoksilapatham, B. (2015). Distinguishing textual features characterizing structural variation in research articles across three engineering subdiscipline corpora. *English for Specific Purposes, 37*, 74–86.

Kim, E. G., & Shin, A. (2014). Seeking an effective program to improve communication skills of non-English-speaking graduate engineering students: The case of a Korean engineering school. *IEEE Transactions on Professional Communication, 57*, 41–55.

Kittle Autry, M., Carter, M., & Wojcik, K. (2016, July). The new WPA: Supporting graduate writing across the curriculum. Paper presented at the meeting of the Council of Writing Program Administrators, Raleigh, North Carolina.

Kuteeva, M. (2013). Graduate learners' approaches to genre-analysis tasks: Variations across and within four disciplines. *English for Specific Purposes, 32*, 84–96.

Kuteeva, M., & Negretti, R. (2016). Graduate students' genre knowledge and perceived disciplinary practices: Creating a research space across disciplines. *English for Specific Purposes, 41*, 36–49.

Kwan, B. S. C. (2006). The schematic structure of literature reviews in doctoral theses of applied linguistics. *English for Specific Purposes, 25*, 30–55.

Kwan, B. S. C. (2010). An investigation of instruction in research publishing offered in doctoral programs: The Hong Kong case. *Higher Education, 59*, 55–68.

Lancaster, Z., Aull, L, & Escudero, M. D. P. (2015). The past and possible futures of genre analysis: An introduction to the special issue. *Journal of English for Academic Purposes, 19*, 1–5.

Lave, J., & Wenger, E. (1991). *Situated learning: Legitimate peripheral participation*. New York: Cambridge University Press.

Lea, M. R. (2004). Academic literacies: A pedagogy for course design. *Studies in Higher Education, 29*, 739–756.

Lee, D., & Swales, J. (2006). A corpus-based EAP course for NNS doctoral students: Moving from available specialized corpora to self-compiled corpora. *English for Specific Purposes, 25*, 56–75.

Lee, S., & Golde, C. (2013). Completing the dissertation and beyond: Writing centers and dissertation boot camps. *Writing Lab Newsletter, 37* (7–8), 1–5.

Li, Y. (2006). A doctoral student of physics writing for publication: A socio-politically-oriented case study. *English for Specific Purposes, 25,* 456–478.

Li, Y. (2017). 'The one who is out of the ordinary shall win': Research supervision towards publication in a Chinese hospital. In M. Cargill, & S. Burgess (Eds.), *Publishing research in English as an additional language* (pp. 187–208). Adelaide, Australia: University of Adelaide Press.

Maher, D., Seaton, L., McMullen, C., Fitzgerald, T., Otsuji, E., & Lee, A. (2008). "Becoming and being writers": The experiences of doctoral students in writing groups. *Studies in Continuing Education, 30,* 263–275.

McGrath, L., & Kuteeva, M. (2012). Stance and engagement in pure mathematics research articles: Linking discourse features to disciplinary practices. *English for Specific Purposes, 31,* 161–173.

Mewburn, I., Osborne, L., & Caldwell, G. (2014). Shut up and write! Some surprising uses of cafes and crowds in doctoral writing. In C. Aitchison & C. Guerin (Eds.), *Writing groups for doctoral education and beyond: Innovations in practice and theory* (pp. 218–232). New York: Routledge.

Min, Y. (2016). Rethinking ESL service courses for international graduate students. *TESOL Journal, 7,* 162–178.

Motta-Roth, D. (1998). Discourse analysis and academic book reviews: A study of text and disciplinary cultures. In I. Fortanet, S. Posteguillo, J. C. Palmer, & J. F. Coll (Eds.), *Genre studies in English for academic purposes* (pp. 29–58). Castello, Spain: Universitat Jaume I.

Murray, R. (2015). *Writing in social spaces: A social processes approach to academic writing.* New York: Routledge.

Naoum, S. G. (2013). *Dissertation research and writing for construction students* (3rd ed.). New York: Routledge.

Neiderhiser, J. A., Kelley, P., Kennedy, K. M., Swales, J. M., & Vergaro, C. (2016). 'Notice the similarities between the two sets...': Imperative usage in a corpus of upper-level student papers. *Applied Linguistics, 37,* 198–218.

Noguchi, J. (2006). *The science review article: An opportune genre in the construction of science.* Bern, Switzerland: Peter Lang.

Norris, C., & Tardy, C. (2006). Institutional politics in the teaching of advanced academic writing: A teacher-research dialogue. In P. K. Matsuda, C. Ortmeier-Hooper, & X. You (Eds.), *The politics of second language writing: In search of the promised land* (pp. 262–279). West Lafayette, IN: Parlor Press.

Paltridge, B. (1994). Genre analysis and the identification of textual boundaries. *Applied Linguistics, 15*, 288–299.

Paltridge, B. (1997). Thesis and dissertation writing: Preparing ESL students for research. *English for Specific Purposes, 16*, 61–70.

Paltridge, B. (2001). *Genre and the language learning classroom.* Ann Arbor: University of Michigan Press.

Paltridge, B. (2002). Thesis and dissertation writing: An examination of published advice and actual practice. *English for Specific Purposes, 21*, 125–143.

Paltridge, B. (2003). Teaching thesis and dissertation writing. *Hong Kong Journal of Applied Linguistics, 8*(2), 78–96.

Paltridge, B. (2016). Writing retreats as writing pedagogy. *Writing & Pedagogy, 8*, 199–213.

Paltridge, B., Harbon, L., Hirsh, D., Shen, H., Stevenson, M., Phakiti, A., & Woodrow, L. (2009). *Teaching academic writing: An introduction for teachers of second language writers.* Ann Arbor: University of Michigan Press.

Paltridge, B., & Starfield, S. (2007). *Thesis and dissertation writing in a second language: A handbook for supervisors.* New York: Routledge.

Paltridge, B., Starfield, S., & Tardy, C. M. (2016). *Ethnographic perspectives on academic writing.* Oxford, England: Oxford University Press.

Paltridge, B., & Woodrow, L. (2012). Moving beyond the texts. In R. Tang (Ed.), *Academic writing in a second or foreign language: Issues and challenges facing ESL/EFL academic writers in higher education contexts* (pp. 88–104). New York: Bloomsbury.

Parsons, T., & Knight, P. G. (2015). *How to do your dissertation in geography and related disciplines* (3rd ed.). New York: Routledge.

Peacock, M. (2011). The structure of the methods section in research articles across eight disciplines. *Asian ESP Journal, 7*, 99–124.

Phillips, T. (2014). Developing resources for success: A case study of a multilingual graduate writer. In T. M. Zawacki & M. Cox. (Eds.), *WAC and second language writers: Research towards linguistically and culturally inclusive programs and practices* (pp. 69–91). Anderson, SC: Parlor Press.

Phillips, T. (2016). Writing center support for graduate students: An integrated model. In S. Simpson, N. A. Caplan, M. Cox, & T. Phillips (Eds.), *Supporting graduate student writers: Research, curriculum, & program design* (pp. 159–170). Ann Arbor: University of Michigan Press.

Pho, P. D. (2008). Research article abstracts in applied linguistics and educational technology: A study of linguistic realizations of rhetorical structure and authorial stance. *Discourse Studies*, *10*, 231–250.

Potter, W. J. (2001). Avoiding writing traps. In A. Alexander & W. J. Potter (Eds.), *How to publish your communication research: An insider's guide* (pp. 13–22). Thousand Oaks, CA: Sage.

Prior, P. A. (1998). *Writing/disciplinarity: A sociohistorical account of literate activity in the academy*. Mahwah, NJ: Lawrence Erlbaum.

Prior, P. A., & Min, Y. (2008). The lived experience of graduate work and writing: From chronotopic laminations to everyday lamentations. In C. P. Casanave & X. Li (Eds.), *Learning the literacy practices of graduate school: Insiders' reflections on academic enculturation* (pp. 230–246). Ann Arbor: University of Michigan Press.

Qiu, J. (2010). Publish or perish in China. *Nature, 463*, 142–143.

Ritter, K. (2017). A question of mimetics: Graduate-student writing courses and the new "basic." In B. Horner, B. Nordquist, & S. M. Ryan (Eds), *Economies of writing: Revaluations in rhetoric and composition* (pp. 112–130). Logan: Utah State University Press.

Robinson, M. S., Stoller, F. L., Costanza-Robinson, M. S., & Jones, J. K. (2008). *Write like a chemist: A guide and resource*. New York: Oxford University Press.

Robinson, P. C. (1991). *ESP today: A practitioner's guide*. New York: Prentice Hall.

Rogers, P. M., Zawacki, T. M., & Baker, S. E. (2016). Uncovering challenges and pedagogical complications in dissertation writing and supervisory practices: A multimethod study of doctoral students and advisors. In S. Simpson, N. A. Caplan, M. Cox, & T. Phillips (Eds.), *Supporting graduate student writers: Research, curriculum, & program design* (pp. 52–77). Ann Arbor: University of Michigan Press.

Rowley-Jolivet, E., & Carter-Thomas, S. (2005). Genre awareness and rhetorical appropriacy: Manipulation of information structure by NS and NNS scientists in the international conference setting. *English for Specific Purposes, 24*, 41–64.

Rudestam, K. E., & Newton, R. R. (2001). *Surviving your dissertation: A comprehensive guide to content and process*. Newbury Park, CA: Sage.

Samraj, B. (2005). An exploration of a genre set: Research article abstracts and introductions in two disciplines. *English for Specific Purposes, 24*, 141–156.

Schratt, G. M., Tuebing, F., Nigh, E. A., Kane, C. G., Sabatini, M. E., Kiebler, M., & Greenberg, M. E. (2006). A brain-specific microRNA regulates dendritic spine development. *Nature, 439*, 238–289.

Simpson, S. (2016a). Essential questions for program and pedagogical development. In S. Simpson, N. A. Caplan, M. Cox, & T. Phillips (Eds.), *Supporting graduate student writers: Research, curriculum, & program design* (pp. 286–298). Ann Arbor: University of Michigan Press.

Simpson, S. (2016b). New frontiers in graduate writing support and program design. In S. Simpson, N. A. Caplan, M. Cox, & T. Phillips (Eds.), *Supporting graduate student writers: Research, curriculum, & program design* (pp. 1–20). Ann Arbor: University of Michigan Press.

Simpson, S., Caplan, N. A., Cox, M., & Phillips, T. (Eds.). (2016). *Supporting graduate student writers: Research, curriculum, and program design*. Ann Arbor: University of Michigan Press.

Soler-Monreal, C. (2015). Announcing one's work in PhD theses in computer science: A comparison of move 3 in literature reviews written in English L1, English L2 and Spanish L1. *English for Specific Purposes, 40*, 27–41.

Starfield, S. (2003). The evolution of a thesis-writing course for arts and social sciences students: What can applied linguistics offer? *Hong Kong Journal of Applied Linguistics, 8*(2), 137–154.

Starfield, S. (2016). Supporting doctoral writing at an Australian university. *Writing & Pedagogy, 8*, 177–198.

Starfield, S., & Mort, P. (2016). Written and oral communication skills support for PhD students at the University of New South Wales. In S. Simpson, N. A. Caplan, M. Cox, & T. Phillips (Eds.), *Supporting graduate student writers: Research, curriculum, & program design* (pp. 239–254). Ann Arbor: University of Michigan Press.

Stoller, F. L., Horn, B., Grabe, W., & Robinson, M. S. (2005). Creating and validating assessment instruments for a discipline-specific writing course: An interdisciplinary approach. *Journal of Applied Linguistics, 2*, 75–104.

Sundstrom, C. J. (2016). Graduate writing instruction: A cautionary tale. In S. Simpson, N. A. Caplan, M. Cox, & T. Phillips (Eds.), *Supporting graduate student writers: Research, curriculum, & program design* (pp. 192–205). Ann Arbor: University of Michigan Press.

Swales, J. (1981). *Aspects of article introductions*. Birmingham, England: The University of Aston, Language Studies Unit.

Swales, J. M. (1990). *Genre analysis: English in academic and research settings*. Cambridge, England: Cambridge University Press.

Swales, J. M. (1998). *Other floors, other voices: A textography of a small university building*. Mahwah, NJ: Lawrence Erlbaum.

Swales, J. M. (2004). *Research genres: Exploration and applications*. Cambridge, England: Cambridge University Press.

Swales, J. M. (2009a). *Incidents in an educational life: A memoir (of sorts)*. Ann Arbor: University of Michigan Press.

Swales, J. M. (2009b). When there is no perfect text: Approaches to the EAP practitioner's dilemma. *Journal of English for Academic Purposes, 8*, 5–13.

Swales, J. M. (2009c). Worlds of genre—metaphors of genre. In C. Bazerman, A. Bonini, & D. Figueiredo (Eds.), *Genre in a changing world* (pp. 3–16). Fort Collins, CO: The WAC Clearinghouse.

Swales, J. M., Barks, D., Ostermann, A. C., & Simpson, R. C. (2001). Between critique and accommodation: Reflections on an EAP course for masters of architecture students. *English for Specific Purposes, 20*, 439–458.

Swales, J. M., & Feak, C. B. (1994a). *Academic writing for graduate students: A course for non-native speakers of English*. Ann Arbor: University of Michigan Press.

Swales, J. M., & Feak, C. B. (1994b). *Academic writing for graduate students: Commentary*. Ann Arbor: University of Michigan Press.

Swales, J. M., & Feak, C. B. (2000). *English in today's research world: A writing guide*. Ann Arbor: University of Michigan Press.

Swales, J. M., & Feak, C. B. (2004a). *Academic writing for graduate students: Essential tasks and skills* (2nd Ed.). Ann Arbor: University of Michigan Press.

Swales, J. M, & Feak, C. B. (2004b). *Commentary for Academic Writing for Graduate Students: Essential tasks and skills* (2nd Ed.). Ann Arbor: University of Michigan Press.

Swales, J M., & Feak, C. B. (2009). *Abstracts and the writing of abstracts*. Ann Arbor: University of Michigan Press.

Swales, J. M., & Feak, C. B. (2011). *Navigating academia: Writing supporting genres*. Ann Arbor: University of Michigan Press.

Swales, J. M., & Feak, C. B. (2012a). *Academic writing for graduate students: Essential tasks and skills* (3rd ed.). Ann Arbor: University of Michigan Press.

Swales, J. M., & Feak, C. B. (2012b). *Commentary for* Academic Writing for Graduate Students: Essential tasks and skills (3rd ed.). Ann Arbor: University of Michigan Press.

Swales, J. M., Feak, C. B., & Irwin, V. V. (2011). *Commentary for* Navigating Academia: Writing supporting genres. Retrieved from /www.press.umich.edu/elt/compsite/ETRW/.

Swales, J. M., & Lindemann, S. (2002). Teaching the literature review to international graduate students. In A. M. Johns (Ed.), *Genre in the classroom: Multiple perspectives* (pp. 105–120). Mahwah, NJ: Lawrence Erlbaum.

Swales, J. M., & Luebs, M. A. (2002). Genre analysis and the advanced second language writer. In E. Barton & G. Stygall (Eds.), *Discourse studies in composition* (pp. 135–154). Cresskill, NJ: Hampton Press.

Swales, J. M., & Najjar, H. (1987). The writing of research article introductions. *Written Communication, 4*, 175–191.

Tardy, C. M. (2009). *Building genre knowledge.* West Lafayette, IN: Parlor Press.

Tauber, D. (2016). Expanding the writing franchise: Composition consulting at the graduate level. *College Composition and Communication, 67*, 634–657.

Thompson, D. K. (1993). Arguing for experimental "facts" in science: A study of research article results sections in biochemistry. *Written Communication, 10*, 106–128.

Tian, M., Su, Y., & Ru, X. (2016). Perish or publish in China: Pressures on young Chinese scholars to publish in internationally indexed journals. *Publications, 4*(9), 1–16.

Tierney, J. (2016). Supporting graduate and professional communications: Yale English language programs. In S. Simpson, N. A. Caplan, M. Cox, & T. Phillips (Eds.), *Supporting graduate student writers: Research, curriculum, & program design* (pp. 272–285). Ann Arbor: University of Michigan Press.

Turner, J. (2012). Academic literacies: Providing a space for the socio-political dynamics of EAP. *Journal of English for Academic Purposes, 11*, 17–25.

Wang, S. H., & Flowerdew, J. (2016). Participatory genre analysis of statements of purpose: An identity-focused study. *Writing & Pedagogy, 8*, 65–89.

Wang, X., & Yang, L. (2012). Problems and strategies in learning to write a thesis proposal: A study of six M.A. students in a TEFL program. *Chinese Journal of Applied Linguistics, 35*, 324–341.

Weissberg, R. (2006). *Connecting speaking & writing in second language writing instruction*. Ann Arbor: University of Michigan Press.

Wenger, E. (1998). *Communities of practice: Learning, meaning, and identity*. Cambridge, England: Cambridge University Press.

White, E. M. (1994). *Teaching and assessing writing: Recent advances in understanding, evaluating, and improving student performance* (2nd ed.). San Francisco: Jossey-Bass.

Yakhontova, T. (2001). Textbooks, contexts, and learners. *English for Specific Purposes, 20*, 397–415.

Yang, R., & Allison, D. (2003). Research articles in applied linguistics: Moving from results to conclusions. *English for Specific Purposes, 22*, 365–385.

Yang, W. (2015). "Call for papers": Analysis of the schematic structure and lexico-grammar of CFPs for academic conferences. *English for Specific Purposes, 37*, 39–51.

Younts-Dahl, S. M., Galyean, M. L., Loneragan, G. H., Elam, N. A., & Brashears, M. M. (2004). Dietary supplementation with *Lactobacillus*- and *Propionibacterium*-based direct-fed microbials and prevalence of *Escherichia* coli O157 in beef feedlot cattle on hides at harvest. *Journal of Food Protection, 65*, 889–893.

Zawacki, T. M., & Cox, M. (Eds.) (2014). *WAC and second language writers: Research towards linguistically and culturally inclusive programs and practices*. Fort Collins, CO: The WAC Clearinghouse.

Index